Barefoot King

The Indian Dalit Who Defied
Caste to Bless Others

HAYLEY BENNETT LYLE

Praise for Barefoot King

"Pulsing with lyrical prose and moral passion, Lyle's *Barefoot King* narrates the riveting biography of a courageous man's struggle to overcome modern slavery in India. Raw anguish and irrepressible dignity collide in this inspiring story of dehumanization, love, and liberation. Lyle's unflinching look into othering paradoxically reveals the highest possibilities for human compassion, equality, and hope. Prepare to laugh, cry, and rediscover the meaning of life."

Dr. Andrew DeCort, author of *Flourishing on the Edge of Faith* and founder of the Neighbor-Love Movement

HAYLEY BENNETT LYLE

Barefoot King

The Indian Dalit Who Defied Caste to Bless Others

Hayley Bennett Lyle

Published by Elyon Press

Cover Design by Jerusha Keziah Isaac

ISBN: 9798367512304

Thank you, Kanni and Anbalagan; may you look down with pride from above.

Thank you, Raj and family, for your generosity and hospitality to me.

Thank you, Debbi Johnson, for playing an integral part in starting this project, Mike Yorkey, for your guidance throughout, and to all those who generously reviewed and offered feedback.

contents

Foreword	*i*		Chapter Eleven	71
Preface	*iii*		Chapter Twelve	78
Chapter One	1		Chapter Thirteen	85
Chapter Two	10		Chapter Fourteen	87
			Chapter Fifteen	95
Part I: Elementary	**16**		Chapter Sixteen	102
Chapter Three	17			
Chapter Four	26		**Part III: Assault**	**112**
Chapter Five	30		Chapter Seventeen	113
Chapter Six	40		Chapter Eighteen	119
Chapter Seven	47		Chapter Nineteen	127
Chapter Eight	50		Chapter Twenty	135
Chapter Nine	56		Chapter Twenty - One	142
			Chapter Twenty-Two	153
Part II: Beginnings	**64**		Chapter Twenty-Three	163
Chapter Ten	65			

Part IV: Life's Bloom   **171**

Chapter Twenty-Four   172

Chapter Twenty-Five   180

Chapter Twenty-Six   188

Chapter Twenty-Seven   196

Chapter Twenty-Eight   204

Chapter Twenty-Nine   212

Chapter Thirty   220

Part V: New Kallar   **228**

Chapter Thirty-One   229

Chapter Thirty-Two   238

Chapter Thirty-Three   244

Epilogue   250

GLOSSARY   ...   253

APPENDIX I   ...   256

APPENDIX II   ...   258

foreword

The question of caste is very alive in India. There are thousands more youth like Raj undergoing the same challenges today that Raj faced in 1986. As a Dalit, one must face hurdles in education, in community, in the political arena, and faith.

There are many like him, craving to learn, to develop in education, and come out of slavery. This is why I feel that this book is very important and will reach at a global level. I am very honored to have been apart of this process, and to have gotten to engage with Hayley. Many foreigners have come India and sympathize, but do nothing more. Hayley has taken her empathy to tell this story to the world. I am very thankful she has told this story so we can come in global solidarity to the Dalit issue.

Rajendran Prabhakar
Founder and Executive Director of Maarga

HAYLEY BENNETT LYLE

preface

I was a twenty-two-year-old blonde American living in Bangalore, India, when I first met Raj. One day I asked about his story and discovered that his family had been bonded laborers, an illegal yet prevalent form of slavery. As I dug deeper, I discovered that Raj had been a sponsor child with a Christian organization and that this had enabled him to climb out of poverty. I didn't know how much more there was to his story at that point, but it was enough. Hearing the circumstances he had risen out of and knowing him for who he is today, I knew this story was worth telling.

This biography's creation involved countless hours of interviews, both with Raj and with other significant people in his life. It included overnight train rides to Raj's rural town and to villages and slums where he has worked. It involved research of Indian laws and long conversations with lawyers, politicians, and academics.

Writing this biography was no easy task because Raj's story exposes humanity's selfishness, prejudice, and corruption. As I worked, it became evident to me that these vices plague politics, the justice system, and even the church. The old ways of thinking and the imbalance of power that led to the most critical events in Raj's life are still very present in India. Yet, in the face of this, Raj's life displays the power that redemption, kindness, and integrity have in the midst of broken systems.

His life has become my roadmap to navigate the tension of existing in broken systems. In writing this story, I find myself in the middle of a paradox: a dire system made up of real people. I have been blessed and formed by my relationships with these people: Christians, Hindus, and Muslims; business owners, politicians, and cleaning maids; cosmopolitan professionals and lowly plantation workers; Brahmin, Sudra, and untouchable.

The love that each has shown me is rich and true; their hospitality is generous; their struggles are real. As a westerner stepping into India, my experience has been contradictory. My heart recoils at the corruption, prejudice, and entitlement I see. And yet, in inexplicable irony, I know that it is Indians who taught me how to love.

I completed writing this book in April of 2020 as a global pandemic, social unrest, and the intense polarizing of politics overtook the world and my own country. The tension and paradoxes I experienced in India were so obviously present in my own home in America. These events pertinently reminded me that I needed the hope and perspective that Raj's story gives.

I wrote this biography because we need this story. We must look at our community with fresh eyes and address the issues we see with boldness. We must step into who God has made us to be and pursue what He has called us to do— regardless of the assumptions or constraints our environment has set. Above all else, we must walk this out in the way of love, mercy, and integrity.

May this story provoke relationship, as any change must begin with true friendship with others. May each of us stretch our realms of empathy beyond our circles of similarity.

And may you find Raj to be a friend by the end of this journey, as he has become a friend to me.

chapter one

A chill breeze hovered over the Indian waters, beckoning dawn. Although it was December, the breeze was thick with tropical humidity. Seabirds thronged the sky above the placid water.

The salty air brushed droplets of sweat and sea off the dark-skinned fishermen. Their muscles strained as they pulled nets brimming with the morning catch into their rocking boats. Their chests were bare and they wore long cloths tied modestly around their waists in a typical south Indian dhoti.

Their wooden boats, painted with faded blues, yellows, and reds, spliced through the gentle waves as they made their way back to shore. They glided onto the hard sand, which glistened in the early light. The fishermen unloaded their catch to barefoot men and gave them instructions to carry the goods to the market.

The urban edifices of Velankanni, a prominent city in Tamil Nadu, towered above the shore. Beyond the city, fishermen's villages dotted the coast and prawn farmer communities lined the inlets and muddy backwaters.

In the city, magnificent white church spires glinted. It was the Basilica of Our Lady of Good Health. Every year, some twenty-two million pilgrims visited the church, and today was the Sunday after Christmas. Thousands of voices lifted in worship, and the music drifted from the basilica out to the sea.

The market stretched from the shore all the way to the iconic church. Pilgrims spilled into the market streets, singing and dancing, each straining to get as close to the basilica as they could in hopes of receiving some of Mother Mary's famed healing grace. The scent of cardamom and chai wafted through the air like sweet incense as the stall owners lit their stoves in anticipation of thirsty fishermen and pilgrims. It all seemed like a perfect day. Nobody could have anticipated the destruction that was coming.

On December 26, 2004, at 6:28 a.m., the exact moment that the sun rose over Tamil Nadu, one of the greatest earthquakes known to man rocked the ocean floor 1061 miles away. The US Geological Survey recorded the earthquake's magnitude as 9.1. It was one of the four largest earthquakes since 1900.

As the fishermen stepped out of their boats, a surge of energy silently raced through the ocean. As they handed their loads to barefoot men for sorting, huge waves amassed off the shores of Sri Lanka.

A chai man lit his stove for a customer, unaware of the alien mass building on the ocean horizon. As he poured dark tea leaves into the simmering milk, an ominous black wave rose. As he grasped a handful of sugar in his fingers, the wave hit an offshore sandbank and grew larger. Before he could splash the tea between his vessels to mix it, a six-meter wall of furiously churning froth pounded the shoreline. At 9:20 that morning, the first of five tsunamis devastated the coast of Velankanni and its entire region.

The chai shop splintered under the weight of surging water. The heavy debris knocked the chai man down. Within seconds, water and wreckage sucked the fishermen, pilgrims, and merchants out to sea.

The tsunamis ripped apart Velankanni and its surrounding coastal villages. The prawn farmers' shanty towns collapsed under the reverberating forces of excess water that flooded the river channels and backwaters they lined. The sea stopped at the outskirts of the church, as if the maiden saint had spared her basilica. However, the roads surrounding the church transformed into death rivers and swallowed all who had been worshipping moments before. All around, the land gagged on water and its own inhabitants.

Within forty minutes, the waves receded. The sky still shone a rich blue. But in a single incomprehensible moment, wives had become widows, sons and daughters had become orphans, families had become homeless, and livelihoods were washed out to sea. A total of 16,389 lives were taken that day from the coast of India.

Splinters of painted wood littered the shoreline where the fishing boats had sat. The basilica stood quiet. There were no traces of the chai shop. Fishing nets held their fishermen in a last embrace, and sand delicately covered the bodies of men, women, and children in an untimely burial.

The clap of a truck door penetrated the commotion. Worn shoes stepped down onto the streets of Velankanni. The man wearing them had dark skin like the Tamilian villagers, but unlike them, he wore long pants, a button-down shirt, and smart-looking glasses. His name was Rajendran Anbalagan, and he was the national coordinator for Samuka Initiative. It was four days after the tsunami, and his goal was to find the leader of the village in order to distribute emergency supplies.

He had just arrived in Kallar, a small fisherman's village that lies only six miles north of Velankanni. The village possessed nothing more than a soft sandy beach as a defense against the tsunami, and like every other village on the coast, it had been decimated.

An exhausted man approached Raj. "Sir," the man said, "I am the leader here, the village panchayat president."

"So far, we have fifty bodies," he continued. "We're looking for a lot more, though." He gestured toward a lone house at a far corner of the village. "The bodies are in that house, waiting to be identified and buried. We don't recognize some of them. The water must have swept them here from another village."

The scene throbbed with intense emotion. All around them were the sounds of mothers and fathers crying out for missing children and children wailing for their mothers and fathers. Animal carcasses floated in putrid puddles. Rubble that once had been houses littered the ground among uprooted palm trees. Cinder blocks and painted concrete were scattered through puddles and splintered furniture.

A sickly white bleach powder dusted the ground. It had been spread by disaster relief workers against the onslaught of diseases they knew were coming: dysentery, malaria, dengue, and others. The odor of decay and chemicals laid siege to Raj's nostrils, and his hand instinctively rose to his mouth to stifle a gag.

"Look at this!" The village leader exclaimed as tears welled in his eyes. "We'll have to rebuild everything. Our village survives on fishing. We're going to be in trouble with all our boats gone. And with all the mud and debris churned up, it may be weeks before we can make a catch.

"We are grieving, but we are also facing an economic crisis. It's going to be a while before we are back on our feet."

"Well, let's start where we can," said Raj. "Will you help us distribute food and build shelters?"

The village leader nodded. "Whatever you need, I will help you."

Raj nodded to his team, and they began unloading packages of rice and lentils to each family and distributing sheet metal and tarps to construct temporary shelters. Raj began to direct some men to begin burying the dead bodies on the village's far side, then paused at the sight of a woman wrapped in a yellow sari amid the rubble and mud.

Her face contorted in anguish. Her dark lips stretched over her clenched teeth, and the tendons in her throat strained. It looked as though she was crying, yet no sound came. By the fourth day of grieving, her vocal cords had given out.

Nobody ate those first few days, due to their grief, and Raj couldn't eat either. Every day, Raj strolled through the sea of meager sheet metal shelters to visit with the families. He started counseling them and gently prodding some life into the heaviness that hung over the village.

One day Raj passed that same woman in the yellow sari.

"Sir," one villager whispered, "For the past six days, she has not eaten. She refuses to eat. We do not know what to do." Her neighbors had been trying to coax her to eat.

"She says her life is over now that her husband and children are dead. She says she has nothing now."

Raj gazed at her for a moment and replied, "Only her heart knows the depths of her losses." He saw that she had a stubborn will, but her body was weak. He needed to convince her to eat something or else her body would fail.

"That will not do," Raj replied, shaking his head. "We must have her eat something. I will see what I can do."

Raj approached her, but she put her head down, disinviting any conversation.

Some of the surrounding villagers chimed, "Raj has come to meet you." "He has come all this way to talk to you." "Such an important official is waiting." But despite their nagging, her head stayed down.

Just as he was about to speak to her, a voice interrupted from behind. Raj turned to see the village leader.

"Raj, sir, everyone is giving supplies to me, and I am distributing it, so I'm speaking with the workers all the time," he began.

"We have received so much care in these past days, but you are the only relief worker who has actually stayed. I see you coming and returning for the past three days. This...this never happens." He paused. "And you are working too hard. We cannot let you go without eating. We don't have much but let me offer you food. Please, have a meal with us."

"Thank you for your kindness," Raj answered, which was a way of saying *no, thank you* in a gracious manner. In India, it is respectful to dance around saying "no," as refusing their offer explicitly could be considered insulting.

The president pressed on, "Please, sir, come—let us thank you. Eat with us."

Raj pursed his lips. The man was persistent. "Okay, okay,"

Raj replied, but he was scheming. If he was going to eat, he was not going to eat alone. The two men looked over at the woman in the yellow sari.

"Perhaps," Raj replied, "we can make this all work together."

Raj stepped toward the woman. "Madam," he whispered, "tell me, how are you today?"

The woman kept her head low, but the villagers immediately picked up on this new strategy. It was the strategy of Indian hospitality. The woman might not have the will to serve herself, but the chance to serve a visitor was something else. In India, there is a common phrase: *Atithi Devo Bhava*, or "guests are equivalent to God." It is a pride and honor to show proper hospitality to guests.

"Raj, sir, you have been working so hard for so many days. You must be thirsty," the villagers said.

Raj consented grimly, and the woman in the yellow sari raised her head slightly. After a pause, she said, "I have some water. I will give." Her eyes lifted toward him. "Sir, did you have food?"

Raj smiled sadly and replied, "No."

The woman seemed to wake from her stupor. "Every day, you are coming here," she said. "Please have food." Her quavering voice gathered strength. "You are here to help all of us. You must take food. If your health is spoiled, then you cannot help us."

Raj raised his hands in a gesture of consent. "Okay, well, if *you* are cooking and giving me food, I will take." He threw a quick smile over to the village leader, who was watching approvingly.

At Raj's acceptance, the woman smiled for the first time. She proclaimed to everyone assembled, "These last six days I would have nothing to do with cooking. But today, I will cook. Not for me, but for you."

Again, Raj consented. "Okay, I will eat."

To the amazement of her onlookers, the woman got right to work. She stoked the stove, fetched cooking water, and grabbed two pots for rice and dhal. Even the simplest Indian meal is quite the operation. It would not be unheard of for an average meal to take at least one hour to prepare. This elaborate preparation is a point of pride for many Indian cooks. As a serving of ghee sizzled in one of the pots, the woman chopped onions, garlic, and tomatoes. She ground an array of traditional Indian spices, and the aroma of cardamom, ginger, and turmeric delicately announced this woman's new inspiration. The rice boiled in one pot, and a creamy dhal bubbled in the other.

In an hour, her neighbors summoned Raj. Gesturing to Raj, the woman said, "Come, sir, it is waiting for you." Raj sat down and smiled at the spread of food.

"Oh, it looks so good!" he exclaimed, but there was mischief in his eyes. "Okay, I will eat the food—provided that you are eating with me."

Surprise lit her face. "No sir, please! I am not eating, I told you. This is for you."

Sighing, Raj replied, "Well then, I do not need to eat. I will be fine. It's okay." And with a little push of the food plate, the joust of wills began.

"No, sir, no, sir," she moaned.

Raj encouraged, "I will eat if you eat with me." Then he smiled and waited.

Soon the neighbors joined in. "Sir wants to eat with you. Look, he is taking care of all of us. He must eat."

Raj's eyes fixed on hers. "I want to sit with you—like family."

She shook her head. "No, sir, no, sir." She was not happy. She moved to protest again, but Raj and the villagers outnumbered her. So she did what she had to. She put a tiny bit of rice and dhal in a bowl for herself and handed a gigantic bowl of rice and dhal to Raj.

Eyeing her suspiciously, Raj asked her to eat. He threatened again that if she did not eat, he would not.

With an annoyed grimace, she took a bite. Glaring at him, she retorted, "This is only for your sake." She finished the tiny bowl as Raj began to take spoonfuls of his meal. She did not eat much then, but at least she ate a little. She had willed herself to starve, but now she was being jostled back into life.

Weeks turned to months. Although this community was one of thirteen projects he oversaw for Samuka Initiative, Raj gave special attention to Kallar. In the first months, he lived full-time with the community. Raj prodded Kallar back into a working and supportive community by gathering the community to play games, initiating leadership classes, and forming a tailor co-op for the women. Raj began to connect the child survivors with outsiders to sponsor their education. Bright Future, another relief organization, partnered with Raj's organization and built a new settlement for the villagers one mile inland from the original site, with one home for each family.

Raj became part of the community. Faces brightened when they saw him, and families competed to welcome him into their homes. To this day, many consider Raj as family and attribute their survival and hope to Raj's presence during those times. The village lived in tenuous circumstances for many years, still rebuilding from their losses, but the children were clothed and in school, men fished again, and women tailored and saved their profits with empowerment they had never had before.

After the first year, Raj continued to visit for a full week every month, so often that the village gave him a permanent home to stay with them. Year by year, the village regained vitality and hope.

Four years passed and Raj strolled through the new Kallar village, greeting everyone by name. Then he stood just outside the village along the main road, lost in content thoughts as he watched carts, motorbikes, and people move past him.

A small girl across the road caught his eye. She met his

glance with beautiful wide brown eyes, framed by sun-kissed hair. But Raj felt a chill run through him. Something was wrong.

Her hair was matted and her dress was tattered. She wore no sandals. And she looked terrified. Two even smaller boys tottered by her, completely naked and dirty. Raj had never seen them before.

Disturbed, Raj followed them as they passed the new Kallar settlement. They continued along a pitiful dirt path by one of the backwater channels. Tangles of sticks and brush enclosed the trail. It was clear from the smell of stagnant scum that the channels of water flowed to the prawn farms nearby.

Suddenly the brush opened into a different sort of tangled mess—one of thatched shanties and rotting wood. It was a village that belonged to a prawn farming community that had squatted on the undesirable land beside the backwaters. Its disarray gave an alarming cry of distress.

It looked like this village had also been decimated by the tsunami four years prior, but unlike the town of Kallar, it had never recovered. It looked as though no relief efforts had ever reached this place.

Before him lay shambled homes and people in ragged clothes. There was no drinkable water, and no leader. The grim presence of desolation covered the entire community. He could see in their eyes a look he knew all too well from his own childhood—of a will caught in the ruthless dance between survival and fatal despair.

Any westerner stumbling upon such a sight would be shocked and wonder how relief had not been given to this village. But Raj knew that what he saw before him was not some logistical failure.

This was a social issue, a caste issue.

Raj had stumbled upon an Untouchable village.

chapter two

A breath and a cry. Every life enters the world in the same way. The heart beats. The lungs breathe. Skin, eyes, hands, and feet: the same basic body carries every human. Lips break into a smile; eyes water into a tear. Every person feels joy and sorrow, humor and affection, anger and confusion.

But look closely in India, and you will notice that some wear shoes and others don't. Some women draw water directly from a well for themselves, while others are not allowed near it. You may wonder why one person receives a job promotion before another who has worked longer and brought the organization more success. If you're incredibly perceptive, you just might notice that there are some people you don't see, and may never see—as there are certain people who are not even allowed outside in the daylight. All of this *could* seem like tragic coincidence, when all the while restrictions and customs silently enforce a system that guards a strict hierarchy of power.

Caste is an identity one is born into based on family occupation. To date, there are an estimated 3,000 castes with 25,000 sub-castes throughout India. While specific castes, with their dynamic array of professions, vary according to each region, they all adhere to a four-fold hierarchy.

The Rigveda, a sacred Hindu collection of poems dating from 1500 BCE, explains the caste system's origin in a whimsical tale. It says that there once lived a cosmic being named Purusha, who the Hindu gods sacrificed to create all living things. From his mouth were made the Brahmin, who preside as priests and intellectuals. From his arms were made the Rajanya, the warriors. From his thighs came the Vaisya, the laborers, and from his feet came the Sudra, the servants. These are the four broadest segments of caste to this day. Each caste has its duty or *dharma*, and it is right that each person fulfills the duty given to them.

Historical documents such as the Laws of Manu reveal just how long these customs have been in place. It was used to decide legal and cultural disagreements and dictates each of the four castes' duties. In these writings, society is rigid and straightforward. For example, the laws write, "A Sudra, though emancipated by his master, is not released from servitude; since that is innate in him, who can set him free from it?"

Today, the castes have become more fluid. Some Sudras are founding businesses, while others remain workers for the businesses. A select few chosen by the Brahmin have become political leaders and lead loyally according to their supporting aristocracy's guidance. Still, their title remains the same, as does their relationship to the other castes. The government acknowledges the distinction between Sudras by defining Sudras of humbler means as "Backward Classes" (BC) and those of better means as "Other Backward Classes" (OBC). These two categories comprise the most significant percentage of India's population.

The four castes of India respect one another's status. The fervor of religious devotion entwines duty and being. They adhere to tradition adamantly. They marry within their caste, respect their own places within the temples, wear the clothes and eat the foods of their castes. These traditions have organized and maintained society for hundreds of years. And with this, a fifth group emerges.

To the lowest of the castes, the lowest of tasks are assigned. These are the street sweepers, the sewage cleaners, and the gravediggers. To those unfortunate enough to receive the dirtiest of duties, their very existence becomes dirt. Their breath, their blood, their saliva, and their very bodies, so immersed in the uncleanliness of their demeaning tasks, have been deemed polluting to society. Thus, 16 percent of India's population is designated so low that they have been placed outside the caste system.

Their very being has been dubbed impure; society works together to protect itself from their presence. Those who exist here must forge a livelihood out of the little opportunity and resources given to them. They have been called Untouchable, Dalit, and Scheduled Caste.

The caste system turns human ambition inward, away from pursuing better prospects and toward protecting what little entitlement a person is given. The top of the scale rests safe from threat, while the lowest of the strata is burdened with enabling the entitlement of the classes above. And so, driven by the noble cause of protecting the sacred duties that their gods and ancient texts so passionately urge, India is locked into a rigid regulation of entitlements, expectations, roles, and—most importantly—marriages.

A net of social customs and expectations, often brutally enforced, has encased the scheduled caste's prospects for over a millennium. The scheduled castes became socioeconomically immobilized and openly degraded. Any actions that question or protest the caste system have been criminalized.

The 1900s saw the advent of constitutional law, sparking a paradigmatic shift in the very definition of justice and rights. However, while the concept of inalienable human rights rules on paper, old ways still reign in reality. Scheduled castes may be denied work promotions because those of higher castes have refused to work under them. Intermarriage with higher castes is often forbidden and violently fought. Caste-based violence is still common.

A person told anything enough times might just believe it, and any person treated a certain way enough times might just live it. Fatalism swiftly permeates the dreams, self-respect, and self-efficacy of the scheduled castes. Alcoholism, abuse, disorganization, and lack of self-discipline confirm their fate. By the time a child is old enough to understand, his or her hope is blackened by the fatalism of his or her people.

Only the hope of a higher reincarnation flickers dimly for these souls and gives them the gumption to tread onward. They say, "better one's own duty ill-done, than someone else's, well performed." To fulfill one's duty is one of the highest values in the ethics of dharma.

Caste is the decider of their economic opportunity, spiritual deliverance, and human value. In the region around Velankanni and Kallar, the workers who carried the fishermen's catch to the marketplace could never be fishermen themselves because they were not allowed to touch the ocean. Many people worshipping outside the basilica were not allowed inside the church, so they were all swept away in the tsunami. Being of a higher caste, the fishermen claimed first status for relief and, as a result, the scheduled caste communities along the backwaters did not receive emergency supplies.

All of this—the lack of economic opportunity, the deaths in the tsunami, the lack of aid—might well appear to be tragic coincidence until you look deeper.

In 1966, about 260 miles south of Kallar by the sea, a young woman named Kanni clutched at the mud walls of her hut and cried out to the gods for mercy. Her water had just broken, and the contractions had begun. She was giving birth to her fifth child. Should the baby die, it would be a tragedy. Should the baby live and be a boy, her family would be cursed.

Poverty had levied its burden on her body. In her first labor, her bones and muscles had borne the strain, but her little boy lost the fight for his life in the womb. His mother's sweat and blood ushered him into the world, and he arrived silent and lifeless. After that, three more boys came and survived—the fight for life was won three times.

However, an ominous superstition threatened the family. In India, everyone wants to have boys because boys grow the family rather than being given to another family (as girls are in marriage), but if a woman has five boys in a row, it is believed that the whole family will be cursed. After their fourth son arrived, Kanni and her husband, Aandi, began to worry.

When she conceived again, a seed of angry fear took root. She could not learn if the child was a boy or a girl. In those months, her anxiety swelled along with her abdomen. She, her husband, and all her children could be subject to torment by the existence of a cursed child.

The woman paced outside her hut, facing each wave of pain with resolved strength. The clouds were dark with monsoon rains, and the sticky air drew her long hair to her face. She had the beautiful dark skin, hair, and eyes of her Dravidian ancestors.

She grasped the edge of her sari, worn from many washings, in her hands. Although pressed and elegantly draped, it betrayed the menial subsistence of the woman it covered. White cracks were etched into the soles of her bare feet from a lifetime of wear. They betrayed that she was untouchable. She was Paraiyan, one of the scheduled castes in south India. Her people were people of the graveyard, handling the funerals and burials of deceased people or livestock.

Her name, Kanni, means "beautiful eyes." When she was eighteen, her parents found Aandi to be a husband to her. They figured, *Better that he take care of her than us.*

Aandi was of the same scheduled caste, Paraiyah, and lived just a few miles away in a neighboring Paraiyan settlement, or *cheri.* "Aandi" means "worthless," which is perhaps how his parents felt about themselves and their family at the time. Still, the young man worked hard. Aandi had labored on a plantain plantation a few miles away as a bonded laborer since he was twelve years old. Kanni barely knew him at the time of their marriage, but he seemed kind, diligent, and a quiet sort of man.

The families came together in a meager ceremony to

commence the marriage. They lacked the money to hire a ceremonial drummer but still exchanged flower garlands. Aandi fastened a gold chain, called a *thali*, around Kanni's neck. As his fingers opened and closed the clasp, she joined her life to his. That thali signified she was married and would stay with him the rest of her life. His home became her home; his gods, her gods; his job, her job; his future, her future.

Ten years and four children later, Kanni braced herself against the mud walls, gasping for breath. With a surge of maternal defiance, she faced the intensifying contractions. They became more frequent. The baby was coming.

Aandi paced nervously outside while the women of the cheri crowded around Kanni defensively, patting her sweating brow and stroking her dark hair.

The child came, but there was no celebration. They named him Natarajan, the name of a Hindu god, and called him Raj. He was the fifth male child born to an untouchable bonded laborer in a small town in rural Tamil Nadu.

He was born as a curse to his family.

And in a way, Raj was indeed a curse because he cursed the way things were. He would challenge the system that prolonged his community's state. He would contest the unchecked power of the higher castes.

He would curse untouchability.

I
Elementary

There cannot be a more degrading system of social organization than the caste system. It is a system which deadens, paralyses, and cripples the people from helpful activity...

All are slaves of the caste system. But not all of the slaves are equal in status.

—*Dr. B. R. Ambedkar, Dalit, Lawyer, and Father of the Indian Constitution*

chapter three

1971, Anaigudi cheri, five years old

Moonlight danced among the swaying plantain leaves as the boy raced through the plantation. The early morning light was only just beginning to fade the stars. Natarajan's deep brown skin blended into his surroundings so that only his curious eyes gleamed through the darkness.

He'd woken up to a rustle as his father stepped out for an early start on the plantation. Mischief overcame the young boy. He had untangled himself from the limbs of his sleeping brothers and sisters, causing only a few yelps and groans, and stepped from the sari laid out on the mud floor that his family slept on. He'd pushed past the cloth tied over the opening of the home and scurried after his father.

Natarajan followed his father stealthily, his heart pounding. Ahead of him, his father stretched his arms as he moved through the grove of plantain trees. A worn white cloth was wrapped around his waist and another like it tied around his head. Many days under the sun had reddened the whites of his eyes and blackened his skin. A mustache protruded from under his nose, and he patted it while he walked.

He paused near a tree. Raj ducked into the shadows and held his breath against his fluttering heart. If Raj were caught, the game would be lost. His target continued toward one of the far groves.

Raj rubbed his eyes and opened his mouth in a wide tiger yawn. A soft breeze began to move through the grove with the warming sun. The large plantain leaves shimmered, and tamarind trees waved their delicate seed pods above him. The birds were waking with a flurry of quips, and in the distance, the shrill cock sang his morning song. Raj's mother would be awake by now, preparing breakfast for the family before they, too, left to work. Kanni would bring his father a bit of the leftover breakfast in a couple of hours.

Leaves rustled just behind Raj and he jumped, only to look down and see a yellow gecko returning from his night venture back to some unknown refuge. Then he raised his head and found himself staring directly into the beady eyes of a bonnet macaque monkey. Raj stood still, his wide eyes meeting hers. She glared at Raj, but her attempt at intimidation was tragically thwarted by the ridiculous tuft of hair on her head. A splutter of laughter escaped Raj.

Raj had lost sight of his father and was blissfully out of range of his mother. His bare feet sank into the soft red earth, and his fingers danced across the waxy, low-lying plantain leaves. He felt like a king. Clad in tattered shorts, he lifted his chin and breathed in the earthy air of his domain. He decided he would be a gentle and gracious ruler over all ants and geckos and monkeys, and they would love him. The green leaves tickled each other in the breeze like tiny applause all around him. A butterfly, black with a bright blue stripe, danced near Raj. He closed his eyes as the early morning light cascaded onto him.

A piercing voice shattered the moment. It was the voice of a boy a few years older than Raj, and his words were crude. Raj crept through the bushes to watch. His father stood with his head bent low and his shoulders bent even lower, as if he were trying to dissolve into the earth beneath him. He could go no lower without kneeling, so he stayed where he was and bore the onslaught of insults. His assailant stood a couple of feet shorter than him: a stout, verbose nine-year-old boy. It was the plantation overseer's son.

Raj watched his father closely as he bore the insults with tiny nods of acknowledgment. Raj could just make out what his father was saying.

"Yes, *Ejamaan*," he said, which essentially meant, "Yes, Master." He had taken off the cloth that wrapped around his head and tucked it into his *dothi*, the long cloth wrapped around his waist. It was a peculiar sight for Raj, seeing his father, an adult man, making himself so small before this boy.

Shame came over Raj. The magic of the moment before dissipated. Shrouded in the bushes, Raj hung his head and saw his feet. He thought about the time he'd asked his brother if he could get some sandals in the market. His brother had briskly shoved the question away. "Better one's own duty ill-done than someone else's, well performed," he had said.

Raj looked at his father's bare feet. Then he looked at the lovely, sturdy sandals that the overseer's son wore. The shame that had grown inside him soon felt like it was coming over him from all sides. He did not know what he was ashamed of, but something was very wrong, and it was somehow his fault. Everything inside of Raj wanted to hide.

Behind them, the sturdy stuccoed walls of the high-caste town loomed through the stalks of plantain trees. Smoke billowed generously out of chimneys from warm cooking fires in the homes below. It looked warm and inviting, but Raj knew better. That was where the overseer and his son lived.

Raj ran all the way home through the long shadows cast by stalks of plantain trees. Soon home came into sight. The row of scantily constructed mud huts and thatched roofs brought relief to Raj as he scurried into his refuge.

Scheduled castes, such as Raj's Paraiyan caste, created satellite settlements called "cheris" just outside the town they worked. They were not allowed to own land, so the landowners permitted them to settle on the unwanted land. It seemed fitting that the land the owners did not wish to touch be settled by the people they did not wish to touch. The townspeople would not venture near the cheri, and the Paraiyans would only enter the town with the proper acknowledgment of their place: eyes down, men's chests uncovered, and no shoes.

Raj's Paraiyan cheri sat just three hundred meters outside the town of Anaigudi. The cheri was shaped like an L. At the top, a main dirt road led into the town of Anaigudi.

This cheri had a strange look about it, however, for one line of the L, Raj's side, was lined with mud huts, crafted out of whatever resources the families could find. Meanwhile, the bottom of the L was lined with concrete homes that had tiled roofs. They were not elegant by any means, but they could withstand the monsoon rains without any need for repairs. Families in these homes didn't get sick as often because the dwellings were cleaner and drier, and the roofs did not catch fire accidentally, as the roofs of the mud huts sometimes did.

Raj had asked one of his uncles once why his cousins had such a nice house. The man explained that not long before Raj was born, his community had moved off land beside the town graveyard to this land, closer to Anaigudi.

"They told us to settle anywhere in the place. One of the parcels of land was from the government and another, your part, was from the Christian church in town. I think they wanted to convert us Hindus to their god or something. We just settled wherever." His uncle contorted his face as if he were trying to untangle the memory. "Well, anyways, you know that fellow Kumaresan in the town with the fancy house and the fancy cars? He is what you call a *politician*. He wanted our folk to vote for him, so he built them fancy houses on the government land."

"But why not where I live?" Raj had asked.

His uncle sat there for a long time, squinting his eyes and thinking hard.

"Deeds," he finally said, matter-of-factly. "The church kept the deed to the land you live on. They ain't never gave the land, really. Since they owned it, the politician couldn't build houses on it. The church would have to." Raj didn't know what a "deed" was or what a "vote" was or why the man with the fancy house and the fancy cars would care, so he had walked away puzzled but less concerned.

Heart racing, Raj ducked inside his hut and stood, panting. Home for Raj was a ten-by-ten-foot structure, mud-walled and mud-floored, with a leaky thatched roof and a rag-cloth door. It was just large enough for the family of eight all to lay on the floor to sleep. Still, home was home.

Two of Raj's brothers, Chelladurai and Petchimuthu, were wiping their faces with their shirts before running to the nearby school. They were nine and seven years old and would stay in school until ten years old. Then they would join their oldest brother, Antony, in the landowner's other plantation. The plantation lay twenty kilometers away. Antony, now eleven years old, lived on his own out there and took care of the cattle and coconut trees on the plantation. He would return home once a year during the Hindu festivals.

Petchimuthu glanced up at Raj. "You gave us an early wake-up this morning," he grunted.

Chelladurai shook his head with a playful grimace, agreeing, and then added, "Well, get some breakfast while you can." Some *gunji* sat in the clay pot. Gunji was soft, fermented rice, saved from the previous night's dinner, and it was the staple breakfast for the family. Raj had three older brothers and two younger sisters, and the food went quickly. Petchimuthu and Chelladurai left while Raj dipped his hands into the pot to grab a few mouthfuls.. His mother's voice rang from just outside.

Mouth full of rice, Raj gingerly crept up to the doorframe. The cloth that hung in the doorway lightly danced in the soft breeze and brushed his face.

Kanni knelt just outside the hut singing an old Tamil song to herself. A pot of water sat with a puddle around it, and a small stack of cleaned clay dishes sat just next to it. Her dark braid fell down her back and flowed down the folds of the orange sari that enveloped her. Her threadbare hem dipped into the muddy puddle where she washed. The golden thali that her husband gave her on the day of her marriage glimmered like the morning dew.

Raj's two younger sisters, Jothi and Selvie, toddled behind

their mother. Jothi was proclaiming something to her sister as she stroked her mother's sari. They were three years old and one year old and stayed close to their mother.

Kanni stood and wiped the dust and water droplets from her sari. "Come on, girls, time to get ready to work," she said as she began to prepare to join her husband on the plantation.

Kanni and Aandi worked hard as "coolies," crass jargon throughout south Asia for manual laborers. Through this, they provided for the family. At times, relatives would need Kanni and Aandi to take in their children, and then the family they had to provide for expanded to a full dozen people.

The family existed in perpetual hard times. Aandi and Kanni worked the plantation, and the landowner provided their groceries and paid them an annual dividend. However, the amount he paid them was barely enough for them to scrape by, and the grocery payments were deducted from the yearly pay, sometimes resulting in debt to the owner.

The landowner resided in distant Chennai, so his overseer saw to enforcing the work. In theory, the labor was fairly exchanged for the groceries that the owner provided and the small percentage of the plantation profits at the end of the year. In reality, living costs were deducted from the already insufficient pay, and when the farm lost earnings due to drought, flood, or storm, that loss would be taken out of Aandi's pay as well. In those years, the owner did not pay the year-end salary but instead deducted from it, charging for the groceries and demanding they pay back their loan with interest.

Aandi and Kanni were caught in a centuries-old system of debt bondage. They went by what the overseer said, perhaps knowing that even if they argued their pay and the deductions, they had no better options. Since Aandi and Kanni didn't know arithmetic, these deductions were lost in a cloud of ambiguity that lingered uncomfortably above the young family. All they could do was shrug and say, "Thalai Elutho" ("it is written in our heads; this is the fate") and

"Thalai Vithi" ("God's command").

A letter from the village administrative officer in 1986 gives insight into this situation. He wrote that the family's annual income, which by 1986 referred to Aandi, Kanni, and their first son, Antony, was "3,600 rupees by means of doing cooli work." To put this in perspective, in 1986, a new shirt alone would cost 500 rupees.

When factoring in the conversion rate and inflation, this amount would be equivalent to $658.26 today for one year's work. The 1986 amount split among three people meant each would be living on twenty-five cents per day, four times lower than the international poverty line set just four years later (see app. II).

Families like Raj's struggled through a threadbare existence. When times became hard, Kanni would plead to the landowner to give her a loan. She would rather go deeper into debt than not be able to provide for her family. She believed her employer was gracious to give to her when she really needed it. Everyone thought that way.

The landowner was a man by the name of Subbaiah Nadar, who'd made his humble beginning selling pots. He was clever with his resources and used his profits to purchase land for a plantain plantation. The existing social structure had set the standard of pay for the plantation workers so low that the owners often accrued wealth exponentially. After all, in most business ventures, employee pay is the most costly expense on the books.

Capitalism had tipped unevenly in favor of the landowner, and this imbalance was reinforced by the society's norms. Raj and his family were forced to survive on subminimal wages while Subbaiah Nadar used his profits to gain more land, plant more plantations, and become a millionaire. Today, Nadar's family owns one of the largest steel manufacturing businesses in Tamil Nadu. Nobody would think twice about the poor wages he offered his Paraiyan laborers, and the Paraiyans had no better options. To Raj and his family, this was their duty; this was their fate.

"Ah, Natarajan, there you are!" Kanni exclaimed, catching sight of her son.

"Yes, Ama?" Raj exclaimed innocently, smiling to himself because she hadn't noticed his morning absence.

"Raj, take this to your father when you take the goats out," she instructed, handing him some leftover gunji breakfast wrapped in a plantain leaf.

"Yes, Ama," Raj replied, taking the package. Each morning Raj would deliver breakfast to his father in the plantation, then care for the landowner's sheep and goats. Raj set off for the fields, hoping the overseer's son would be long gone.

"*Ayya!*" Raj called, looking for his father. He led his little herd through the plantation as he carried the plantain leaf package delicately in his hands. In the near distance, he heard the squealing of a rusty water pump. He pushed past some trees and saw his father wiping his brow then his hands on the dothi wrapped around his waist. The last of the water flowed out of the spigot into some small channels dug to irrigate the trees. Aandi gave a gentle smile as he received the breakfast, then gestured to his son.

"Natarajan, come, walk with me," he said. Curious, Raj left the docile herd to munch on grass while he followed his father to a nearby shed. Raj watched his father take a key from a black rope called an *arana kayiru* tied around his waist. Carefully he unlocked the door and stepped in. Entranced, Raj entered behind his father into a room filled with rusted pipes. The machinery hummed as it operated the water pump outside.

Aandi rested his arm against the rusted pipes, then turned to Raj.

"Son, I have worked for this plantation ever since I was a boy," he explained. Raj nodded his head.

"The highest honor shown to me was the day the overseer

gave me this key." He lifted a fold of his dothi to expose the key once again, tied securely around his waist.

He stooped down, shut off the pump, then took from a corner a long garden hoe called a *manvetti*. As they stepped out, he locked the door and carefully stowed the key back around his waist.

"Soon, your brothers will join Antony to work on another part of the plantation," he continued. "Your brothers have been working hard, you know." Raj nodded his head obediently.

Aandi sighed. "My father's father was a coolie, my father was a coolie, I am a coolie." As he spoke, his eyes implored his young son. "I don't want you to use the manvetti. Natarajan, I want you to use the pen."

Raj looked up at his dad with wide eyes. At five years old, Raj could not have possibly understood the significance of his father's words.

His father added with a smile, "The school will give you lunch too."

The somberness of the situation escaped Raj, and a goofy grin erupted over his face.

"When can I go?" Raj asked. Free food was just as good an incentive as any, and to a boy who had only eaten a cup of rice twice a day, every day, for his whole life, free lunch sounded like a feast. Moreover, Raj could sit inside a classroom instead of working hard in the fields. Raj bounded back to his herd with new excitement.

Aandi leaned against his manvetti as he watched his son ramble away.

The overseer would fuss; he always did. "Why are you sending him to school? It will be a waste. After all, he's not going to complete school—he'll be in the fields soon enough." There was just too much to do, the overseer would add, and then he'd mutter something about deductions of pay and the debt Aandi still owed him and how the world isn't very nice to people of his status, and aren't they fortunate to have an overseer who takes care of them?

Nevertheless, the overseer would relent, and Aandi would get his wish. Aandi had worked for the overseer long enough to know that he could outlast him in patience on this request.

Even if Raj just learned to sign his name, that would be far more than Aandi had ever known.

chapter four

A British missionary named Bishop Robert Caldwell founded the Caldwell Primary School back in the 1800s, when India was still under the British Empire. While colonialism's legacy certainly had its negative and disturbing consequences, some of the most positive contributions were the countless schools and hospitals created by Christian missionaries. Driven by the conviction that people should be able to read the Bible, have access to health care, and, at the heart of it all, understand the gospel message, hundreds of missionaries ventured into the Indian subcontinent to create these institutions. Many still operate today.

Bishop Robert Caldwell resided and built a church in Indiayagudi, the town next to Raj's. However, he constructed his primary school in a unique location. Rather than placing the elementary school in between Anaigudi and its neighboring town to the north, Bishop Caldwell placed the school along the outskirts of Anaigudi on the opposite side. This meant it would be closest to the cheri. Perhaps he hoped this would enable the children of the cheri to attend school, which it most certainly did.

Clad in his only shirt and shorts, Raj bid the sheep herd farewell and headed for his first day of school. Chelladurai and Petchimuthu sauntered ahead of him.

"Come on, Raj!" Petchimuthu yelled behind him.

Raj stepped out of his cheri onto the lone road that ran beside it. He turned to see the little huts lining the single street, with the younger children playing and the parents making their way to the plantations. His rag door wagged in the breeze.

Raj could barely contain his excitement, and it spilled into a white toothy grin. He breathed in the fresh smell of surrounding plantain trees and palmyra fronds and thought of the other boys and girls he had seen walking to school every morning. Today he could be like them. Today he was getting lunch!

Raj ran after his brothers, but as he turned away from his home, he suddenly felt nervous. He couldn't explain it, but he always felt the hairs on his neck rise when he walked on the road toward the town of Anaigudi.

Soon enough, he saw the school. It stood as one large building, washed in a gray-blue concrete finish with a high clay-tiled roof. A plaque just to the door's side read, "Bishop Caldwell Primary School," impressing the bishop's legacy upon all who entered.

Raj stepped past a flagpole standing at the school's front, took a deep breath, and entered. The chatter of all the students filled the building. Inside, two thin walls with open windows sectioned the space into three large areas. The excited voices of a hundred students sang over the barriers. Blackboards on the walls distinguished each class.

There were so many students. A queasy uneasiness burst into Raj's naive bliss. He walked into a sea of bodies that felt like it was closing in on him from all sides. He must have been the smallest one there. There were so many people, and they all knew where they were going.

Raj caught sight of the overseer's son. In shock, he backed up to one of the walls with his head down. Most of these children were upper caste. Suddenly Raj's heart began to pound, and the rest of his body wouldn't move.

"Can I help you, child?" asked a stern, motherly voice from behind Raj. He turned to see two shiny shoes in front of him. Rigid, Raj slowly raised his eyes to see one of the teachers. She allowed her taut mouth and hard eyebrows to relax into a smile.

"My name is Miss Esther. If you're in the first standard, then I'm your teacher." She smiled reassuringly. "Come with me." Miss Esther beckoned Raj toward a group of children sitting around a blackboard.

Raj stumbled after her and was soon comforted to see other children his size.

"What is your name?" asked Miss Esther.

"Natarajan," Raj answered sheepishly. He wished he could be back with those sheep.

Her eyebrows furrowed pensively. "Natarajan, you say?"

"Yes, teacher." Raj started to get nervous again. A familiar feeling swept through Raj, the same one that overcame Raj the morning he watched his dad grovel in the plantain grove.

She didn't like his name.

"Natarajan..." she repeated.

"Yes, teacher, but everybody calls me Raj."

An odd look came over her. Was it confusion? No. Her eyes grew soft, and she leaned closer to him. Her brow turned down in gentle sympathy. Then she lowered her voice to have a private conversation with Raj.

"And...are you from the cheri?"

Raj wished he could melt into the cracks in the floor.

"Yes, teacher," he cried. His brown eyes began to water, and he nervously inspected a button on his threadbare shirt. Everything in Raj wanted to escape. He could do without the lunch. He felt like he didn't belong here, and he didn't know what the teachers would do to him.

The school had a twenty to eighty ratio of Parayians to upper-caste children. All the teachers were upper caste; however, quite a few teachers attended the Christian CSI church in town. Miss Esther happened to be one of them.

"What are the names of the landowner and overseers your family works for?" Miss Esther asked. Raj stood up straight and started to list them as if this were his last chance to prove himself in school.

"Rajendran, you say?" she asked, repeating the second-to-last name.

"Yes, teacher."

"Well, then we will call you that from now on. Go along,

Rajendran, and find a seat. Don't worry, I will talk to your parents about this, but I'm sure they will be all right with it."

Rajendran? Raj wandered to a seat, bewildered. This teacher had just given him a privileged caste name. His parents could never have given him that name, being themselves untouchable. That day his name in the schoolbooks was Rajendran, and he would be Rajendran every day thereafter.

Esther, a devout Christian, was probably responding against the fact that the name was that of a Hindu god. However, she also had to know she was doing far more than removing the name of a Hindu god. She thought differently than most; she thought outside the system.

A Hindu untouchable name like Natarajan would condemn Raj to stay in his caste forever. No matter what he did or where he went, people would know his low caste as soon as he introduced himself. If education were his way out of the system, she wanted him to have a fresh identity to go with it. With a single swipe of a pen, she redefined Raj's entire reality in a way that would allow Raj himself to forge his own role and prospects.

And she chose for him a beautiful new name. It meant *king*.

chapter five

1976, Anaigudi cheri, ten years old

Four monsoons, four harvests, and four years of study had passed since Raj's first day of school.

By the time Raj left school that day, night had settled over the sky like a dark blanket through which the stars dimly shined. A symphony of insects hummed, mice chirped, and soft wind brushed against the trees, blending into a rural evening ballad. In the distance, a dog barked. The small mud walls and thatched roof of Raj's house stood as a dark silhouette against the sky and landscape. Raj gently pushed by a lime tree that grew behind his family's home.

He had grown a few inches since his first day in school. Now the leaves of the tree softly touched his eyelids, and he giggled as they tickled him.

At age ten, Raj wondered if he would have to join all three of his brothers in the plantation now. His younger sisters, Selvie and Jothi, attended school with him but would soon drop out to work in a rice mill that had just opened near the village. However, Raj loved school and happened to be pretty good at it. In fact, he consistently had the best test scores in his class.

The glow of his mother's cooking fire emanated from underneath a clay pot next to the hut. Kanni emerged through the cloth-shrouded doorway. She carefully selected sticks from her pile outside the house, then stoked her cooking fire. The sticks were a costly commodity, and she carefully added them one by one. Kanni scavenged through the forests, but inevitably one of the landowners would chase her off. She would plead, "Next time I will not come, but this time, please allow me..." And if she begged enough, they might permit her to take some sticks off their land. It was humiliating, but she had no alternative.

The clay pot held more costly commodities yet: rice and water. The village well had given a pitiful amount of water before it dried up. Kanni would trek one kilometer to fetch water from the neighboring cheri, then repeat the one-kilometer walk back to the house with her heavy, sloshy load. She used every stick, every drop of water, and every kernel of rice to keep her family going. Into the late hours of the night she would make food for the family, then work all during the day on the plantation. She was motherly in the most practical of ways.

Kanni caught sight of him. "Raj!" she called. "What are you doing out so late at night?"

"The teacher wanted me to clean his house after school," Raj replied. Raj knew he was asked because he was from the cheri, yet he couldn't help but feel that the teachers trusting him to do these chores gave him some prestige. Nobody else from his cheri would even be allowed into some of those houses.

The family's cock strutted in front of the home, pecking at some seeds in the dust as the cooking fire smoldered. Dinner was almost ready.

Raj turned to go inside, but another pot caught his eye—batter to cook *idlis*. The soft, steamed, sourdough-tasting buns took hours of preparation; they consisted of a batter made from rice that had to be turned and turned. They were for only the most special occasions.

"*Ama!*" Raj cried in joy. Kanni answered with a grin.

She would make them once a year for the festival to celebrate their god. Raj had almost forgotten that the festival started tomorrow night. His heart leaped with excitement. His brothers were home from the fields, and tomorrow they were going to have a feast!

"Raj!" two small, girlish voices cooed from inside the

home. Raj poked his head through the doorway. Jothi and Selvie were smashing rice for the next day. The kernels had been picked straight from the paddies, then boiled. The heat softened the rice enough for the girls to smash the hard husks off. Doing this took a great deal of time and effort, but was far more affordable than buying already prepared rice.

Next to them sat Raj's three brothers, grinning.

"You're back!" Raj cried as he flung his arms around them.

"Raj, look at how you've grown!" his oldest brother Antony exclaimed. Antony was now sixteen years old, and his voice had become low like a man's. The three boys' skin had turned dark from their long days working in the sun.

Aandi brushed through the doorway and quietly draped his towel back over his shoulder. He must have walked through the town on his return from the fields. He was not allowed to walk through Anaigudi wearing sandals or a towel to cover his chest. Instead, he would walk with his head bowed, nodding in submission to the upper-caste people he passed. Raj looked down. He had often accompanied his father through the town and endured mockery from his classmates as they demanded his father to bow to them. "Yes, *Ejamaan*." That was Aandi's only reply. Embarrassment flooded through Raj at the thought. He did not like to walk through the town with his father.

Aandi sat in the hut's corner, holding a special drink that Raj was not allowed to touch. A palmyra tree grew on the land Aandi worked, and the overseer had allowed him to take some of the juice home this day. The plant gave a sap that would become more and more fermented throughout the day and naturally turn into an alcoholic drink called *toddy*. It would provide just enough buzz to relax Aandi after a long day of work. Aandi rested his tired head against the mud of the hut and sighed. The wrinkles around his eyes softened. Here in the enclave of his domain, the red and white cloth lay across his shoulder, threadbare but demonstrative of the respect he was warranted. As the father of the house, he would eat first.

Kanni brought a steaming clay pot of rice from the cooking fire outside and dished some out to Aandi. Suddenly Antony, Chelladurai, and Petchimuthu were beside the rice, each clutching their clay bowl. Raj moved quickly to grab his own bowl, lest he be left out.

"So you come just for the food, *huh*?" Kanni complained—though beneath the quip was satisfaction. Kanni dished out a bowl of rice and one green chili to each person. They may not have had much, but they could indulge in some spice. Rice was the standard for the family. Morning and night, it was what they had to be content with.

"Ah, Ama," Antony said, smiling, "of course we love the cook of the food as well." He stood up and hugged her.

"Hey! I helped too!" little Selvie protested indignantly, but by then, the boys had immersed themselves in their food. Raj started to knead the rice between the fingers of his right hand, then pushed the rice ball into his mouth with his thumb.

Petchimuthu scraped his plate along the ground, and Kanni shot him an annoyed glance. He always did that when the food wasn't enough. Chelladurai rubbed his ear. Although nobody wanted to ask for more food, they each had their "tell." Ticking her tongue, Kanni dished a small extra portion of rice onto the boys' plates. Selvie burst into laughter. She couldn't help but make fun of her brothers' gestures. She was the life of the family, and the giggles bubbled out of her. The rest of the family chuckled with her.

Soon Jothi and Selvie were served. Kanni oversaw the intake with a keen eye. Though they had little, she took pride in cooking for her family. As the family moved away from the fire, she took the scant remainder for herself and ate. It was considered a woman's honor to cook for her family, and her seat of honor was to eat last: the sign of a job well done.

She kept the rest of the rice in a clay pot with some extra water to settle into gunji during the night. The rice would become a thick porridge for the morning. Occasionally they would have some vegetables like eggplant, but this was their usual diet, day after day.

Raj changed out of his shirt and shorts to go to sleep. He set them down on the floor when he heard an emphatic noise behind him. "*Aiyo*, Rajendran!" exclaimed his mom when she saw the shirt. She shook her head in motherly disapproval. She tightened her lips and tongue and released them in a loud, disapproving smack. "All these clothes we get through the years, all the cleaning and mending, and look at this new hole!"

Raj grimaced, looking at the muddy, patched-up thing.

"We played cricket in school today, and I fell in the dirt." He left out how his friend had managed to tag him, but he had hit a winning run. A smug smile betrayed his lack of remorse.

"*Aiyo*." His mother shook her head as she surveyed the once-white shirt. Raj owned one pair of pants and one white shirt, which he would wear six days out of the week.

With wearing it every day and washing it every night, it was no wonder that the shirt looked bedraggled. He heard Antony and Chelladurai chuckle from behind him. They, too, had gone to primary school for a couple of years before dropping out to work in the fields. Now they wore a dothi like their father.

"Don't worry about it, Ama," chided Antony. "He could learn in school even if all he wore were a *lungi*." Chuckles chattered in the hut's corner as the children lay a sari on the mud floor and jostled into position to sleep.

"These things, they cost too much," Kanni complained.

Raj's mom took the shirt for washing, along with the vessels, and after she was finished, she hung the shirt up to dry for the night.

The shirt didn't dry completely; it never did.

Raj awoke to a new day, threw on his soggy shirt and

pants, ate some gunji, and started off to school. The morning air was already warm with thick humidity and pressed his moist clothes to his skin. His legs chafed against the wet cloth uncomfortably. The buttons had come off his pants long ago, and he held them awkwardly as he walked so that they would not slide down. With his other hand, he grasped his precious, fraying books close to him.

"Hey! Where'd you go last night?" One of the older boys from the cheri pressed something into Raj's hand with a nod. "You missed hanging out. You're with your books too much." Raj opened his hand to see a *beedi*, a makeshift cigarette of a pinch of tobacco rolled into a leaf. He knew if a teacher caught him, he would get a beating. Or maybe Paulraj, the school's headmaster, would catch him. Raj shivered. The headmaster was known to give a nice beating to any student who repeatedly broke the rules. But Raj's friends were doing it. He slowed to put the beedi in his mouth and drew in its foul air. Then he pulled his sagging shorts up one last time and ran to catch up with his friends.

Raj wished he could hide by himself with his books. Unfortunately, Raj couldn't hide much in school.

"Hey, Post Box!" The usual banter had begun. Raj stepped past the freshly painted "Caldwell Primary School" sign that gazed so regally upon all who entered and braced himself for the bullies.

As hard as teachers try to coax creativity and love for learning out of their students, there's nothing like bullying to inspire incredible flights of imagination in children. In a moment of sheer brilliance, one of the boys surveyed the holes in Raj's clothes, and the words "post box" escaped his lips. His eyes widened as he slowly realized the cleverness of his analogy—after all, both had holes. As he looked to his neighbor for affirmation, a smile and another pair of mischievous eyes answered. The name was catchy. He was a hero. And Raj was christened "post box" for the rest of the year.

They all knew Raj was from the cheri and would keep

themselves away from him except for when they saw an opportunity to throw chiding insults. Raj tried to stay near his own people, the others from the cheri. This morning he sat on his usual bench with a little squelch as his sodden shorts met the polished wooden seat. He scooted over, leaving a residue of water where he had just been.

"Ew, he peed again!"

Embarrassment seeped out of Raj like the water from his clothes. He could feel all eyes on him, piercing through the holes in his shirt. He glanced up. A girl in front of him was inspecting the blue ribbon on her pigtail. A boy to his left picked his nose, then caught his glance awkwardly. *Good*, he thought, *the fewer people who notice me, the better.*

But it was difficult not to be noticed. All the students and all the teachers knew he was from the cheri. A degrading tone, a withheld smile, an order to clean and fetch supplies— each interaction silently affirmed that every student from the cheri was simply in a different category than the other children. If the other children were asked to clean their teacher's house, the parents would fuss. Raj couldn't help but ask himself, Why only me? No explanation was given; no questions were raised—at least not aloud. This was simply the way things were.

Nevertheless, the school did maintain equality in one most integral way. Most likely, it was the fruit of a legacy of fairness that grew from Bishop Caldwell himself. Caldwell Primary School strove to *grade* fairly, regardless of a student's background. These equal standards laid a foundation that would enable any student of ability to succeed. Raj continued to excel in school. By the fourth standard, he rose to be one of the best students in his class.

Teacher Madam Thangam entered the room and began to pass out exams. Her name meant "golden," and she positioned herself to achieve gold in whatever task was before her. Her forehead bore a red bindi, a dot marked on her forehead by the temple priest that morning.

She carried with her an intimidating aura of excellence,

and a disdain for anything less emanated from between her eyes and down her nose. Her loyalty to integrity defined her and gave her a certain transparency. She walked with purpose even when she had nowhere to be, and the children found themselves straightening their posture and their clothes whenever they entered her presence.

Her family was well respected and deeply religious. Her husband presided as headmaster in a different school. They were quite well-off and contributed generously to the esteemed Anaigudi Youth Association. The Anaigudi Youth Association tried to enlighten the upper-caste children about the richness of their culture and the importance of its preservation. In this way, they affirmed the children's superior status in their society. Everyone from the cheri feared her husband. He was known to be a leader in the community and an enforcer of caste violations. The high-achieving headmaster and schoolteacher put a premium on acquiring an excellent education for their sons, Vinoth and Perumal, and their younger daughter, Vanitha, who sat a few desks away from Raj.

Madam Thangam placed the exams on each desk, one by one, but slowed at Raj's desk.

"Class," she said, with a dreadful stiffness in her tone, "let's honor Raj. He has scored the highest marks on this exam." She continued to pass out the other exams as the silence in the room lingered uncomfortably. Then she came to her daughter, Vanitha. The silence grew even more tense.

Vanitha was a quiet, sweet girl and most certainly the prettiest girl in the class. The entire town adoringly called her the "angel of Anaigudi." She was a smart girl and had scored well, but not to the level of her parents' expectations for her.

"You have scored…" her mother and teacher lingered on the last word, provoking unbearable suspense. The students stared at their desks as if too preoccupied to pay attention, but they were captivated. The entire room held its breath.

"Second, Vanitha. Second. You let this boy from the cheri do better than you?" A couple of students raised their eyes to survey the scene. Vanitha fingered the corner of her exam paper. Her eyebrows furrowed, and her mouth turned down as if she were concentrating very hard. In reality, she was trying not to cry.

"I'm sor—" she began.

Her mother smacked the girl's knuckles with a wooden ruler. "This should not happen. There are no excuses."

The judgment had been passed, the gavel brought down, and the teacher satisfied. The students relaxed, but Raj's heart wrenched. He would have felt better if the teacher had beaten him instead of her.

The class resumed, and Teacher Thangam discussed various math problems, then read, then talked, then read, then discussed. Vanitha had sunk into her chair and was tracing the wood grains that ran along her desk. One of her friends leaned over to whisper something, then stopped herself and awkwardly stared at her desk for a moment before turning to a girl on her other side.

At recess, Raj waited at the door while the rest of the students exited. At last, Vanitha stepped out.

"Vanitha—I'm...I'm sorry." Raj didn't know what else to say. He felt like he should do something, but there was nothing to do. He saw her older brother, Vinoth, wrestling with some of the other high-caste boys, then looked at the ground. If the other kids saw them talking too much, they would give him a hard time.

"Rajendran, it's not your fault." She was only nine, but she spoke like she saw her mother do. Breathing in, she straightened up and looked Raj in the eyes. "It's not your fault—it's just how it is."

They stood there for a little while, watching their classmates run around the yard and the Indian flag gliding aimlessly in the slow breeze. Despite the outside pressures, or maybe because of them, a friendship began. The soft moment lingered, then passed. Vanitha ran to be with her friends, and Raj split to join the boys from the cheri loitering in the corner of the field.

Raj walked home that day, imagining himself with his new friend, Vanitha. However, as he turned the corner to his cheri, all his thoughts shattered as he nearly smacked head-on into a brutal reminder of who his people were.

The man was a Paraiyan from a neighboring cheri and stood with a thick, four-foot metal rod pierced through both of his cheeks. Puss oozed from the untreated punctures and mixed with crusted paint on his cheeks. His eyes were crazed with the suffering of a man who has not eaten for days while at the same time enduring immeasurable pain.

The festival had begun.

chapter six

Ominous drums pounded from the cheri's little temple, and people busily finished preparations. The man with the rod through his cheeks gestured with open hands as Raj pressed past him.

"Any money for the man?" an older man asked Raj. He had been designated as the *Poojary* and would conduct the coming rituals. "He has endured the pain of the *Alagu Kuthuthal* for the gods now for an entire week. What he collects will be given to the Brahmin priest. The gods might have mercy on us if we do so." Raj shook his head but hoped his parents had given some. They said the gods could bring droughts and disease if they were angry.

The Brahmin priests would keep their distance from these interactions but would encourage them all the same. No Paraiyan would ever be allowed to enter high-caste temples nor take part in Hindu functions as those gatherings' purity was vigilantly guarded by the Brahmin and other high castes. Unworthy to even spectate the rituals and sacrifices that gave salvation, their only hope glimmered beyond the horizon of death.

That faint hope was that, if they performed their duties well, they might return in a better position for their next life, and if they pleased their god, he might make life on Earth a little easier. Thus, the Paraiyans dutifully worshipped their god, and they would do whatever their god asked to grovel for mercy.

Whether or not the Brahmins believed these traditions appeased the gods and helped the Paraiyans secure a better next life, these primitive and gruesome traditions would keep the Paraiyans in their place and deliver a nice gratuity to the priests.

The drums beat louder and louder from the temple, and the elder looked over.

"We are beginning. Come," he said to Raj.

Some three hundred people had gathered around the temple. Raj found his family and stood close to them. The gates had been swung open, revealing the idol of their god: Sudalai Madan.

All Paraiyans worship this god, the god of the graveyard. He stands with his sword drawn, eyes crazed, and fangs unfurled. Painted garlands of flowers and golden necklaces adorn his chest as trophies of his prowess. His skin is black like the people who worship him, and he is savage, like the worship he demands. Tradition tells that Shiva, one of the main gods in the Hindu cosmos, created Sudalai Madan to protect his graveyard from evil spirits. However, other stories say that he was banished to Earth after he was discovered to prefer eating human flesh over the gods' divine nectar.

The latter seems most in line with the worship he receives. The Paraiyans had little to give to their god, but what they had, they gave. And even when their resources were gone, they could give their pain.

Raj strained his eyes to see through the swaying bodies.

"The spirit has come!" the old painted man shouted as two men beside him began to dance wildly. The rhythmic cacophony of drums and shouts resonated through the people's souls and demanded reverence like the crack of a whip to a steer.

A clay pot, flaming out its top from the coals inside of it, was passed to one of the dancing men. He grasped it, rolling his eyes back with pain as the hot pot scalded his hands, but he continued to dance.

"See how he grasps the pot with his bare hands!" the painted man shouted. "It is the spirit of our god that lets him do this. The god is pleased."

Elated cries ran through the audience. The drums

continued to beat as glowing coals, still smoldering from the fire, were laid out in a ten-foot path.

"Now the firewalk!" the man exclaimed.

Men from the cheri lined up in front of the coals. Then in self-abusive surrender, they tread on the ten-foot trail of burning hot coals. Raj watched with wide eyes as Antony joined them. The men's calloused feet blistered with the heat, but the god was pleased.

Now the drums beat more slowly, menacing like the soft steps of a tiger before he makes his kill. The methodical beating had lulled the crowd into a communal stupor. Now families brought whatever savings they had to set on a stage at the idol's feet. Plantain stalks were set beside pots of rice on a fire. The rice was prepared as a dish called *pongal*, which boiled over, the creamy excess cascading down the sides of the clay pot. What boiled over was said to be offered to the god. Then the Poojary handed the food back to the families to eat.

Raj's family brought their cock along with a pot of rice. Every sacrifice the family had made throughout the entire year to raise and care for the cock culminated in the crack of the cock's neck.

Then a young goat was led through the crowd. One of the dancing men stepped up to the goat, and the wrestle began. Two pairs of widened eyes met: man's and goat's. The thumping drums sped alongside the racing hearts in the crowd.

The man now held the goat down with his bare hands. With the gnashing of his teeth against the warm hide that covered the goat's fragile, pulsing neck, he broke the throat and drank the blood.

As if delighted by the man's actions, the spirit of their god, Sudalai Madan, seemed to manifest in the man. The warm red blood flowed down his dark lips as he ran around the village in frenzied mania, then disappeared into the night.

Suddenly Raj's mother began to move beside him. Kanni was overcome with dancing, and the crowd ushered her to the front. She convulsed with the beating of the drums uncontrollably as more throaty cries rang through the crowd.

"The spirit of her sister-in-law!" the Poojary exclaimed. Years ago, Aandi's sister passed away. Because she died a virgin, the cheri believed the gods had taken her to become a goddess with them. The community hoped that her spirit would be willing to function as the conduit between the people and the gods. Now every year, Kanni was overtaken by her spirit.

"Let her speak!" the Poojary called out. The crowd hushed, and the drums slowed. In a trance, Kanni danced and then began to prophesy.

"Good…" she slurred. "Good crops, good rain. This year we will be safe from sickness and death." The crowd cheered. Whether or not the prophecies were fulfilled, they held enough power over the people to direct their steps.

The man who had split the goat's throat reappeared, wilder than before. The goat's blood had dried in his matted hair and in dark trails running down his neck. Freshly turned earth clung to the dried blood. In his hands and mouth, he carried human bones. He had just returned from the graveyard. Now he flung himself into the crowd. His yellowing teeth crunched the dried human bones, producing chilling cracking sounds.

The people feasted on rice, plantains, goat meat, and chicken meat until late into the night. Then Raj and his family settled into their sleeping places on the ground of their hut, but Raj did not sleep very well. He felt like a different person from the one he was at school. It felt like here, in the festival, his people were acting as the savages everyone else deemed them to be. Raj drifted into a restless sleep with images of blood and gnashing teeth surfacing through his dreams.

The brutal tragedy of the situation was that even the Paraiyan god was inferior to their other gods. Even he was subject to the caste system: presiding over the graveyard was deemed polluting to the other gods. For all the gifts, all the sacrifices, and all the pain, the cheri's situation remained the same. For generations, they suffered as landless laborers, unable to move up because of their untouchable status. Perhaps this god delivered them from small hardships, but could this god, who himself was subject to inferiority, deliver them from their ultimate plight, the system that preserved their painful vulnerability?

Raj and Vanitha tag-teamed scoring the best grades for the rest of the year. By the fifth standard, Raj scored the best marks overall in his class, which made him the class leader. It was a weighty title, because fifth graders were the oldest kids in the school. Because of his position, he was assigned to watch over the ingredients that would be used to cook the midday meals.

As Raj shut the kitchen storeroom, the latch gave an ornery creak. Raj inserted the key into its lock. Every day the cook would come, and Raj would ration the ingredients: 5 kg wheat, 1 kg sugar, salt, and curry, and give them to the cooks. Then he would track each coming and going in the register and finish with his signature.

All too often, his friends would ask him to swipe some food for them. Raj thought of the first time he had been so tempted. It would be so easy. And yet, he had never been given such trust before. The teachers' confidence in him inspired him to retain it. Against the grumbles of his stomach, he shook his head and latched the cupboard. Raj checked the books often and kept the key safe.

One day Raj locked up the storeroom at the end of school, only to jump at the sound of a clearing throat just behind him. Then he jumped again, for it was Paulraj, the headmaster. Paulraj's bald head shined like a scepter of righteous judgment. Panicked, Raj scoured his memories to see what he had done wrong. Discipline seemed imminent, but Raj had no idea what to confess. His heart raced; his thoughts fumbled. Raj resigned himself to his fate and stepped toward the man, still trying to identify his transgression.

It was then that he realized Paulraj was smiling at him.

"Do you know what tomorrow is?" he asked.

How could he not? Green, orange, and white ribbons had been placed around the school in preparation for the biggest day of the year. Tomorrow was India's Independence Day.

"Yes, sir," Raj answered.

"Very good. And do you know what that means?"

Raj looked away, searching for what he was supposed to say.

The headmaster could tell that Raj was struggling to answer, so he sighed and continued to speak. "Every year, we have a ceremony where we gather around the flagpole."

Of course, Raj knew this, but he could not understand how this was important enough for the headmaster to tell him personally.

He continued. "I, along with"—he gestured toward Raj—"the class leader, raise the flag. It is an honor, and I will not do it without you."

Raj's eyes widened. He knew the tradition well; he had seen it every year. But never in his dreams had he imagined he would stand in front of the entire school and raise the Indian flag. Part of him was excited, the other part of him terrified.

The headmaster chuckled as Raj processed it all. "You'll be ready by tomorrow, won't you?"

Raj, speechless, nodded his head.

"Excellent. Then I shall see you tomorrow at the flagpole."

That Independence Day, August 15, 1978, a hundred best outfits and perfectly tied ribbons on impeccably braided pigtails gathered around the courtyard to honor their country.

Raj stood side by side with the headmaster by the flagpole. Raj shouted into the crowd the first line of their nation's pledge, "India is my nation," and a hundred little voices echoed back. Then he yelled, "I love my nation." And again, a hundred voices echoed back, "I love my nation."

The exulting tune of India's national anthem, "Jana Gana Mana Athi," shrilled throughout the town, falling irreverently flat while small orange, white, and green flags waved exuberantly through the crowd. The teachers sternly corralled the excited children, and the music conductor wiped his brow in fretful concentration.

In somber dignity, Raj took the weathered rope in his hands. Together he and the headmaster pulled the rope down, little by little. The schoolchildren followed the movement of his hands with wide eyes in their tiny faces and raised their own hands in salute. Raj glanced through the crowd, and his eyes met Vanitha's. She was smiling at him. To her left stood a group of his friends from the cheri, waving their flags. They beamed, and so did Raj. They could never have dreamed a Paraiyan from the cheri would be raising the national flag with the headmaster.

The orange-, white-, and green-striped flag rested, sheltered from the wind. With every thrust downward, the flag ascended. Two hundred eyes watched him as Raj, a Paraiyan, scheduled caste, raised their emblem of national pride. The strip of saffron caught the shimmer of the afternoon sun first. It stood for courage, and the green below it, fertility. The wind gathered in the cloth's folds and slowly revealed the blue chakra wheel on the middle white stripe. The circular blue wheel represented unity; the white background symbolized peace and truth. Thirty-one years after India's independence, Raj hoisted the ideals that the founding fathers so longed to grasp. Could that ideal be reached, that to every human, even an untouchable, belonged the freedom of India?

That day, the schoolchildren clasped their hands together in a huge circle around the flagpole. If people could have looked down from the sky, they might have thought they saw the chakra wheel forming on the school grounds. And yet, in some of those that day, an uneasiness began to simmer. For in that small boy from the cheri, honored and elevated, they saw a threat.

chapter seven

"In those days, the dog was freer than his master." A dwindling cooking fire cast light on the grimy faces of cheri children as they crowded around one of the oldest men in the village, Raj's uncle, who sat cross-legged, stoking the small fire as he entranced the children with stories of old.

"The south Indian mutt—bony, and with short, coarse fur—they may not be pretty, but these are survivalists. They survive on the good graces of the local god and the bones tossed their way."

The children nodded.

"Should any person toss the scraps from their table to them, them dogs'll quickly turn on each other. They know their survival depends on the food people give 'em, and they'll beg. Their loyalty is to the one that fed 'em." The old man stared into each of the children's faces to make sure his point had been made.

"Every once in a while, a human comes along and adopts a stray one. Such was the dog of my father, Raj's grandfather," he said, gesturing toward Raj, "back when Raj was just a boy. We all named the dog 'Puppy' and there was no person this dog loved more than Raj's grandfather. The dog barked at intruders and fawned over his master's children. That dog prided himself in his family.

"Now, then there are the *purebreds*. Before they are even weaned, they are wanted and chosen. The value of their breed attracts wealthy owners. They are cleaned, brushed, pampered, and secured with the collar of their weighty pedigree. The perks come with expectations. They are to be well-behaved, stay by their masters, and protect...which they do.

"They know who they belong to and know that their master has power…which they figure is somehow endowed upon them. They aren't scared like the other dogs—*they* are scary! Such were the two dogs of Velpandi."

The children knew the name well. When the British East India Company arrived in the 1600s, certain Indians of the high castes fell into their good graces. Sometimes the alignment proved to be incredibly profitable, as was the case with Velpandi's family. His ancestors collected taxes, and when the British left, they gave a large piece of land to Velpandi's family. Most of the land around Raj's village belonged to Velpandi, as did the wealth extracted from it.

The man saw to it that his children studied and married well. His son became a headmaster and his daughter-in-law became a teacher—none other than Raj's teacher, Thangam. Vanitha was their daughter, and they had two sons.

The people of the cheri feared Velpandi, and now that the man was old and confined himself to his home, the people's fear of Velpandi lived on in the fear of his son, Vanitha's father.

There were reasons for this fear.

Satisfied with the children's wide, scared eyes at the sound of "Velpandi," Raj's uncle continued.

"Now, Velpandi grew very fond of riding his horse around his land every afternoon, and so every afternoon the beautiful purebreds would parade their sleek coats and white teeth through the plantations with their master and his horse.

"One day, the entourage trotted by the cheri. It was that area we call 'no man's land' which, as you know, means no man really spends time there. However, in the same moment that Puppy happened to be wandering there, Velpandi came around with his horse and dogs. The dogs saw each other first. All ears were up, tails straightened, and fur bristled. The horse whinnied. The dogs threw themselves into each other, for master and for country. With one large stick, Velpandi separated the squabble, but that was not enough to stifle the fury swelling in 'im. He took out a pistol and shot at Puppy. The bullet missed."

Now the children gasped.

Raj's uncle contorted his face to mimic the wealthy landowner. "'When I come back, I should not see this dog alive!' he shouted to the nearest person around. He gestured with the tip of his pistol, just like that. 'Tell the owner to kill this thing! Otherwise, I will kill him,' he said. With an icy slap of the reins, he galloped off, his purebreds running with 'im. The people who had seen it all told Raj's grandfather.

"I remember that day when I watched Raj's grandfather look sadly down at his dog, panting by his side.

"He buried Puppy under the lime tree just behind Raj's home."

The children got up, disgruntled by the sad ending. Raj, however, stayed. He couldn't help but feel like the story meant something more than just a dog buried under the lime tree.

He realized he himself felt like one of those mutts.

Which made the end of the story all the more unsettling.

chapter eight

The sun gently warmed Raj's skin as he roamed through the tamarind trees. The woody stalks stretched just over his head, not high enough to block the sun but enough to block his vision. The branches drew themselves into a cocoon around him. The heat swallowed his energy, but he felt peace in the tiny hollow. Hard times had hit him and his family, but here he could hide away from reality. *Just half an hour*, he thought to himself—half an hour to be anywhere but school. Raj was in eighth grade now.

His stomach churned uncomfortably, searching for something to gnaw on. His mind muttered through anxious thoughts. A betel vine grew next to him, and he plucked one of its green, heart-shaped leaves. He rolled the betel leaf into a makeshift beedi and lit the end. Raj and the others from the cheri had started smoking beedies, and Raj liked it. It took the edge off his hunger. The real ones had a pinch of tobacco inside. At least this one made him feel like he was smoking.

Raj sunk into the hollow, drifting through memories. Fifth grade had been a glorious year, and his last day at Caldwell's Primary School had come all too quickly. The teacher had shared the final scores of each student—Raj's at the top—then described how to enroll in the next school. Like Raj's older brothers, most from the cheri would drop out after primary school—if they even made it that far. But as the teacher spoke, Raj felt a hand rest lightly on his shoulder. He turned to see the beautiful face of Vanitha, her eyes silently imploring. Then she whispered in his ear, "You'll enroll, won't you?"

Raj had stayed deathly still, startled at her forwardness. Yet, he couldn't help feeling a flutter in his heart. She gently shifted away from him before anyone else could notice. But her urging was all Raj needed to make his decision. The fact that a beautiful high-caste girl was encouraging him to enroll in the next level of school may not have been the *only* reason he did it, but it was certainly a major factor.

He had returned home that day, nervous about asking his parents to stay in school. He was shocked by his father's answer.

"Your mother and I have been talking. We want you to stay in school too and will do what we can. Maybe you could be like your Uncle Selvaraj one day. He is the only man from this cheri who ever made it to high school." Selveraj lived in the city of Tirunelveli. It was the closest major city to Raj's cheri but was still miles away. "We do know that his education helped him get a good job. Maybe one day you will be like him, a man of the pen. We will see what we can do."

Raj and his family decided he would attend Caldwell Centenary Memorial Higher Secondary School in Idaiyangudi, the neighboring village to Anaigudi, that taught grades six through ten. Vanitha was to be sent to Ignatius Convent in Tirunelveli. Though far away, it was one of the best prep schools in the area. She would return home only on school breaks.

A pang of sadness ran through Raj at these memories as he brushed through the low-lying branches. Continuing his schooling had seemed so wonderful then….Raj turned around in the expanse of dust. The yellowing, thorny trees seemed to shrivel in the heat. It was the dry season now, and the earth had begun to crack.

The last monsoon had brought little rain and the parched plantain trees had struggled to bear fruit. The plantation had lost money, so the landowner took the bulk of the profits and withheld most of the share promised to Raj's family—this way he sheltered himself from taking the loss.

The overseer, in turn, shoved the old account book in Aandi's face, muttering about the negative balances and how Aandi and his family now owed the overseer for loss, in addition to the groceries the owner had purchased for them that year. The family was in debt to the plantation and would have to pay the debt back with interest. Aandi stared at the scribbles on white paper, bewildered and unable to read them.

"We have all the accounts," the overseer had said, raising his hand in patronizing reassurance. "Don't worry, I have maintained all the accounts for you." It seemed like every other year, the family was in debt. This drought had hit the plantation particularly hard, and the family couldn't afford the annual school tuition for Raj. His school fees amounted to twenty rupees per year. In today's money, that would be about $7.86: small for a yearly fee, yet completely unaffordable for Raj's family at the time.

Kanni had been begging the administration, promising to pay as soon as she had the funds. She had begged her landlord to loan her more money. She had done all she could.

Raj had hoped that he could get through exams. Every day he had feared he would be asked to leave. He just hoped he could make it to finals and complete the semester. It was nearly summer; exams would be in a few weeks.

Now anxiety and hunger swirled through him. If his family couldn't afford to pay for his classes, they certainly couldn't afford for him to have lunch. His lunch meals had ended with the fifth grade. Now lunch was simply a luxury his family could not afford. Every day around noon, he left the school while his classmates ate and then slipped back in before the next class began.

He just had to get through finals. Then he could return to the fields to help his family.

Raj had made the mistake of staying around for lunch during some of his first days in that school. He and his Paraiyan friends had all sat down and begun the usual ritual of unpacking their lunches, or dabas, and announcing what

54

food they brought. The sharing and distribution of goods began, then always came the dreaded question, "Raj, where is your food?" "Do you need food?" And they would make him eat with them. Raj didn't have it in him to tell them he would never have food. As kind as their sharing was, Raj could never be on the giving side, to share with them when they needed. Their generosity was sweet in the moment, but Raj's need was not a single event, it was his life. He could never be that friend back to them.

So now he hid.

Raj took one last puff of the beedi, then stood up. He pushed through some low-lying palm leaves and slipped back onto the school grounds. He quietly shuffled into the classroom with the others. His absence had been unnoticed.

The afternoon waned as school rambled on at a dull pace. Arithmetic, history, and their native language, Tamil. A single fan brought relief to the teacher at the front of the class. The children sat in their desks, enveloped in heat. An occasional breeze was their only respite. The children yawned as flies buzzed and clocks ticked. Finally, they came to the last hour, then the last half-hour, then the last fifteen minutes.

Just five more minutes, Raj thought.

Suddenly a school administrator entered. He trotted to the teacher, and they murmured to one another.

"Class, stay one moment," the teacher commanded.

"Rajendran?" the administrator inquired, looking at a paper.

Raj froze.

"Yes, there you are. Rajendran, you have not paid for your tuition, so you will not be able to write your exams if you do not pay in time."

The class gasped, and Raj couldn't breathe. All eyes fixed on him. Raj was the top-ranked student in the class. They watched to see what he would do. Wide-eyed and petrified, Raj blinked, trying to hold back tears.

"Sir, please," Raj whispered, devastated. His cheeks began to burn. His heart pounded, and his thoughts raced. Raj grasped the fraying book on his desk. He couldn't bear to look at the shock on his friends' faces. All he could think of was how hard he had worked that year to do well in class and how hard his parents had worked to let him be there.

"Sir, please," he pleaded again. His eyes were fixed downward to his desk.

"You will not be able to write your exams unless you pay for your tuition," the administrator repeated, this time exasperated. With a click of his hard shoes, he turned and exited.

The class scurried awkwardly out of the room while Raj crumpled into his chair. He was crushed. He felt every inquisitive eye burn deeper into his humiliation. He wished he could be alone and invisible.

"Raj?"

Raj turned to see one of his classmates from the cheri.

"Raj, you're our best student. This—this shouldn't happen to you."

Raj looked hard toward the ground. He couldn't bear the sympathy. A dreadful pain was welling in his throat, and his eyes had become hot. Any more sympathy, and he wouldn't be able to stop the tears that welled in his eyes.

"Thank you," Raj croaked. It was all he could manage.

"Raj," the boy continued tentatively.

Raj turned away, wishing the boy would leave him alone.

"Raj, did I ever tell you about my sponsor?"

The voice weakly penetrated through the deafening maelstrom of emotions and thoughts swirling inside Raj. Raj sighed. Maybe whatever his friend had to say would distract him from his pain.

He could use the distraction.

"It's part of this program where somebody in another country provides everything I need for school. These two men run the program, and they give me breakfast in the morning, tutor me. The best part is, they even pay my school fees. I'd be out working the fields if it weren't for them!"

Raj slowly raised his head.

"You mean that somebody in another country would pay for *me* to go to school?" Raj asked, doubtfully. He did not believe it.

Nevertheless, his friend continued to assure him it was true. "Yes, they *want* to."

Raj was incredulous. He knew he was a nobody. No, he was less than a nobody; he was a Paraiyan from the cheri.

"And there is this man, you see, who runs these morning meetings. Every morning he feeds idlis to the students."

Raj's eyes widened, and his stomach grumbled. Idlis were the special steamed patties of rice served with spicy coconut chutney that Kanni would only make once a year for the cheri festival. She would spend the whole first day of her labors in preparation, collecting the rice from the paddies, boiling and unsheathing them, boiling the rice and lentils, then mixing them for hours by hand to create the batter. The children would excitedly crowd around their mother as she fussed with and turned the batter. Raj would always be too excited to sleep the night before.

The boy continued to describe the morning meeting. "He tells us stories about self-discipline. He reads some wise things from a big black book. He even helps me with my homework. When one boy's family began to struggle and kept him home to work in the fields, this man came to his parents and encouraged them to send their boy back to school."

"What is this?" Raj asked. It sounded too good to be true.

"It's called…" and with a flourish of wide-eyed wonder, the boy declared, "Bright Future."

Raj couldn't have known it then, but what he'd just heard was about to change his life.

chapter nine

The Bright Future center was in a building just behind the old Bishop Caldwell Church in Idaiyangudi, the town where Raj attended secondary school. It looked welcoming enough, graciously doused in the shade of a grove of sheltering trees.

Raj sheepishly stepped into the courtyard and stood in front of the building, a large wooden structure with a porch on the front. "Bright Future: Caldwell Karunai" had been painted on the side of the door. Raj's heart pounded. Slowly, he climbed the few steps up to the porch, wincing slightly with every squeak the steps made. Then he took one last deep breath and stepped inside.

Before him sat a desk piled with papers, and behind the papers, a young man. The man had the light caramel skin and features of a north Indian, handsome eyes, and an impressive shock of shiny black hair. He looked like one of the north Indian heroes in the comics Raj would pass by in the marketplace. He couldn't have been older than twenty-five. Raj stared at him awkwardly and in awe.

The man raised his eyes from his work and smiled.

Raj stepped back uncertainly.

"You must be Raj. Your friends have told me about you," the man said reassuringly. He stood up and walked around his desk to offer Raj a handshake.

The social worker carried himself with dignity, and he spoke like a well-educated man. But Raj noticed the man's clothes were faded from much wear and washing, quite like his own. And the man's smile surprised Raj—it was as if the man *wanted* Raj to be here. Raj relaxed a little; he felt that he could talk to this man.

"I am Sujeevan Dass. I am the Bright Future manager for this area. Your friends tell me that you are standing first in your class," he said.

Raj straightened himself and said, "Yes, sir."

Sujeevan sat on his desk to get closer to Raj's level and looked him up and down with softly pursed lips.

"Now, what is this I hear? You must drop out due to nonpayment of fees?" he asked.

"Yes, sir," replied Raj. He looked down at his bare, calloused feet.

The man turned to sift through some papers behind him. It was only a moment, but that moment was unbearable. Raj shifted uncomfortably. Finally, Sujeevan spoke.

"We will pay your fees—provided you are willing to keep studying in school." Sujeevan looked up toward Raj inquisitively, a smile betraying his kindness.

Raj's heart leaped. Willing to keep doing school? How was that even a question? Raj's future had been a dark, murky cloud, and now hope broke through it like a sunbeam. He didn't have to go to the plantation. Not yet. Perhaps he might just graduate from high school! He might just be the first person ever to graduate in his entire community. A grin erupted over Raj's face.

"Now there is one stipulation," Sujeevan explained. "You must attend the morning meetings. We conduct a story lesson and have a time of tutoring. We'll provide some breakfast for you as well. Idlis."

Idlis! His friend had been right after all. Raj could not contain his astonishment. It seemed impossible, yet this Bright Future seemed to want to take care of Raj and bestow upon him all they had to give.

As Raj turned to leave, Sujeevan rested his hand on his shoulder. Raj stiffened, shocked. Nobody ever touched people from the cheri. This man didn't seem to care.

"I will see you tomorrow morning then," Sujeevan said.

They bid each other goodbye, and Raj skipped all the way home.

The next morning, Raj arrived at the meeting extra early, and as he saw what waited for him, an uncontrollable grin spread over his face. Sujeevan's promise was delivered on a plantain leaf: chutney, *sambar*, and two beautiful idlis.

The compound was full of some five hundred children, varying from untouchable like Raj to high-caste, but all needy. They happily grabbed their idlis and made their way to different rooms. Raj navigated to a room with his age group. Another social worker, Jose, began the meeting with a clearing of his throat. He flipped open the big black book that Raj's classmates had mentioned and asked, "Can anyone tell me the Bible verse we read yesterday?"

A girl in the back stood and, in a quavering but determined voice, recited, "For God so loved this world that he...he gave his son Jesus...that who believes in him will not perish but have eternal life."

Raj recognized those words. At Caldwell's Primary School, they had also memorized verses and heard stories about Jesus. Back then, a piece of candy provided more than enough incentive for Raj to memorize whatever they asked.

"Very good. This verse is saying that Jesus is the one God, and Jesus is your friend if you will have him. He is always with you, watching over you, and he loves you." The morning meeting transitioned into storytime and homework. Soon Raj and the other children set off toward school, but the words of the lesson lingered in Raj's mind.

Raj walked home that evening deep in thought when a raucous noise pierced his thoughts. The compound emitted earsplitting music through squealing speakers to announce the cultural evening. The night was sponsored, most likely, by Vanitha's family. The Anaigudi temple had been dressed in golden lights, and people garbed in their best outfits swayed toward the entrance.

Inside, people sang and danced. It was beautiful. The

glowing lights shimmered through swaying silks, and shadows danced across the compound. All the women had swathed themselves in their newest saris and gleaming gold jewelry. They glided gracefully in the dim light.

Forty dark faces watched shyly from outside the compound. A five-foot wall surrounded the temple compound, establishing its cold boundary between pure and defiled, a blunt reminder to the Paraiyans of their place. They would not dare venture inside, as their presence would defile the sacred space. Still, they could watch. Raj grabbed a large stone and placed it by the wall to step onto so that his eyes rose just above the wall.

In the center of the compound stood a small portico. A Brahmin priest had come into the portico where the idol stood to mutter his inscrutable sacred mantras to the god and wave incense. Only the Brahmin priests were allowed inside that area. The rest of the townspeople stroked the wall of the sacred enclave and danced around the other shrines in the courtyard. They garlanded the shrines with flowers and fruits and danced to the beating drums in whimsical worship.

The Paraiyans leaned against the wall that separated them and the ceremony and swayed longingly with the rhythms inside. To Raj's left, a father held his son on his shoulders. His shoulders began to droop, and he shifted under the weight of his son. The father rested his son carefully on the wall.

"Hey!" one of the townspeople inside the compound called out. Suddenly he rushed to the wall and shoved the child off. Immediately all ceased but the ominous pounding of drums. The townspeople inside fixated on the wall. On the other side, the child whimpered as his father brought him to his feet and held him closely.

A cluster of infuriated men came outside of the temple. Their dark eyes flashed in the unnatural light, and they grimaced, showing their teeth. With a loud smack, they hit the child again, and then the father. Both fell to the ground.

"How dare you let your child sit here!" one yelled.

Quaking, the father stood, took his child, and quickly left. Slowly, the rest of the Paraiyans slunk away. Raj slipped out with the rest of them, back into the night.

A man by the name of Mr. Williams adopted Raj as a sponsor child through Bright Future. Although Raj knew little of the man except that he lived two oceans away in America, the man was a savior to Raj. He provided for his school fees, which meant more to Raj than anything else in the world. He felt like he had a guardian looking out for him and knew no other way to communicate his gratefulness than to continue to try his hardest in school.

Raj completed his exams and finished, once again, first in his class. The morning meetings broke for the summertime and Raj joined his family working on their landowner's plantation.

Raj thought often about the morning meetings and this Jesus man they spoke of. Raj decided he would venture to church and see if he could find out more about this god.

Down the road and to the right of the Anaigudi temple stands the CSI church, still to this day. With its disproportionately tall bell tower and bright pink exterior, it is quite hard to miss. Raj had grown up hearing about the church from his elementary school teachers and one uncle, the only Christian convert in the Anaigudi cheri.

One weekend, Raj convinced his father to come along. After a cold early morning bucket bath outside their house, and dressed in two pairs of the family's best pants and shirts, they set off for the town.

Under the clang of the church bells, the town's Christians walked into the church in their vibrant saris and ironed suits. Squeaky shoes added to the symphony of rustling silk and turning papers as the congregation sat and stood in obedience to the service program.

There were a few other Paraiyans in the congregation, and

they stood in the back, behind the pews. Raj and his father quietly slipped in next to them.

The preacher's voice echoed authoritatively within the modest concrete walls of the church. A sad figure of a half-naked man tied on two crossing planks of wood gazed out over the congregation. Raj grimaced at the thought of any person being forced into that man's position.

A sea of heads loomed over Raj from his position on the floor, everyone dutifully watching the pastor. As the sermon continued, the most reverent maintained their solemn stare, and a little girl who sat in the pew in front of Raj swung her short legs idly back and forth. An old man cocked his head as if suddenly intrigued, but then surreptitiously cleaned earwax out of his ear.

"And that concludes today's homily on James, chapter two. Now let us prepare our hearts and minds for the Eucharist," announced the pastor. Suddenly the entire congregation stood. Raj jerked up in an unsuccessful attempt to blend in. The members in front of him began to stand in lines, but the Paraiyans stood still. He stayed in the back with the others. The pastor served the Eucharist, and the service ended. The little girl who sat in front of Raj jumped down and exited. The pastor removed himself—Raj had the impression he needed to wash or change or something—but the Paraiyans still waited in the back.

Raj exchanged confused glances with his father. They stayed for some time. Eventually, the pastor reemerged and began to serve the Paraiyans communion.

Raj shuffled up to the pastor. The man smiled down at him, his two eyes blurred through thick glasses. The pastor handed Raj a bit of bread and said, "Be blessed."

Neither Raj nor his father spoke as they left, even though Raj's thoughts overwhelmed him like a flood. In some ways, the church felt strangely like the temple. He didn't quite understand what was going on or what he was supposed to do, and he didn't quite feel good enough to be there. Even though the pastor spoke about the same things, it felt nothing like the morning meetings the social workers led at Bright Future.

But then again, he was allowed inside the church—that alone made it different from the temple. The statue at the far end of the church was like no other god he had seen before. Raj's curiosity lingered within him.

He decided he would return the next week.

As they exited the town and neared their cheri, Raj noticed three girls standing outside under a tree.

"Raj!" one called.

"Vanitha?" Raj asked. It must be a school break for Ignatius Convent. Raj shyly shuffled over to greet her.

As he approached her, Vanitha teetered on her feet as if wanting to step forward, but held back by an invisible fence. When Vanitha visited her home, she would gather a few of her treasured friends, announce she was going for a stroll, then steal away to the tree in the middle ground around the cheri. She knew better than to venture too close to the homes of the scheduled caste. Nor could she invite Raj to her place. Her grandfather and her father ran the house, and they were powerful men. If a Paraiyan from the cheri were to step even just inside the threshold, he would be thrown out, and then they would wash the entire house, to purify themselves from what they saw as the corruption of his presence.

"I came this way just to see you," she said, smiling. "I am doing quite well in my classes. My parents are already looking for a college in Tirunelveli for me. Oh, you will go to college too, won't you?"

"Well," Raj faltered. "Well, yes, I hope to." He looked around self-consciously. Her two friends lingered a little way away and Aandi had disappeared into the cheri. He couldn't help but feel excited to see her, and he hoped with all his might that nobody noticed that. Why did she have to be so beautiful and so kind? And why was she always so kind to Raj?

"Well, you most certainly should. You're smart enough!" Vanitha replied.

"Thanks." Raj smiled and looked at his feet.

Vanitha gathered her long, dark, braided hair in her hands and stroked the ends absentmindedly. She looked toward her friends, who smiled at her, then said softly, "Hey, I am dancing in the village tonight. My parents are hosting the evening by the temple. They are keeping seats up at the front for my friends and family. You'll come, won't you? Come and sit at the front."

If Raj even thought about sitting in those front seats, he would be beaten.

He didn't know what to say. She beamed at him in excited anticipation and somehow just didn't seem to understand Raj's uncomfortable position. Her parents had painted a beautiful world for her, and she was a beautiful person who thrived in it. But Raj knew if he entered that world, or ever got too close, either it would shatter, or he would.

Raj's heart wrenched inside of him. "Yes, Vanitha, I would love to come," he lied.

That evening, she danced to the rhythm of drums and *veena* and voice. The village swooned over her light feet and delicate smile, and as she gazed into the audience with her shining eyes, she almost thought she saw him.

II
Beginnings

My final words of advice to you is educate,
organize, agitate; have faith in yourselves.

—*Dr. B. R. Ambedkar, in an address at the All India
Depressed Classes Conference, July 18, 1942*

chapter ten

1980, Anaigudi, fourteen years old

Raj walked through the town's center with his sandals in his hand. Mud from the well-trodden road bonded to his bare feet as he walked.

No shoes, head down, don't attract attention. Towel down, uncover your chest. Nod, but don't look. The familiar thoughts rumbled through Raj. Every day he passed through Anaigudi to go to secondary school in the neighboring town, then returned through Anaigudi to get back to his village.

A concrete electricity pole leaned unstably next to a village shrine. Raj's gaze followed its lean toward the town temple. People were cleaning up chairs and marigold petals from the cultural evening the previous night. Raj turned to go the other way, walking left around the shrine. He passed the town's one bus stop, then its beautiful well. A shiny vehicle drove through the gate of a house just in front of him—Kumaresan's residence.

Raj heard his name as a child and learned to walk quickly through the part of town beside his mansion. Now that Raj was older, he understood.

Kumaresan was an influential political figure for the *Dravida Munnetra Kazhagam* political party, also known as the DMK. In 1967, he was the runner-up for the government position of the Member of the Legislative Assembly in the Radhapuram constituency. In the next election in 1971, he secured victory. The person with this political title, abbreviated to MLA, is elected to represent a district to the state government. While Kumaresan only served in that position for one term, he was recognized as "MLA" from that point onward. He drifted through other prominent roles, from panchayat president to the DMK party president in his area. Although his office lay in Thisayanvilai, the largest town in the area, he conducted many meetings in his home. Kumaresan was arguably the most powerful politician in the entire area for a full twenty years.

The house towered majestically over most of the other homes, just like Kumaresan's political influence. The only other house that stood as tall was Vanitha's. Raj wondered what important person might be in the automobile. Raj quickened his pace to duck past the CSI church and the remaining houses.

Although less than a quarter of a mile separated Anaigudi from the cheri, a familiar relief fell through Raj as he passed into the wilderness of shrubs and plantain trees that separated the settlements. Still, Raj continued to look down with hunched shoulders as he walked. It had become a habit. The area's undesirability provided refuge to Raj. After all, the townspeople only ventured through here when they had to. Raj glanced up as he passed by Caldwell's Primary School. The flagpole stood empty out front.

Beyond the school, the smokestack of the rice mill spewed its black dust. Its owner constructed the mill next to the cheri to spare the town from its ash. Now the huts in the cheri were grimy and gray. The people of the cheri constantly breathed in the ashen air. It mixed with their sweat, creating a gray mud that smeared across their dark bodies.

When the mud finally dried, it was hard to tell body from ash; they looked as if they were one. Raj turned into his village. With a sigh, he sank into the dust outside his home.

Raj suddenly jerked his head up at the sound of a squeaky bicycle. To his surprise, he saw Sujeevan Dass from Bright Future ride into the cheri. The man smiled and waved.

"Raj!" he called.

Raj leaped to his feet and ran to him. An unexplainable joy welled in his chest. Then Sujeevan clasped his light-brown arms around Raj's dark shoulders.

"Raj," Sujeevan began, "you know the storytime we have every morning?" Raj nodded. "I want to do the same thing with your village today. What do you think?" Raj nodded again, still too astonished to speak. Raj could not believe a man like Sujeevan would come to his village.

"Would you gather the children for me?" Sujeevan asked. A smile burst across Raj's face.

"Yes, sir!" Raj replied. "Mani!" he called to a younger cousin playing with an abandoned rubber tire. "Selvie, Jothi!" he called to his sisters. Some of the other children were just arriving from working in the fields or the mill. One by one, Raj called the children over to a spot by the front of the village. With the parents occupied in the fields during the day and then either busy cooking meals or drunk during the night, the children of the cheri were usually left to their own devices.

In the shade of a tree, Sujeevan sat with them and began to tell a story about a man who helped his neighbor, even though the neighbors' families didn't like each other. Then he asked the children who their neighbor was and who they could help. Raj beamed with pride as he listened with his peers.

Sujeevan was a wonderfully strange man to Raj. He couldn't understand why such an attractive, educated man would want to bother with him or his people. Most of all, Raj couldn't believe this man, this North India Hero, would care to know *him*. Yet Sujeevan seemed delighted to come. He genuinely wanted to befriend the Paraiyans.

Raj enthusiastically served as his right-hand man and, as Sujeevan returned to the cheri day after day, Raj continued to gather the children together for him. Eventually, Sujeevan trusted Raj to teach some of the classes. Raj involved himself in every way possible in the Bright Future sponsorship program. Every morning before school, he attended the early meeting, then returned for the tutoring sessions after school. Then he would walk home, call his peers together, and help them with their homework. Sujeevan's wonderful life had collided with his own, and now Raj was beginning to see himself differently. Raj started to dream that one day he could be like Sujeevan.

Sujeevan visited the village every week to tell stories and encourage the children to love their neighbors, be good to their parents, bathe and brush their teeth, and, if they were in school, to study well. Soon all the children picked up their heads at the sound of his bicycle. Sujeevan would greet them by name and clasp his hand on their bare shoulders. Raj would sit by his side.

They had never heard the kinds of things Sujeevan shared with them, just as Raj had never heard them before joining the Bright Future sponsorship. Even the simplest practices of hygiene were new to them. The children started to wash the dust off their bodies more often.

"Boys," Sujeevan called as the Bright Future meeting concluded for the morning. Raj raised his head curiously and gathered with the other boys around Sujeevan's desk.

"I understand tomorrow is a holiday," he started. His eyebrows raised playfully. "I would like to invite you over tomorrow to spend the night. We can play games, share stories, what do you say?" The boy's faces lit with excitement.

The next night, wide-eyed and silent, they shuffled into Sujeevan's residence. His home was small: one room with very modest furnishings. To the boys, however, it was a palace.

Suddenly one boy squealed. Then they all squealed. Just outside Sujeevan's home stood a shiny red motorbike. The boys rushed out to see it. Sujeevan followed, grinning.

"Yes, yes, go ahead, you can touch it," he said. "I use it to go to and from the city. It's been with me a while." Raj stroked the glossy side in awe. The metal glinted beneath his touch. Suddenly Raj frowned.

"But you could ride this everywhere! Why don't you?" he asked.

Sujeevan chuckled. "I suppose I just wanted to be friends with your village. If I came on this bike, they'd treat me differently. I wouldn't get to be just a friend."

Raj had never heard of such a thing. Sujeevan put his arm around Raj, as he often did, then said, "Everything I do is because of Jesus."

That was the only explanation he ever gave.

He called the boys back into his home, and together, they told scary stories and laughed for the rest of the night.

The summer baked on. One weekend, Raj joined Bright Future and the others in the sponsorship program for a short vacation. For three days, they danced, played games, and listened to stories about Jesus. Just before the end, the leader stood up and shared, "If you want Jesus to be your God, just ask him to be."

Raj sat there on the concrete floor, mesmerized by the possibility.

Raj had heard about Jesus in Caldwell's Primary School. But now, Raj wondered if he had seen Jesus and felt him. It was all in Sujeevan—that wonderfully strange North Indian Hero who had waltzed into the cheri with no thought for how it might be beneath him. He gave himself to the children he taught. And he made Raj feel like he was worth something.

For the first time, Raj dared to imagine following a different god.

He thought of all the sacrifices, all the dancing, all the *poojas* given to the Paraiyan's god, Sudalai Madan. All the ceremonies in the high-caste temple—so much sacrifice and devotion. He had once thought of their devotion as love and the god's giving as grace.

Yet when his people had nothing to give, they would be punished, even if the reason they had nothing to give was because of a previous punishment from the god. For so many years, his people had pleaded for this god to give them mercy, at the cost of all they had. Was their situation any better than before? Even the higher castes prayed and gave money and sacrificed to their own gods to please them.

This didn't seem like love and grace anymore. Now it seemed like a game of flattery and fear, the gods and the people alike, jockeying to get what they wanted, or in the cruelest moments, what they truly needed. It felt like slavery.

Jesus was different.

Could it be true that this god wanted good for Raj? This god did not demand any sacrifice that he had not already made himself. He had come to the dirtiest of places and brought what? Love? *Maybe for a rich man, a god would do this,* Raj thought, *but for me?* Raj came from a shoeless, worthless people. What sort of god would see a nobody like Raj, willingly suffer for him, and actually *love* him? He didn't know what it all meant, he couldn't have known, but he did know one thing—there on the cold concrete floor he whispered, "Jesus, I want to live for you."

chapter eleven

Transformation spread through Raj like wildfire. Ever since Raj began attending the morning sponsorship classes, he had been different. Either the idlis were just that good, or something about those classes inspired him to be a better person, to care about other people, and to want to help other people. At least, that was what the people in his village saw.

However, Raj not only acted differently, he *felt* like a completely different person. First of all, he simply could not grasp that another person, who had never met him, and who he was sure lived in a much higher caste than he, actually cared enough about him to pay for his school fees. All Raj knew was that this sponsor lived far away in America.

Raj knew he didn't deserve to go to school, Raj knew he didn't deserve someone to sponsor him, and yet Sujeevan assured him that this sponsor wanted Raj to go to school and was proud of him.

Nobody had ever treated him like he could be disciplined, or succeed in school, or look outside of himself to give to others. The morning meetings taught him a new way to see the world and to see himself. Something in him now believed his own life meant something and that other people's lives meant something too. His heart held an unshakable conviction that there was some God who knew him and loved him and was always watching him. Something had happened—Raj didn't know what, but he felt so much joy and love that he couldn't bear to make this God unhappy. It changed his whole character.

Now he gathered children of the cheri together and taught moral-education classes, led tutoring sessions, and aided whoever was in need in his village. Raj just couldn't help himself. The cheri was dumbstruck and started wondering where this new Raj came from. Curious, more children began to join Raj's weekend storytimes with Sujeevan in the cheri.

His transformation sparked curiosity. Mothers, fathers, sons, and daughters decided they wanted to be different like Raj, and whole families started following Raj to church. To the dismay of the more devout Hindus of the cheri, these families slowly began to realize that they didn't have to worship their old god anymore. They could be free from the painful worship Sudalai Madan demanded.

Aandi continued to accompany Raj to the CSI church, curious but reserved. As more and more people began to join, he decided he would like to be baptized with the others from the cheri. One afternoon, over one hundred members of the cheri—fathers, mothers, and children—asked Raj to baptize them and pledged themselves to Jesus.

As Aandi raised his face to the water sprinkled over him, he declared his new name—a Christian name. Though people would always refer to him by his original name, his legal name would no longer be Aandi, meaning "worthless." From that day, his legal name would be Anbalagan, "man of love and beauty."

Kanni would nod guardedly as she listened to the others in the village talk about her son. For so many years since her sister-in-law's death, Kanni had been led to dance and prophecy for the spirit, but she was tired. She wondered if perhaps this God could stop the spirit from descending upon her.

When the festival came, the village gathered in anticipation of Kanni's prophecy. She was a valuable connection to the spirits, and they needed her to appease the gods. The cheri began to beat drums in expectation. But it never came. Raj emerged from the fields later that evening. He had been praying to his God that the spirit would not come, and it never did, from that day on.

As Raj brought people from his cheri to church, it became

so packed that the Paraiyan community constructed their own little church at the entrance to their cheri. It felt like a necessary move. Once a month, the CSI pastor would visit to give them communion. On the other Sundays, Raj or one of the others from the cheri would give a sermon.

All families enjoyed Raj's storytime, the songs, and the skits performed at the church, whether they were Christian or Hindu. However, when the Christians opted out of the Hindu rituals for Sudalai Madan, tension smoldered. Anger released in short bursts of arguments, and a line of demarcation formed in the middle of the L-shaped town. The portion that had settled on government land remained Hindu, and the portion that had settled on land from the church, where Raj lived, and where the new little church stood, became Christian.

The Hindus said the Christians had turned their backs on their ancestors' god, on their tradition and people. The Christians said they had found something better and urged the Hindus to join. The conflict finally manifested in a brick wall constructed at the fulcrum of the L, separating the Hindu section from the Christian section. That wall still stands to this day. But tensions ebbed and flowed—after all, they were family, and they still respected Raj.

"'Why can't you be more like Rajendran?' That's what she said to me. I mean, come on, mapile." Raj's cousin Chitravel took a beedi from his mouth in order to release an exasperated sigh. The smoke rose lazily from his lips and lingered below Raj's nose.

It was true—the mothers loved Raj. "Raj" had become the household name for excellence.

And Raj himself wasn't quite sure what to do about that.

On the other hand, Chitravel was the delinquent boy who rolled his beedis in the corner and let his teenage angst seep out through various profanities. He'd suddenly found himself at a terrible disadvantage whenever Raj came around. He felt like he was nothing when compared to Raj—Raj who was always tutoring small children, inviting children to storytime, and volunteering to run errands for the parents without even asking for a peppermint as commission.

Chitravel wouldn't have cared about all of that, except that all the girls liked Raj too.

Chitravel ran into Raj as he was returning home from working in the fields. He complained to Raj, "I mean, my own mom compares me to you now. What am I supposed to do about that?" Then, as he took the sizzling beedi from his mouth, his dark eyes brightened. "And the girls like you. Why?"

Raj stiffened. He knew Chitravel was tough; his father was one of the angrier alcoholics in the cheri and was known to give a good beating. And Chitravel could be just as volatile. "What?" Raj asked cautiously.

"They like you. They walk with you to school, and they want to hang out with you after school. I can't figure it out." Then the boy added sulkily, "They won't let me near them."

The tension in Raj dissipated.

"That's because you're mean to them," Raj replied. "Girls don't like it when you're mean."

"Really? Aw, but I'm only teasing!" Chitravel exclaimed.

Raj shrugged and started to walk again.

Chitravel followed closely behind. "What, you mean I should…help them and stuff?" he asked, cringing at the notion.

Raj laughed. "Yes! That is what I mean." Raj turned and looked at his cousin. He was taller than Raj, and lankier too. His hair was shorn unevenly; his teeth were yellow from betel leaves; his shirt was, impossibly, even more ragged than Raj's. He was only a couple of years older than Raj, but the days working in the fields had already weathered his skin. He might have been a tough kid, but then, he had to be in order to survive. Raj felt a new compassion for the boy.

"Come on," Raj said.

Happy, Chitravel walked beside him. Their feet sloshed through the mud from the previous night's monsoon rain.

"Hey, Vanitha's in town, I hear," Chitravel said. It was an awkward conversational switch, but the subject never failed to intrigue Raj.

"Is she?" Raj replied, in another lame pretense of ignorance.

"Yeah, she came by again yesterday with her friends. Her friends don't like you, you know. They're mad you didn't come out to see her."

Raj concentrated harder on the path and didn't say anything.

"It's okay, mapile, I got your back. Just watch out for her brothers, Vinoth and Perumal, okay?" Chuckling, he gave Raj another boisterous slap and shook his shoulder. "Nah, I know you guys are friends."

Raj laughed uncomfortably. Vinoth had become a state champion in the discus and javelin and sometimes passed by the cheri on the way to one of his father's fields. He would grab Raj, and in the cool of the afternoon and the shade of the cashew trees, he would throw, and Raj would fetch. They got along well, and Vinoth often gave Raj a bag of cashews as thanks. Raj knew that would all change, however, if he ever initiated anything with Vanitha.

His laugh petered into silence as some school peers emerged around the corner. The attractive, foreboding figure of Prakash appeared in the middle. He was the son of Anaigudi's political authority, Kumaresan, and always made sure everyone knew that.

Prakash prowled nearer with an air of authority. He looked over Raj, unimpressed. The other students trotted close to his side, panting excitedly to do his bidding. They all belonged to high-caste families and were stepping into their families' prominence as they came of age. The Anaigudi Youth Association was grooming them for their coming roles in society.

The Anaigudi Youth Association was funded by Vanitha's

father and other influential families. Being the son of Kumaresan, Prakash had been designated the youth leader in the association as a soft induction into his father's political vocation. He was already a charismatic and intimidating leader, and the other children rolled over for him any chance they got.

Raj and Chitravel quickly passed to the other side of the road. The high-caste girls glared as they passed by.

The boys were less couth.

"Sewer boy!" one of them jeered, and his buddy snickered at this bit of eloquence, then stole a glance at Prakash for approval. Prakash strolled on, unbothered.

"Hey, watch out up there," another threatened, nodding up the road. They laughed and continued into the town.

All of them were angry with Raj. The girls hated him because he had stopped coming out to greet Vanitha—they had been looking forward to the spectacle of forbidden romance. The boys hated him because they were all in love with Vanitha too and were jealous of her affections. Even the cheri was afraid of Raj, or afraid of what could happen to all of them should Raj make a wrong move.

Raj couldn't help but be mad at himself, too. He knew what he wanted, and he knew what was wise, and he could not reconcile the two. Somewhere behind the large stone wall of Raj's heart lay seedlings of love and affection, but he refused to allow them to grow. Raj was aware of every time Vanitha came to visit; he could count every single one. But he simply could not go to see her.

Raj and Chitravel slowed their walk. Ahead, a small but boisterous crowd gathered along the dirt road. An ominous foreboding overcame them as they saw the police standing nearby. They got as close as they dared, hoping to get a glimpse of what was going on.

The public justice officers were trying hard to maintain the peace, but the crowd yelled and jeered and smacked, swarming around a nearly naked figure cowering in a fetal position. It was a man from the cheri, and his head had been shaved and painted. Purple bruises were forming all over his bare skin, and a small ragged cloth covered only the most vulnerable part of his body. He had been adorned with a garland of dirty sandals, a sign of dishonor.

Chitravel let out a quavering whisper. "That's our uncle, Mutihiah."

chapter twelve

Mutihiah's chief accuser angrily waved a coconut above his head, yelling something. To the side of the jeering crowd stood the quiet, intimidating figure of Vanitha's father, surveying the situation approvingly.

Mutihiah cowered on the ground, but he was not allowed to stay there. An enthusiastic onlooker brought his donkey, and the crowd thrust Mutihiah up onto the beast. Then they paraded him around the high-caste village so that everyone who wanted to could join in hurling insults and spitting at him.

Raj stared shame in the eyes that day when he looked at Mutihiah. His eyes, dark brown with yellowing whites, were tense, petrified. Mutihiah's hands feebly tried to cover himself. Under his rags and garland of sandals, his shoulders hung low. There on the donkey, all he could do was endure.

A hushed but emphatic whisper behind Raj urged, "Chitravel, Raj, get back!"

Raj turned and could just make out the whites of someone's eyes glinting in the dark jungle.

"Come here," the voice urged the two boys from the shadows. "You can't help him now—you know better than that." It was one of the men from Raj's village.

"What happened?" Chitravel asked.

"This morning, a few of us were walking to the fields and found these old coconuts on the roadside that had fallen days ago." He held one of the coconuts in his hands. It looked a few days too old to be good.

"What were you thinking?" Chitravel asked incredulously. Every Paraiyan knew that the landowners would not take kindly to them taking fruit from their land—even if it were days old. "You were asking for trouble."

"We didn't think anyone would see, but we weren't thinking straight either. We were, well, you know, we started early on the *arrack*."

Raj shuddered. Arrack was a horrible drink, at least when the Paraiyans made it. They used battery acid and all sorts of waste items to blend into toxic, illegal alcohol. It was no wonder the men had not been thinking straight.

"We had only just picked up the coconuts when that man saw us and yelled. In moments, they had grabbed Mutihiah. I only just barely got away." He looked down at the old coconut for a moment, shook his head, then threw it into the jungle.

The crowd of mockers grew tired as the sun dipped low in the sky. Eventually, owners reclaimed their sandals, the donkey was returned, and the town slipped into a peaceful slumber. Mutihiah was left lying in the street, a wilted figure of a man. When a Paraiyan took too much liberty, a mob like this was a common reaction. Raj knew that.

However, watching it happen was something else. Raj's nausea grew with every step he took toward the man. Together, he and Chitravel led Mutihiah back toward the cheri.

"Looks like the Anaigudi Youth Association is finally ready for the next festival," remarked Chitravel as they passed a freshly painted stage.

The sharp scent of drying paint made Raj's belly twist with nausea as they walked back home.

Everyone was quite surprised when two men clad in nice pants and button-down shirts strode into the cheri one day. No outsider ever came into the cheri—except Sujeevan. And these men's mannerisms and dress were completely out of place in the cheri; it was clear they were professionals.

"Selvaraj!" The cry of shock and joy pierced the cheri. Raj's Uncle Selvaraj had returned. The man was the first of the cheri to get to tenth grade, before flunking out. He had moved to the city Tirunelveli, forty miles away, and nobody had heard from him for years. The villagers shook their heads in disbelief and ran to embrace him.

"Friends! Family!" Selvaraj exclaimed. The initial greetings paused. "Everyone, please meet my friend. This is Sollalagan. He is the leader of the Ambedkar Association for our entire state of Tamil Nadu." The villagers looked at the man in awe. He looked educated and professional, yet bore himself with an ease that said he was exactly where he wanted to be.

"Thank you, comrade." Sollalagan bowed. Then he spoke with eloquent fervor. "You are all close to Selveraj's heart. In the city, he has devoted himself to the Dalit cause, for the Dalits of the cheris. This is how we met. We want to make your lives better."

They did not know what the Ambedkar Association was, but they believed this man must be important. In a frenzy, the women dashed inside to prepare chai and fruit for the guest. The eldest members of the village were summoned. The children stared.

Whatever gifts the village had to give were given to the guests, including arrack and beedies. Then with nervous smiles and much scratching of their white-haired heads, the elders turned the visitors in the direction of the one literate and responsible person they could think of: Raj.

Raj was squatting outside his door, advising a younger student in her arithmetic, when the man approached him. "So now, when you take three away from six…"

"Are you Raj?" Sollalagan asked. Some of the elders had accompanied him, curiously watching the events of this strange day unfold.

Raj looked up, puzzled at the odd sight. "Yes, I am he." Raj caught the bewildered eye of his dad, then the short, smiling figure of his uncle, Selvaraj.

"It's a pleasure," the man said. "My name is Sollalagan."

He offered his hand for a shake. "They tell me that you are the one to talk to around here." The man beamed toward Raj.

"Well, thank you, sir, I guess." Raj awkwardly stood.

Sollalagan stood by Raj's side and moved to address the villagers standing around them. "I am one of you, I am a Dalit, and I know the hard issues that plague our people. I travel through Dalit villages to share with them the noteworthy teachings of our dear founding father, Dr. Ambedkar." He turned to Raj. "Are you familiar?"

Raj tilted his head. He had heard the term "Dalit" only rarely. It was what social changers called the scheduled castes because it meant "broken" and "oppressed."

"No, sir," Raj replied. The little crowd around them murmured similar confirmation.

"Not a problem. You will soon, I hope." Sollalagan smiled down at the young teenager. His tone turned fatherly.

"Raj, you are young, but you have a lot of respect in this village. I value that."

Raj took the compliment in silence, trying to figure out who this man was and who this "Ambedkar" was. Sollalagan spoke with authority, but at the name of Ambedkar, his voice softened. Raj decided Ambedkar must be a great man.

"You know, Ambedkar was quite like you. The same thing happened to him. As a small boy, he was treated very badly in school. But he decided he would grow up to be different from his peers."

Raj tilted his head curiously.

"Ah yes, this Ambedkar was a great man. He went to America and became a lawyer. They didn't care that he was untouchable. Ambedkar came back to India when we needed him most. India was becoming a nation—we needed a constitution. He wrote our constitution and made sure that the untouchables were looked after. His whole life was devoted to his people and his nation.

"You are a shining star, just like him. The respect you've earned will allow you to do good for your community. You should use it." He paused, eyeing Raj. Sollalagan was a patient and levelheaded man, but he also knew when to push. He gave Raj a moment to take in his words. Then he asked the question he had been leading up to.

"I am looking for a leader to bring these people together to make their home a model village. Raj, I want you to lead the initiative. When you and your village are ready, I would like to conduct a meeting in your village to talk about Ambedkar and his philosophy. Will you organize this?"

"Model village?" Raj asked.

"Yes. I want you to make your home village so clean, organized, and healthy that other villages will be inspired. I will guide you. We will go through Dr. Ambedkar's teachings together. You must educate...you must organize...and..." Sollalagan paused with a glint in his eye. "You must agitate. I will be your guide, and Ambedkar, your father. You need not worry."

"Thank you, sir, but I—I need time," Raj replied.

"That is not a problem—when you are ready, send the word." With a handshake, he left.

News about the visitor spread quickly. "A state-level official, you say?" "I hear he was very impressed with Rajendran." "Our Raj? Our very own Raj talking with a state-level official?" The rumors ran through the village.

Then something amazing happened. The children Raj brought together each week for stories with Sujeevan gathered around him expectantly. The parents he had helped gather groceries for nodded their heads in approval. The boys Raj had tutored into the late hours of the night came around him with admiration. As Raj looked around him, he realized that the three hundred people of the cheri looked to him with trust—and were ready to follow him. Raj was in disbelief.

Somehow, he had been catapulted into leadership.

"I need to think," Raj said to the crowd around him, and he stole away to find some peace. He sat under his family's lime tree behind his house, and it gently stretched over him, making a soft shelter. Dusk came for a little while, then shook the dust off her feet and made way for night. Raj felt as though he were sitting on the edge of a giant turning ball, and he was going to have no other choice but to slide off into the unknown. These people counted on him to do something, and Raj was terrified.

Raj struggled to imagine his cheri different than it was now. He knew the problems they faced, but how could he change it? What if he failed?

"Why me?" he asked into the darkness. Why had this responsibility come upon him of all people? He hardly felt equipped to do anything, and he hardly felt worthy of leading anyone. He didn't deserve this responsibility. He didn't know what consequences would come with this. Thousands of excuses turned through his mind.

The swollen, yellowing eyes of the man stripped and paraded on the donkey stared back at him, helpless but searching. Raj saw despair in his eyes.

He saw despair in everyone's eyes.

And yet Raj could see the despair because he himself wasn't in that place anymore. Raj had been loved. He had been given a chance to climb out of the cheri existence. And through that Raj had begun to hope and imagine his life could be more. He was beginning to believe that his life was worth caring about and that other people were worth caring about. He didn't have to just try to survive anymore.

He wanted the people of his village to have that hope too.

A slow-burning wave of emotion welled in Raj's throat and behind his eyes. Suddenly his body quaked as the tectonics in the deepest extremities of his heart broke and shifted. Tears poured out the most secret longings of his soul, and he gasped for breath as the droplets flowed into a river down his cheeks and onto the dry earth where he had collapsed.

He looked up through the lime tree leaves. The dark monsoon rain clouds were dancing with higher wind, and their edges began to glow. The moonlight broke out and doused the earth in a silver kiss. Somehow, he felt reassured.

His fear gradually evaporated into the warm glow of

inspiration. He could see it all unfolding in his mind. He might be a raggedy fifteen-year-old but he had behind him a raggedy band of boys with a yearning to question the way their lives were and had always been. They had the fortitude to look beyond their parents and childhoods and to dare to imagine—then to dare to look beyond their cheri, past no man's land, past the upper-caste village, and dare, dare, dare to imagine life past the farthest plantation.

Chitravel emerged from the shadows. He tentatively pushed aside the low-lying leaves and sat next to his cousin.

"It sounds nice, huh? This model village idea," he began. He looked over at Raj, who still stared past the leaves. Chitravel smiled and, nodding his head, said, "Hey mapile, I'm with you. Whatever it is you have to do, I'm with you."

chapter thirteen

Arrack was a putrid and illicit alcoholic drink beloved in Raj's cheri and throughout south India. It did not discriminate between high caste or low caste; it was a friend to all. Through arrack, the plantation workers found peace from their hard labor and hungry stomachs. They could live with the violent, alcohol-fueled outbreaks and the pains of long-term drinking.

They had to, because they were addicted.

The landowners loved arrack for the fun. They laughed and jested under its rousing touch and sunk happily into its soothing embrace. Some gave the laborers free arrack to distract the men and disarm the women, so they could take advantage of them.

Centuries of consumption had refined a genius economy for arrack production and distribution—and production was not only illegal, it was dangerous. Thus, the landowners conjured creative ways to persuade their low-caste counterparts to produce the drink *for* them. The usual route was to hold some old debt over the Paraiyans' heads or to entice them with some meager pay for their services. Brewing facilities were created out of trash containers, tire tubes, and wood fires. There they would ferment and distill a concoction of various wastes and battery acids into alcohol. Gradually, the cherished liquid, with its 25 percent alcohol content, would flow out.

The toxic fumes spread their foul incense over the entire yard and home of the maker. Sometimes the vapors would catch flame, destroying the whole facility. Nevertheless, the drink was irresistible. The Paraiyan distillers would fill rubber tire tubes with the arrack and share it with their high-caste patrons.

Because this type of arrack was illegal, needy police officers and thirsty landowners forged a brilliant, symbiotic relationship. The police were often low in their case numbers each month and would push for extra arrests at the end of the month to ensure ample income for the next. The landowners did not want to be penalized for conducting an illegal operation, so they gave the names and addresses of each of their arrack makers to the police.

Under the cover of night, police officers would sweep through the low-caste communities and capture their targeted arrack makers. Each month, the police would round up a minimum of five cases in their region of villages. The Paraiyan distillers would be impounded in the local jail until they agreed to a statement of guilt and paid a fine for their crime. They would choke up the funds they had accumulated through selling the illicit drink and pay the penalties, or else be jailed and beaten until Lady Justice had drunk her fill.

Then the officers would execute justice by fire, burning the alcohol and the distilleries used to make it. The Paraiyans would count their losses and get to setting the distilleries back in order. The landowners were safe, the deputy happy, and the officers paid. The high-caste townspeople would settle back into their beds, thankful that justice had been done. The officers would wipe their hands, congratulate themselves on a job well done, and celebrate with a glass of arrack.

chapter fourteen

Raj's uncle Mutihiah stumbled back into the village in the early morning light. Another police sweep had been conducted during the prior night. The Paraiyans never knew who would be ousted that month, and this time it happened to be him. He had paid the minimum fine in court, accepting that he was guilty. Raj watched his uncle trudge to his house. His wife came out, nodded her head sadly, and together they walked inside.

The rice mill coughed its ash out of its tall chimney. Dawn cascaded through the dust and ash, illuminating the people of the cheri heading out to the fields.

The cheri's little church stood proudly at the entrance to Raj's side of the village. However, beyond the entrance, mud houses stretched along both sides of the dirt road. The community well had long since dried up and sat uselessly in its place. Raj shook his head as he surveyed the dilapidated shelters of his community.

The section of cheri that had settled on government land, the Hindu section, was not much better off. Although they lived in the sturdier, cleaner concrete structures that the government had built for them years prior, the robust exterior could not protect them from the economic vulnerabilities shared by their sister cheri. The police sweep certainly did not discriminate between the cheris.

They all labored in the plantations with all their strength, and still, they could not afford to make their houses sturdier, their clothes cleaner, nor their children healthier. *There must be a better way*, thought Raj.

"Hey—why don't we make our own 'Youth Association'?"

he blurted.

Chitravel stood next to him, groggy. "What?" he responded a couple seconds later.

"Well, the Anaigudi Youth Association has all these cultural evenings for festivals, has nice buildings, and runs programs for the community, but we can't be part of it. Why don't we make our own?"

Chitravel yawned, took out a beedi, looked at it, then shook his head and threw it in the mud. Slowly he tried to catch his mind up to Raj's, but Raj had already moved into a sprint.

"They have the Anaigudi Youth Association…we'll make the *Ambedkar* Youth Association," Raj continued. Fifteen other boys from the cheri had pledged to help Raj, so they had a team; now they needed a plan. And he could envision it all.

"We need a sign. That's where we'll start. And we will read Ambedkar's teachings to one another and make a constitution for our community, then help our village follow it. That's how we will become a model village."

"A sign? How on earth are we going to get a sign?" Chitravel asked. Neither had any money; in fact, the entire village had no money.

But Raj was already determined to do it.

"We will have to work. See those tamarind trees?" One swayed gently next to them, hanging low with its burden of hundreds of seed pods. People would harvest the pods, grind them, and then use the powder to season their chutneys and curries. "We'll start with those. We can sell them and make some money for a sign."

In India, a sign was essential to existing. Any group of people who wished to designate themselves as a group absolutely had to have a sign. The louder the colors, the larger the font, and the bigger the total amount of space that the sign enveloped was seen as being in direct proportion to the group's prominence.

The *Anaigudi Youth Association* had a sign.

Raj and his band of boys set to work. They negotiated with the landowners and began to climb the tamarind trees, harvesting what they could. The owners took most of the harvest, but allowed them to keep a small percentage of the seedpods they collected as their pay. These the boys sold to the village shopkeeper. The harvesting was difficult work for menial pay, but the collection of money slowly grew. The boys were proud of their hard-earned rupees.

It also happened to be the time of year that the plantain trees needed to be cut down, as they were every year to make way for a new crop. Raj and the boys had an idea. They approached the plantation owners and offered them a deal they couldn't refuse: to clear the old stumps *and* remove them. Free of charge.

The owners eyed them suspiciously at first, then with bored disdain. "We won't pay you, but you can take them," they said. They chuckled, thinking they had the better half of the deal.

The boys collected the stumps and threw them into the old, dried-up well in their village. Then they gathered cow dung and other wastes and threw those down the well too. They mixed it. Then, lo and behold, they had high-quality compost, ready to sell.

The landowners shook their heads with amusement. They needed the compost for their plantations. Could they stoop so low as to buy from cheri boys? Sure, they were dealing with untouchables, but then again, they had the power. They agreed to buy at a suboptimal price, satisfied with the discount. But that was enough to ignite the young boys' spirits. They were making money. In the midst of their sweat and ambition, a brotherhood had begun to form.

Raj walked through Anaigudi one evening on his way home from the Bright Future center. The place had become a refuge for Raj. Raj breathed in the fresh scents of dusk.

Sujeevan continued to encourage Raj immensely. His pride in Raj helped Raj believe in himself and look beyond himself. The deeper Raj stepped into leading the Ambedkar Youth Association, the more deliberately he watched Sujeevan's leadership. Raj didn't have many role models in his community, and what he had embarked on was unprecedented. Moreover, the leaders he had known were not leaders that looked after the cheri communities. Sujeevan was the first that had wanted good for them, and the way he showed it was like no one before him. Sujeevan once called it "servant leadership." Raj determined to be a leader like him.

It had been a day of uprooting plantain tree stumps, and Raj could feel the satisfying ache in his muscles from the successful day. The Ambedkar Youth Association was working hard. Raj passed through the main square of Anaigudi. The sun had just dipped below the horizon, and the sky turned deep purple. Raj stretched his sore muscles as he walked.

"Hey, you," a figure called. The light was so dim that Raj could barely see him, but then the man moved in front of him. The hair on Raj's neck began to rise. The man was intoxicated and aggressive and looking for a target.

"Why should you study?" he growled. "What do you need to keep going to school for? You should be in the fields, with the rest of your kind."

Instinctively Raj bent his head down. "Sure, sir," he mumbled, then briskly moved around the man. Raj would often be stopped when he passed through the town. These days he had been receiving more threats than he normally did. His success and leadership had been noticed by more than just his own village.

Raj slipped into the dark shadow of a house for cover. The pathway bent at the temple grounds and wound past homes and a shop or two on its way to the cheri. Now his heart quickened. He glanced at Vanitha's house, standing regally on its corner. The lights from the house shone harshly through the open windows. He glanced through an open door and saw the figure of his mother in their kitchen. The family would occasionally pay her to clean their home. Kanni would finish her work in the fields late in the day, then begin her work in their home. She was finishing mopping the kitchen floor.

He wondered if Vanitha would be home from school. He tried to push the thought out of his mind and shielded his eyes to see the dark road.

"Rajendran!"

His heart leaped at the loud whisper. He turned his eyes, looking for her.

"Rajendran, come, come. I'm over here," Vanitha called from a black window in the shadows.

His heart began to race with longing and conflict. Raj took a step forward toward the dark alcove.

"Thank you, thank you, madame..."

Raj stopped in his tracks. His mother's voice rang from the other room. This evening the family had allowed her to take home some of their leftover food. Raj felt his stomach cave at the cruel juxtaposition.

"Rajendran, come, it has been so long," Vanitha continued.

He felt reality prickling through the hard earth beneath his bare feet. He wished he could forget the world at that moment.

An insect chirped loudly from nearby, rousing Raj to his senses. His heart broke as he let go of what he longed to be.

"I'm sorry, Vanitha. I can't," Raj whispered.

He retreated into the shadows of the night.

At last the day came. The Ambedkar Youth Association had gathered enough funds to purchase the long-anticipated sign, and it was a beautiful sign. It was made of sturdy metal, with elegant Tamil letters stamped proudly in red paint. The words read, "Ambedkar Youth Association." Below the sign, the boys wrote the well-known urging of Ambedkar himself, "Educate, Organize, Agitate."

Together, the boys fixed it on two wooden poles. They wove together leaves from the coconut palm to create a shade covering to meet under. Their smiles stretched past their faces that day as they stared at the culmination of their hard work.

None of the boys could sleep that night in their excitement. Instead, beneath its progenitor's guiding words, the Ambedkar Youth Association excitedly talked late into the night. They began to question what had once seemed to be normal and unavoidable hardship in the lives of the people of the cheri. It was as if a light had spilled into the boys' worlds and poured vibrant color into their dull existence. Together, they began to imagine.

They discussed the alcoholism that their parents and friends coped with. It helped them get through fifteen-hour days of intense labor yet decidedly perpetuated their poverty. Half of the women and all of the men depended on drinking. The intoxication spread its greedy fingers into their tiny wages and regularly caused domestic violence. It broke apart relationships between husband and wife, father and child, neighbor and neighbor.

One boy cleared his throat uncomfortably. "My father comes home every night from the fields and strikes my mom. It's happened ever since I can remember. She has the scars and bruises." He hung his head low. He had plenty of his own scars and bruises.

Then, another boy opened up. "Both my parents use arrack to survive. My father doesn't beat my mom, but he's stopped eating any food. I'm afraid of what will happen if he keeps going on like this."

With every anecdote shared, the boys drew closer. Then Chitravel spoke. "Well, you all know…my dad beats my mom almost every night, and she usually runs out of the house to get safe. The streets are safer for her than the home when Dad's back."

Raj thought of his own father. He never beat his family, and he was a kind man, but still, he drank like he needed it. Raj's mother had begun to hide the jars that Aandi would take to fill with alcohol back when Raj was a child. His brothers drank too. Everybody did.

"All of our parents work hard—much harder than we did to make this sign, and yet nobody can see the money at home. Look at how the children dress, look at what we have to eat. Brothers, what can we do about this?"

The boys became silent. To confront alcoholism in their village would be daunting. The youngest of them was twelve years old. The oldest only fifteen. Would the rest of their cheri support the initiatives they took? What if they had to defy their brothers, mothers, and fathers to fight for such change? It seemed far easier to let it be, to say nothing. And yet, each boy knew if anything were to get better, they would have to step out. Raj spoke again.

"Our village is suffering, and they know it. I think they'll be with us on this." His mind raced. "We can't ask people to stop drinking. And we should not interfere when that happens inside the house. But we will protest anyone who beats his wife and children in the streets."

This was answered with nods of agreement.

"And there must be a consequence for beating," Raj continued. "We'll have them pay a fine that will go toward making the village better."

"And if they keep beating?" one boy interjected.

"Well…I guess then we will have to file a case with the police."

The crowd shuddered. Everyone feared the police. The thought of going to them was nearly unthinkable.

"Hopefully, the threat of that will be enough," Chitravel added.

More heads nodded in agreement. The first rule for their constitution had been made: no domestic violence would be tolerated on the streets of the cheri.

They presented the rule to the cheri elders, who said they

agreed with it. But the boys were aware that they could not know who was truly behind them until the association had to step out and enforce the rule.

It was not long before their first opportunity arose.

Chitravel's father often returned after dark from work in the fields. Wearily, he cracked open his creaking wooden door and trudged in. He kept his arrack in a safe place: a clay pot in the corner of his hut. Instinctively he reached for the pot and, with a sigh, drank relief from that day's hard labor. His tongue recoiled at the bitter taste. It stung his throat but warmed him as it flowed down. He wiped the dirt and sweat from his brow. He felt peace, just for a moment.

Chitravel and the Ambedkar Association decided they would be ready that night. They sat under their sign in nervous anticipation. Sure enough, they soon heard the screaming. They looked toward Chitravel. "Are you sure you're up for this?" one boy asked.

Chitravel grimaced. "Yes, I'm sure."

So they all rose and ran toward the noise.

Chitravel's mother had come into the street crying, and his father followed, grasping her wrist. He yelled some slurred words and raised his hand for another blow. She sheltered her face in her hand, gasping for breath.

Suddenly, Chitravel flung himself into his father, breaking his father's grasp on his mother's wrist. They exchanged a wide-eyed glance while the rest of the boys came around and separated the man from his wife. By then, several villagers had gathered. They began to calm Chitravel's father down while women from the cheri attended to his mother. Chitravel's father slowly came out of his rage. And then something amazing happened. He apologized.

"I'm sorry," he said. He shook his head, ashamed, and whispered, "I don't want to be this way."

Chitravel's father returned to his hut, and the crowd lingered in hushed awe. As the Ambedkar Association turned to leave, one of the elders stopped them. He put his hand on Chitravel and shook his head in disbelief.

"For the first time, we are all coming together," he said. "We are helping each other." He nodded at the small crowd, squinting his eyes as if contemplating a profound realization.

"You are doing a good thing for us, Rajendran," he said. "And I think we will be much better for it."

chapter fifteen

The boys often discussed issues in their community in the late hours of the night.

"There must be more we can do. People are drinking less, and beatings have gone down, but we still have many other problems. We still struggle to get food. What can we do?" one asked.

"We keep growing food for the landowners—why aren't we doing it for ourselves?" another said.

"You're right. And remember how we managed to make money for our sign? It took work, but it also took saving. We haven't been thinking about saving money. Every day we spend all that we have and—"

"Guys, guys!" A cry from an approaching comrade interrupted their planning discussion. He ran to them, breathing hard. "There's another situation. We have to go."

The boys stood up, ready to go.

"Where?" one asked.

But the boy stood there, silent and kneading his hands.

"What is it?" another boy asked.

Finally, the newcomer answered. "Raj, it's your brother, Antony."

Raj froze. Dull nausea rumbled in his stomach as dread trickled in.

Raj hadn't seen his brothers very much in the past few years. They had left home to work in the plantation's farther regions and would stay out for months on end. Their work had, in part, allowed Raj to remain in school. And where friendship may have lacked, respect remained. They were his older brothers, and Raj honored them as such. Antony now lived in the cheri and had married a woman named Saroja, and together they lived in the village, working as full-time laborers. They, too, had begun to attend the little church in the cheri.

Raj's thoughts raced. Antony drank, but, like their father, he had never been violent. He took care of his family; he was kind to them. And now this? Everything in Raj screamed to not go. *Antony is a good man*, Raj pleaded in his mind. *I can't...I cannot humiliate him...*

Expectant stares answered his anxious thoughts. The entire association waited, watching to see what he would do. Raj buried his face in his hands.

Then he felt a hand rest on his shoulder. "Come on, Raj. It's okay." Raj looked up to see Chitravel staring back at him with soft, reassuring eyes. Chitravel had been through this with his own family. He understood.

Raj took in a deep breath and stood. In unison, the association stood with him. A new boldness flowed through his veins. Nodding his head, he told the others, "Come," and started toward his brother's hut.

Raj pushed through nervous onlookers to see Antony pacing. He wavered in his balance, then lunged toward an onlooker who had ventured too near. Saroja, his wife, had collapsed near the opening to their hut. She had been struck and covered her face with her hands as she murmured prayers. A couple of villagers had attempted to pacify him with food and drink but that had only fueled his drunken belligerence.

"You!" Antony suddenly yelled as he caught sight of Raj. Raj stepped toward him with his hands raised protectively. Antony swung in impulsive rage but missed. "Are you the king for this village? Should we listen to your rules? You're still a baby." He staggered again, then muttered to himself, "I'm gonna do what I want."

Saroja lifted her head. Her deep brown eyes were glossed over with tears, and she bewilderedly took in the new crowd that had come. Then her eyes locked with Raj's. Suddenly she struggled to her feet and cried, "Don't hurt him, don't hurt him!"

Antony shook in his anger and suddenly swung a punch toward one of the association boys. Raj reacted before he could think, lunging toward his brother. The crowd stepped back in shock as Raj pushed Antony down to the ground and pinned him in the dirt. Raj held his older brother there, sitting on top of him with his hands cuffing his brother's arms to the ground. Suddenly Antony lay deathly still. Fear seized Raj. For a moment, their shocked eyes stared into each other's. Raj could smell the arrack on his brother's breath.

Suddenly Antony's wife sprung toward Raj, trying to pull him off, but she was too weak to force Raj to loosen his grip.

"Raj, don't kill him! Please don't kill him! He didn't mean any harm. Raj, he won't do it again. Please…" The other boys in the association gently took her aside. The entire situation was awful. Every part of it felt so wrong. Raj stared into his brother's eyes again and watched anger turn to shame.

Antony calmed and did not even try to fight back anymore. As his muscles loosened, Raj felt Antony's rage dissipate. Antony looked away from Raj.

"Let me go," he whispered. His eyes turned from Raj's. "I am sorry, I will pay the fine." Raj gently lifted his arms. The two brothers looked at each other, both disturbed. Then Antony lifted himself up and walked into his home.

Saroja's cries penetrated through Raj's fog of adrenaline. "Couldn't you have done this privately?" she cried. She brushed the dust off her sari and limped back into her house.

Raj let out a slow breath. His heart ached with conflicting emotions of fulfilled responsibility and shame. He hung his head and exhaled a sigh of relief.

An entire year passed from the day Sollalagan had first stepped foot into the cheri. During that time, the boys put more plans into action: they started growing some of their own food and earning and saving money again. Ambedkar Youth Association's teamwork sparked tremendous change in the community.

The cheri had never had cleaner streets and the whole village buzzed with rented lights, a mic system, and anticipation. Today Sollalagan would return to see the village…in a car.

"Who would have thought a state-level leader would ever come to our village?" Raj overheard one villager say.

"An automobile is coming to our village!" another exclaimed. Each household had pitched in seven rupees to honor the guests. Marigold flowers covered the stage excessively, and fresh garlands of marigold lay hidden in preparation. The cheri had set aside travel money for the visitors. Nearly every person living in the cheri, three hundred of them in total, stood outside to watch the rickety automobile pull through the village to the stage. Four well-dressed, smart-looking men stepped out and into an elder's house.

Children gingerly crept up to the car. The boldest of the group gently touched the sleek metal and jumped away with a cry of excitement. Soon all the children were stroking the side and poking at the wheels. They wondered who these fascinating and incredible men were to be able to drive a car.

The adults were more coy in their excitement. They congregated around the elder's house, hoping to catch a peep of the conversation inside.

"The elder is telling them about our gardens!" one man whispered. "Now he is describing how we save money at the post office, and how many children go to school and are tutored, and about the village discipline…" The words spread rapidly through the captive audience.

Sollalagan, Raj, and the elders emerged from the hut. They were smiling. The village quickly gathered around the stage that had been prepared, and Raj welcomed the visitors on stage. Sollalagan shook Raj's hand, then took the mic. The mic whined. The people hushed.

"Your god of the graveyard, he is your god," he began. "Every single one of you belongs to him, and so you are god's children." Sollalagan's boldness and authority echoed through the straining mic system. The people turned their ears to listen.

"Maybe this town Anaigudi is not allowing you to worship their god? But they cannot stop you from worshipping your god, from honoring your ancestral traditions."

The crowd leaned in, curious.

"And who are the ones really taking care of the fields? So, your neighbors own the land and are taking the fruits of the land while you sow and plow and reap. For centuries your people have worked, but the owners have gotten all the benefits. It is your family, for *generations*, that has tilled this land. The land should belong to you."

The crowd stirred uneasily.

"Our great father Ambedkar is one of us, a Dalit. And he looks over us. He tells us three things. What are they? Educate, organize, agitate. Educate—there are government provisions for Dalits. There are laws made to protect you. Know the rights that have been given to you!" Heads perked up in the audience.

"Organize—the higher castes have divided the lower castes. They have set you up against one another, brother against brother, so that you do not rise against them. They keep you believing that you depend on them. They give you arrack to turn you against your neighbor and then take advantage of you." Angry murmurs of agreement rumbled through the audience.

"Do you see it? Tell me, are you beginning to see? Now agitate. Agitate the government, agitate the landowners, because you are exploited and abused for centuries yet you accept it. For centuries, you accept the abuse, accept the manipulation, accept them taking advantage of your women and starving your children. How long can you tolerate this? This injustice? If you keep quiet, it will never stop.

"You must organize and agitate so that it will stop. You

are the workmen. They will not have the strength of you. If you all stand up, they cannot oppose you!"

The villagers stood and responded with deafening applause. Three hundred imaginations were lit with a dream, for that day they truly believed.

Raj placed the marigold garlands around Sollalagan and his three comrades. Suddenly, to his surprise, Sollalagan placed a garland around Raj. The town cheered even louder. Sollalagan waved his hand and the crowd grew silent. Then he put his arm around Raj.

"We are seeing Dr. Ambedkar in Rajendran. Within a short time, he has been able to bring healthy discipline to this village. He and his association have managed to clean up this village. You are saving your money, your children are in school." The crowd murmured in enthusiastic agreement.

"I want to honor this young man. What he and his Ambedkar Association have accomplished will be an inspiration to many cheris. We are excited to honor you all and declare this a model village."

Cheering erupted once again. Raj looked past the stage and into the crowd as tears welled in his eyes. He couldn't believe the transformation from one year ago. He couldn't believe he had been a part of the change. His eyes fell on the rest of the Ambedkar Youth Association. They beamed with pride. Chitravel's eyes met his—he was nodding with a huge white grin on his face. *They should be up here too*, Raj thought.

Under the guidance of Sollalagan, Raj and the Ambedkar Youth Association visited cheris in the area, sharing about the model village of Anaigudi cheri. They told stories of their vision and the obstacles they overcame to make it a reality. They told the villages that they could do the same. Soon they were influencers throughout the entire region.

Sollalagan visited the meetings often. He and Raj became close, mentor and mentee. Sollalagan would often put his arm around Raj and say to those around, "See this man? You should be like him." Raj couldn't help but be inspired by Sollalagan's attention, and he drank in the praise. Sollalagan often told Raj, "One day, you may be a community leader just like me. The people of the cheris need a voice in politics— you will be that voice." Sollalagan told Raj that he saw a bright future unfurling for Raj and that he would do what he could to propel it forward.

Sollalagan informed a political party named the India National Congress, or INC, about Raj and his work. They wondered at it. "A Dalit who's well educated...who's a leader?" Delighted, they recruited Raj to be their youth representative for the Dalits of one subdistrict, called a *taluk*. They too saw his potential and gleefully took the chance to pull this rising leader into their own realm of influence.

The opportunity astounded Raj. He could never have imagined a Dalit like him would have such an honor. They named Raj the youth taluk president for the INC party.

When a community issue arose, Raj would meet with the appropriate government official to represent the people's interests, from the most local governing body, the village panchayat, to state officials like the district commissioners and ministers.

At fifteen years old, in the tenth standard, Raj oversaw more than two hundred villages.

chapter sixteen

Whereas it is necessary and expedient to facilitate the donation of lands for the Bhoodan Yagna initiated by Shri Acharya Vinobha Bhave for the transfer and settlement of such lands for the benefit of landless poor persons or for community purposes and to provide in Gramdan villages for the vesting of lands in, and the management of those lands by, the Sarvodaya Panchayat in the State of Tamil Nadu.

— *The Tamil Nadu Bhoodan Yaagna Act, 1958*

The words of the Tamil Nadu Bhoodan Yaagna Act of 1958 articulated a fiery conviction that had swept through India behind the revered footsteps of Mahatma Gandhi. Gandhi's word of "Sarvodaya" (Sanskrit for "universal uplift" or "progress for all") was whispered throughout the land. It was a novel ideal for new India: equality. And that led to an even more novel action: working toward progress for all.

But how could there be equality when so many citizens could not even own land? Small embers began to glow in a tiny village in central India in the year 1951. A wealthy man voluntarily gave a large allotment of his land to the landless. Then the inconceivable happened: the embers grew into a noble flame that spread throughout India. Landowners everywhere began donating allotments of land to be redistributed to the landless. The influx of donations was so great that the Tamil Nadu government was driven to draft a new law to organize the distribution of these lands and so, in 1958, two years after Raj was born, the Tamil Nadu Bhoodan Yaagna Act was made law.

In a bewildered frenzy, the men of Anaigudi cheri

gathered themselves together. They had been summoned to the town bank, and they did not know why. Nervously, they cleaned off their grime with cold bucket baths, patted their quivering mustaches, and straightened their dhotis. As a crowd, they gave off the smell of bar soap and apprehension. Together they trudged to the local bank.

On the steps of the bank stood the Anaigudi accountant from the local panchayat. Smiling, he bowed and welcomed them in. The men tilted their heads, stepped inside, then felt a thrill of joy. Before them, a vat of biryani steamed next to beautifully sealed bottles of toddy, the best alcohol in the area. "What is this!" they exclaimed to each other.

"It is for you," the accountant replied.

Dumbfounded, the men stared at the feast again.

"Now we have just one formality to deal with first," said the accountant. "Here are some papers which the government has issued and which we need your signatures for. This meal is our thank-you for you coming in and helping us with this."

The cheri men looked over the papers. The paper was nice and smooth, filled with black swirls joined together line after line. They knew it said something, but none of them ever learned how to read. Mouths watering, they placed their thumbprints on the bottom of the paper as instructed. With a knowing smile and a curt nod, the town accountant thanked them and left them to enjoy the feast.

The illiterate men could not have known that the government had just issued them land. It was the first time in Paraiyan existence that they owned land to cultivate for themselves.

But with a stamp of their thumbprints, they had just given their land away to the men of the high-caste town.

The incident remained in the memories of Raj's people as a distressing and perplexing day. It left them with a distaste for dealing with government provisions. If they just had one person with them who could read and write, perhaps this could change.

Following Indian independence from Britain in 1949, the Indian government created various provisions to carry India into the modern age. For those in rural and underdeveloped settings, government programs enabled access to basic amenities like clean water and electricity, to raise communities in India to an appropriate standard of living. Additional provisions were granted to those in the scheduled castes, to compensate for and attempt to offset the societal obstacles that had cemented over centuries.

The Protection of Civil Rights Act of 1955 was one such provision. It protected those of the untouchable and tribal castes from a plethora of injustices—at least in theory. It created a faster and simpler court process when cases of caste-based violence or abuse arose. The Indian Constitution wove into its fabric a reservation system that held seats in the government for scheduled-caste representation. Various provisions were given for jobs in the government workforce and scholarships in higher education.

The forerunners had done what they could to weave equality into the foundations of their country. However, actually accomplishing such a paradigm shift in the nation and system would take many years. Writing justice into the law was a different thing than actually enacting that justice in the streets. The reservation system broadcasted India's modernity to the world, but in many cases, it still left substantial space to maintain a medieval social hierarchy. It was like a man poorly patching up a pipe, wiping his hands clean, and saying he's done something—when all along the pipe is still leaking. And sometimes the plumber is the very one who has ensured that the leaking continues.

To fully realize the constitution's ideals would require a paradigm shift not just in the laws but in the cultural fabric of the nation. It would take the labor of many willing souls to cause that paradigm shift to happen.

Now, the government had recently enacted a scheme to fund borewells for all villages in need of clean water. Each village panchayat oversaw the flow of government funds for this purpose from the district collector to their people. Across India, village panchayats wrote petitions, and wells were drilled.

Now, every panchayat council was elected by the prominent people of the village, and the prominent people of the town happened to all be upper caste. While anyone could petition for a well to be built, these panchayats were the only ones informed and educated well enough to fill out the petition. Only a few from the cheris knew how to read and write. Besides, their interactions with the government had consisted of watching the police stand by while they were beaten by the upper castes or being collected, jailed, and fined during police arrack raids. They had little desire to approach the government. And so, the government funds flowed freely to the high-caste villages like the fresh water of Anaigudi's new well. Meanwhile, the people of the cheri were forced to make long treks for unclean water.

One afternoon, after his village had been declared a model cheri, Raj gathered the elders of his cheri together. The well in the cheri had dried up years before. The people had to trudge a mile to a neighboring cheri's well or try to take water from the plantation's irrigation pumps without being caught. Neither were good options.

"How many of us do not have wells?" Raj asked the elders. "How many of your family members must draw water from their landowner's field pumps?" Eyebrows wrinkled and mutters sifted through long mustaches. The elders were all too familiar with the problem.

"Our women must bathe there because they do not have their own well," one said. "They're vulnerable there. Sometimes they get taken advantage of." Angry murmurs rumbled through the group.

Raj nodded his head. "We must create a petition for a well," he urged. "The government is digging them for anyone who shows they need one. We just need to go to the district collector with a petition."

A familiar fear shivered through the group. Trusting the government for anything presented a risk. Would the district collector actually respond to a Dalit petition? They feared upper-caste retaliation. Even though they asked only for their own well, a request that would not interfere with the upper castes in any way, they were asserting their rights. This had never been done before in that area.

And yet, the need was undeniable. Raj was a young man who seemed confident and capable. If he was with them...

"Okay," they concluded. "We will follow you, Raj, in whatever you decide."

Raj nodded. Suddenly exhilaration and terror alike flooded through him. He looked around him. Tired and worn faces watched him with pleading eyes. The wrinkles that cascaded from the corners of their eyes and down their cheeks had been etched by years of enduring and surviving. They yearned for something better, but for their entire lives, that yearning had seemed futile. This was no small matter they trusted Raj with.

"Okay, I will draft the petition," Raj announced.

Raj set to work writing down the needs of the area and justifying why Anaigudi cheri needed a new well. Then he needed the witness of the villagers. The petition would need to be marked with their signatures or, for the illiterate, their thumbprints with names scrawled underneath. The boys of the Ambedkar Association rose to the challenge and toured the village to collect the signatures.

Raj excitedly called his mother and father out to contribute. Kanni and Aandi looked upon the paper in awe. An old pen was broken open and the ink used to anoint each of their thumbs. In a solemn declaration of sovereignty, they branded the white paper with their prints. Neither knew how to write their name and neither of them had ever impressed their identity on any document. Kanni gave a cry of joy as she watched the ink dry on her print. Curious onlookers had crowded around them and eagerly pressed closer to place their own prints on the paper. For them and many others, the print signified personhood—the first time they had legally asserted such a thing.

The village contributed money to buy Raj a bus ticket to Tirunelveli. Soon Raj found himself on the forty-mile journey to the district commissioner's office, clutching the petition filled with six signatures and over one hundred thumbprints.

Every Monday, the doors to the district commissioner's office opened for grievance day. During this time, the district commissioner and block officers of each district in the community would hear the people's complaints. Raj's pulse pounded in his ears as he strode into the office. At the entrance of the room, police officers of the different districts stood around chatting and sipping chai. At the opposite end of the room, sunlight cascaded onto the desk where the district commissioner sat. He was listening to a man who stood awkwardly before him, pouring out his complaint. The district commissioner nodded his head sideways, as if he were interested, but a bored pout sat on his lips. He muttered something inaudible to his suppliant and then sent the man on his way.

Raj stood, hiding the shaking in his arms by holding them loosely as he approached.

The district commissioner lifted his chin curiously as Raj approached. He smiled. "I don't see many your age around here," he said. "What is your grievance?"

Raj handed him the petition and the signatures, inhaling deeply.

"There is no drinkable water in my village—the well is dry," he began. "We have to take water from the field pumps now, even though all the other communities have wells. We are the only ones without a well. Please help us."

The district commissioner raised his eyebrows and lifted the petition to his eyes. Clearing his throat, he put on his glasses. Then, he slowly turned through the pages of signatures and thumbprints. He looked up at Raj, then back at the papers. Finally, he took one long look at Raj and then called out to the room at large, "Who is the block tahsildar? You know, Anaigudi of Radhapuram Taluk?"

An officer jumped up and scampered to his side. "Yes, sir," he answered.

"Okay, they are asking for a borewell. Is there a working well in Anaigudi cheri?"

"Eh…no, sir."

"Why is there no borewell for the Anaigudi cheri?"

The officer paused. "No funds."

"We sanctioned for seven borewells, no? Why did you not make one for the cheri?" The district commissioner gestured toward Raj.

"Sir, we finished. We dug borewells for the needy villages."

"Do you think this is a needy village?" He lifted the pile of thumbprints and signatures.

The officer looked down. "Yes, sir, this is a needy village."

"Then why did you not dig a well for this village?"

"Lack of funds," the officer started to repeat. But he stopped himself at the look of amused disdain on the district commissioner's face. With a nod of his head, the officer acquiesced. "I will make arrangements."

The district commissioner nodded. "Make sure this community gets safe drinking water as soon as possible."

And to Raj's immense surprise, the government built the well. One day, a lorry arrived at the front of the village, thrust its great drill into the earth, and as it raised it back up again, drew water along with it. They fixed a metal hand pump over the hole, and from that day on, the Anaigudi cheri had their own well.

Everyone had caught a glimpse of something that day—it was a little glimpse of hope that maybe the new government would look after them too.

❖

Raj thrust his face under the cold, pure water pumped out of the new well and sighed with pleasure. He had spent the afternoon in one of the far fields around the village helping Vanitha's brother Vinoth train for discus and javelin. Vinoth had become the district-level champion and was competing to become state champion. He would throw, then Raj would fetch. Raj knew his place, but still, they had mutual respect. Vinoth would often give Raj fruit from the orchard they practiced in as a thank-you.

"Raj?"

He looked up at his mom's voice, wiping the water from his eyes and nose. Kanni's mouth was turned downward, pensively.

"What is it, Mom?" Raj asked.

"Vanitha came by today."

"Really? What did she want?" Raj asked. The familiar, unwanted emotions burned inside of him. Raj wished he could have seen her.

"She wanted to give me a golden necklace to sell so that you can go to college."

Raj's jaw dropped. He quickly collected himself, wiping the remaining droplets from his cheek.

Vanitha. Since she had gone to boarding school, he saw her only rarely. They interacted less now, for as he aged, Raj became more keenly aware of caste distinctions. She must have as well. Childhood offered the protection of naiveté, but in this world, such grace eventually ceased. The sun had set on childhood, and they each emerged into distinct groups. Their friendship subsisted now in memories and fleeting glances—but, somehow, it persisted all the same.

Raj gulped. Somehow, Vanitha cared more about Raj and who he was than what his caste was. She saw him for himself, and she wanted him to succeed. And yet...Raj thought back to that night she had called to him from her window.

"What—what did you say to her?" Raj asked.

"I didn't take it. And I told her we would find a way to send you to college."

Raj nodded, not knowing which emotion to express. Gratitude? Relief? Longing?

Raj moved to leave, then stopped as Kanni let out a soft sigh. She was looking down, thumbing her frayed sari. Her skin had dried during its days in the sun and light wrinkles had begun to cover it. Kanni stood now a full head shorter than him.

She may have been a small woman, but she was strong. She endured so many long days working, late nights cooking, and so many hours working extra jobs. She endured humiliation when she had to plead for money just to feed her children and send Raj to school. She fought for her children, and she fought with flaming tenacity fueled by nothing other than her own love. She had devoted all she had to giving her children the best start in life.

"Ama," Raj started.

Kanni's eyes strained to look up at him.

"Thank you, Ama," Raj said.

The future churned before him as a great expanse of the unknown, but the chance at further education stayed minimally open if he continued to achieve top marks. Raj had concluded his studies at Caldwell High School in Idaiyangudi that year, graduating first in his class. By completing tenth grade, he had gone further in education than any Dalit before him in his taluk.

Raj received a scholarship to fund his year in the eleventh standard at St. John's Higher Secondary School in Tirunelveli because of his top-class ranking. Still, Raj would need to score top marks to secure a scholarship for twelfth standard. The idea of continuing to the university level drifted before him, as a distant vapor of possibility.

The plan was for Raj to attend St. John's Higher Secondary School in Tirunelveli and stay with his Uncle Selvaraj. He also hoped to often visit Sollalagan and to serve as youth taluk president, establishing himself more firmly in the Indian National Congress party. Raj planned to return home when he could, in order to advise the Ambedkar Youth Association's leadership and to further encourage the movement he had begun.

Raj's Bright Future sponsorship concluded as Raj prepared to embark to the city for eleventh grade. The idlis were bittersweet and the storytime nostalgic as Raj attended his last Bright Future morning meeting. As the children exited, Raj and Sujeevan embraced.

"Raj," Sujeevan said. "Raj, I am so proud of you."

"It all started with you," Raj replied.

Sujeevan smiled. "Stay faithful. Stay faithful to God. He is with you, and he will guide you."

Raj shook hands one last time with Sujeevan. The two stepped back from each other with soft eyes.

"Before you go, this is a gift from your sponsor," Sujeevan said. He pulled his hand from behind his desk to reveal a pair of leather sandals. His eyes looked deeply into Raj's.

"Your feet have been bare long enough," Sujeevan said.

Raj nodded, too shocked to speak, and slipped his feet into the soft leather. Although thick and calloused, his feet melted into the skin of the sandal.

"Thank you," Raj managed.

For the last time, he stepped off the porch he had been so scared to walk on three years ago. Raj stopped and turned to look back at the old building, swallowing a tear that threatened to fall. With a deep inhalation, he turned, and with a smile, he strolled out of the compound.

With each step, he gained new boldness. He did not know where he was headed, but he knew where he came from. Bright Future had fostered a transformation in him that had marked him forever.

III
Assault

"We, the people of India, having solemnly resolved to constitute India into a sovereign socialist secular democratic republic and to secure all its citizens:

Justice, social economic and political;

Liberty of thought, expression, belief, faith and worship;

Equality of status and of opportunity; and to promote them all

Fraternity assuring the dignity of the individual and the unity and integrity of the Nation;

In our constituent assembly this twenty-sixth day of November, 1949, do hereby adopt, enact and give to ourselves this constitution."

—*The Constitution of India, Preamble*

chapter seventeen

1985, Tirunelveli, nineteen years old

The Indian city welcomes all, enticing the wealthy with more wealth, enticing the poor with a half-true promise that they can reinvent their lives. Cities crave western-style development while still clinging to tradition like a swirling mixture of oil and water.

Caste-based distinctions linger along the economic divide. Rags and suits, bikes and cars, slums and mansions. The wealthy hide behind high walls and guarded gates. They have people to ease their way forward through burdensome bureaucracy and corruption, while the less fortunate sweat and grind to maintain themselves in their place.

Traffic is the great equalizer. Nobody is spared from the potholes or the congestion. There, on the broken, infuriatingly dysfunctional roads, no one is above the immovable piles of cars. All are forced into the mayhem at some point. Ticking auto-rickshaws, ambitiously decorated with names of loved ones and gaudy prayers and idols, spit out dark clouds of smog. Motorbikes dodge through narrow passages when they can but still run into the standstill of traffic on the other side. Occasionally, a nervous horse trots by, pulling an archaic carriage. They all manage around each other, honking like chattering monkeys as they crawl through the traffic ecosystem. Pedestrians are everywhere, on the sidewalk and in the road.

In the city, anonymity gives any person the space to create a new identity and provides an opportunity to excel. Under the shroud of obscurity, some belonging to scheduled castes manage entrepreneurship. Some become domestic house workers, vegetable salesmen, or taxi drivers. Perhaps their children will stay in school and go to college. Perhaps their children will be able to get a good job. Perhaps their children will climb out of the slums. But they'd better not let their hopes skew their clear perception of the present reality. It's not all safe out there.

Raj arrived in the city of Tirunelveli in the eleventh grade with nothing more than a scholarship, brains, and a work ethic. Good grades granted him another scholarship for twelfth grade. After breaking the record for highest marks in twelfth grade, he was awarded yet another scholarship to continue his education at the university level. In 1985, Raj attended St. Xavier's College, located in Tirunelveli, for a bachelor's in economics.

College expanded Raj's world immeasurably. Raj drank in provocative ideas, the ideals of society, and stories of happenings around the world. In the city, he could be whoever he wanted, and he liked it that way. He felt more equal to his classmates than he had ever felt before. They fondly joked with each other and called each other anna, "brother." And to Raj, they felt like brothers, like the boys in the Ambedkar Youth Association.

His involvement with the Indian National Congress grew as he succeeded in mobilizing the people of his community back home. Now a shiny automobile with INC flags would pull up to his hostel and take him to important meetings with prominent leaders in the city. On some occasions, the car would come all the way to the Anaigudi cheri to pick Raj up during a visit home.

It was wonderful.

But it did not come without provoking shifty-eyed glances and wary whispers. The rural townspeople did not think like those in the city. The car, a shocking display of favor, always rolled out of the village like a flashing alarm to all those around: this young scheduled-caste man was gaining power.

Only brief eruptions of threats alluded to a tension that was silently intensifying in the high-caste townspeople. Suspicious eyes and mutters followed close behind Raj as he stepped through town.

"What are you going to school for?" they would ask him. With a disdainful look at his uniform, they would sneer, "What do you need these nice clothes for?"

In the cheri, Kanni would open her mouth hesitantly. "Raj, I'm scared for you. I'd rather you didn't walk through Anaigudi at all but…just please be careful. It will be good that you go to college. You'll be safer away from here."

It was good that Raj lived in the city now.

School had just let out for the weekend, and Raj happily navigated to the Tirunelveli bus station through a disorienting crush of cars, bikes, wagons, horses, cows, people, and the noise of haggling and the choking smell of smog. He was going home for the weekend.

Buildings protruded from the urban tangle, straining toward the sky. Every pause in traffic provided beggars and sellers the opportunity to tap on the automobile windows, raise their hands in prayer with pleading eyes, or display their impressive products. Occasionally, an elegantly garbed transgender person would glide through the traffic, offering to give a blessing for pay.

A disheveled man turned his head to spit out a red liquid from his mouth. Raj dodged the squirt only to nearly walk over a crippled man sitting on the street. The man's clothes were unkempt from days spent on the side of the road, and his eyes stared at nothingness before him, reddened from the sun.

The multitudes of people steered Raj onward. Women in black dresses and hijabs giggled secretively to each other as they passed. A man and his young wife passed in suit and sari, both of their foreheads painted with a red dot from a morning pooja.

"Sir, sir, please buy!" A beggar child thrust a pad of stickers in Raj's face before the foot traffic ushered Raj forward. Bartering, shouts, and laughter in five distinct languages bubbled out of the colorful crowd, who represented a mix of religions, wealth, poverty, tradition, and progress.

Raj reached the Tirunelveli bus stop and climbed on board the bus to Thisayanvilai, the largest town by Anaigudi. Settling into his seat, his thoughts drifted to his family. He wondered if they would have any news about his two brothers, Chelladurai and Petchimuthu. They had moved to find manual labor jobs in another village.

Antony and Saroja lived in the cheri, working for the same landowner as Raj's parents. Raj thought of his brother's sad, placid eyes on that day Raj intervened to stop Antony's drunken raging. He could have sworn he smelled his brother's intoxicated breath on the breeze from the bus window. Familiar guilt welled inside of Raj. After the incident, Antony could not look at Raj for a week, and it had taken a month before they could speak again. Raj felt he had done what he needed to, but he still wondered if there could have been a better way.

The bus jolted as cars swerved around the bus and the bus swerved around the cars. It squealed forward, voyaging from the city into the rural expanse of India. Gradually an entirely different country emerged.

In the rural areas, tradition held dominance over the new. With everyone knowing everyone and everyone's mother, old tensions breathed and reproduced. No matter what Raj accomplished outside of Anaigudi, he would always be a boy from the Anaigudi cheri.

After one and a half hours of near collisions, the bus slowed to Raj's stop, Thisayanvilai. Raj squirmed through the sea of bodies and hopped off. *Just three more miles to home*, he thought. Raj walked through the bustling marketplace, looking for a bicycle to rent.

It was methodical mayhem. Goats and sheep paraded

alongside the carts, bikes, and people in a colorful, moving kaleidoscope. Vegetables were tossed from basket to cart and weighed on shiny scales. From huge pots, large enough for a small child to crawl into, wafted the tantalizing scent of fresh biryani, causing the mouths of anyone who walked by to water. Chatting and honking and mooing all swirled together, as the marketplace bubbled with fresh chai and excitement.

Raj had come to the Thisayanvilai marketplace many times. As a boy, he accompanied his father during the day his father's landowner would permit him to buy groceries. Occasionally, his father would brighten with a smile as he led his son to a shop and told him, "Go ahead, pick whichever candy you want." The candy would cost only one rupee, but it would mean the world to Raj. His eyes would gleam, and his mouth would water as he chose between a red candy or a green candy. Raj remembered how small he felt back then and how just leaving the plantation and coming to Thisayanvilai felt like a privilege.

Now Raj strode with confidence. He scanned the marketplace and found a bicycle to rent. After he paid for it, he looked up and his gaze stopped at a familiar figure: Prakash. The young man strolled majestically through the market: attractive, sleek-haired, and a head taller than everyone else. Every shopkeeper smiled and bowed with a wagging head to greet him. His father, the politician Kumaresan, was still inarguably the most powerful politician in the area. Prakash proudly led Anaigudi's Youth Association for the high-caste youth and formed connections with his father's political allies. Prakash was following in his father's footsteps, and everyone knew it.

The young man wandered through the crowd past Raj.

Instinctively, Raj cooed, "*Anna*! How are you?"

Immediately Prakash's expression grew dark. Raj felt his heart skip a beat. He'd made a mistake, and Prakash's fury confirmed it.

"Who are you to call me that? Are you my brother? Did my mother give birth to you?" he fired back. His eyes narrowed and his jaw clenched. Reality slammed Raj back to earth. Raj couldn't call Prakash brother.

Prakash started toward him and Raj couldn't think of anything to do but run. Before Prakash could get to him, Raj vanished into the crowd. Pedaling his hired bicycle, Raj panted, relieved. It had been a close call—a clear warning that he needed to watch himself more carefully back home.

Little did he know, it was too late now. There was no way Prakash was going to give up his anger that easily.

chapter eighteen

Raj's fear was momentarily forgotten in the splutter of hugs, stories, and chai at home. He loved these days spent in the warm embrace of his family. All too soon, the weekend came to an end, and Raj began his journey home. He could catch one of the few buses in Anaigudi back to Tirunelveli, so he waited in his town's little square.

He thumbed his bus ticket as he stood, wondering how late it would be this time—the buses adhered to the schedule in the most casual manner possible. Raj gazed up at the tall bell tower of the main CSI church and then let his gaze fall to the clusters of meandering townspeople. A shopkeeper sold some chai just behind him.

"Who are you to call me brother?"

Raj froze.

Prakash.

"I'm sorry," Raj said, "I was not thinking. I did not mean to—"

"To insult me?" Prakash stalked toward him. "Oh, did college make you forget who you are? And who *I* am?" An unnatural smile filled his face with menace. "Do you think you're something special now that you're back from college?" Then he slapped Raj hard, across the face. Raj lost his footing and fell onto the nearby shopkeeper. Prakash spat and growled, "Learn your lesson, *Paraiyan*." Then he disappeared.

Raj gasped, trying to reclaim his breath. His arms clutched his abdomen protectively, and his face stung. The world around him spun and then grew blurry as his eyes watered. He gasped again, realizing he had been holding his breath to suppress a cry. A sea of blank faces answered his pitiful plight. Not one person in the crowd stepped in to help him. They moved around him as if nothing had happened. He glanced at the shopkeeper he had fallen against, but he brushed Raj off as quickly as he could and then acted like he was doing his best to forget everything he had just seen. Nobody wanted to fuss over a slight committed by the MLA's son.

Prakash's blow dealt a wound to Raj's pride. The scholarships, the awards, the youth taluk presidency...did those mean anything at all? Or was he still a small, cowering boy from the cheri, watching his father bow down to the overseer's child?

The shame stung worse than the skin on his cheek. Maybe it was better that the crowd ignore him. He could pretend, at least to himself, that it had never happened. He stretched his back to regain some dignity. The bus came, to his relief, and he headed back to school.

"You did what?" Uncle Selvaraj exclaimed when Raj had returned to the city. "Raj, really, what were you thinking?" He nodded his head back and forth, ticking his tongue. "But this should not happen...this should not happen to you."

Raj traced the patterns on his uncle's tablecloth with one finger, doubting that he should have told his uncle in the first place. Uncle Selvaraj was a short man, but his shock of white hair sprung from his head like a flame, mirroring the fire in his spirit.

Many times, he had told Raj his story. The first of the cheri to ever make it through tenth standard. Through the provisions granted to scheduled castes for those who completed a certain amount of schooling, he attained a humble but reliable job as a government typist. However, his incredible educational achievement and moving to the city did not shield him entirely from being treated like an untouchable. He worked in a sea of ambiguous holdbacks, quiet insults, and unreasonable obstacles to promotions.

Still, the spirit and teachings of Ambedkar flowed through his veins. He was a dreamer and an activist and had channeled his angst into involvement with the Ambedkar Association for Tamil Nadu.

Raj's uncle set a tray of south Indian sweets on the table. A clear sugary substance leaked out of the *galub jamun*, and the *baarfi* perspired oil in the heat. Selvaraj wiped his forehead.

"Rajendran, look at you," he began. "You have graduated, you are in college. And this man beats you and says all these vulgar things about you and your caste. We have laws for this sort of thing!" He sighed, but he was just getting started.

"And you, you are a leader! You have led our cheri to stand up for themselves! This country…this country has big dreams." He began pacing around his tiny room. "We want to be so much, and here we are getting in the way of ourselves. These laws that we have, these provisions, mean nothing if you are not willing to use them. Rajendran, you must file this with the police. This sort of thing should not happen anymore."

Uncle and nephew set out that afternoon to the police station. They entered the main building and climbed the stairs as sweat beaded on their brows until they came to the office they were looking for. The words "SC/ST Violations" had been inscribed on the door, leading to the person designated by the government to handle episodes of caste-based violence. They looked at each other, suddenly nervous, then turned the knob to step in.

The door opened to an office with one man at the desk. Raj dutifully filled out a First Information Report, or FIR, to describe the incident and surrounding circumstances. Then Raj and Selvaraj stood awkwardly as the inspector scanned through the report. His thick mustache quivered over pursed lips, and he nodded occasionally.

He calmly leaned back into his chair and blew on the waxy film that had formed over his chai as if he were thinking deeply. Raj watched the droplets of the milky substance leap onto his mustache. Then he stared out his window for some time, thinking. Beside him, a fan lightly pushed a fly carcass across the polished floor.

Finally, he responded.

"So, you were slapped by this man named, eh, Prakash?"

"Yes, sir," Raj replied.

"Ah." He looked over the report again. And again, Raj and his uncle exchanged nervous glances. Then he set the report on the edge of his desk.

"Ah yes, thank you, gentlemen. Have a nice day." With that, he dismissed them.

As soon as the door closed behind them, Raj and his uncle let out nervous laughs.

"That was easy," Selvaraj said reassuringly.

However, Raj was troubled. *It was*, he thought to himself. *Was it too easy?*

Christmas break came like a sunny day in monsoon. Classes broke for three weeks, and the students gallivanted away for long-awaited hugs and home food. Raj took the familiar bus journey to his native place.

He passed through Thisayanvilai and then Anaigudi, grateful to not encounter Prakash. He thought little of the past incident or of the case he had filed about it. Under the warmth of the Christmas sun and the cheer of the holidays, life felt too good. As he passed, the Anaigudi Youth Association blared popular Tamil tunes through the village, welcoming their own students back home.

Before Raj squeaked to a stop and climbed off his bike, the first joyful shout signaled that a villager had caught sight of him.

"Raj!" cried Selvie, Raj's youngest sister. She and Jothi sprung on Raj adoringly and gave him a hug.

"Ah, sisters!" Raj exclaimed. "Let me have a look at you!" They had just returned home from working in the nearby rice mill and were sooty and sweaty from the hard work. Jothi arranged her hair self-consciously over a thin patch. They carried pots of boiled rice on their heads, and the pots were so hot that their hair would fall out. Still, they were beautiful.

Selvie stared at Raj with a gleam of mischief in her eyes. "You're back! So, they finally kicked you out of school?"

Raj rolled his eyes.

Most of Raj's peers, including Chitravel, labored on the land around Anaigudi or had moved to nearby villages to do the same. The familiar ashen shanties stood just as they always had, but now Raj passed by growing flower beds, peaceful streets, and smiling faces. The activity of the Ambedkar Youth Association had dwindled in Raj's absence, but its legacy reverberated through the community. Now they had a working well and drank alcohol more responsibly. More children attended school, and families grew vegetables, saved money, and endured with a resolved dignity.

Christmas exuberantly bounded into the cheri. The little church was decorated with garlands of marigolds. The Christians invited the rest of the cheri to join in their celebrations. Together, Christian and Hindu families enjoyed dancing, singing, and a dramatization of Jesus's birth. Then Raj gave a short message inside the tiny, packed building. Then they indulged in vats of steaming biryani for a joyous feast. The celebrations lasted for days. The new year quickly followed as the celebrations continued.

On January 13, 1987, Raj and his friend Mani rented a bicycle and decorated it for the ride around the neighboring towns and cheris. They wove marigolds into the bicycle spokes and tethered bright balloons to the seats. The two friends balanced on the seat and handlebars and set off to visit the neighboring towns.

The squeaky two-man parade exited the village, trailing balloons behind it. Raj looked ahead to see that a group of young men had gathered along the road to the town.

"Look, it's Vinoth!" Raj exclaimed, and he waved...but something seemed off. It was as if they were waiting.

Then Raj saw Prakash. Suddenly his stomach caved and a chilling realization set in. The group was from the town's Anaigudi Youth Association. Their dark eyes fixed on Raj. They had been waiting for him.

The bike squealed toward the group, now only a couple of feet away. They moved toward Raj, and in an instant, joy evaporated. Panic set in. Suddenly Raj's head spun, and he crashed into muddy reality. Prakash had kicked the bike, and Raj found himself on the ground with the bike on top of him. His face was in the dirt.

"Run! Mani, run!" Raj cried as he struggled to maneuver out from under the bike.

Prakash growled, *"Para thevadiya mavane!"* In other words, "Paraiyan son of a bitch!"

And twenty young men of the Anaigudi Youth Association, hair bristling and teeth bared, came upon him. Raj glanced up to see Mani slip away. *Good*, he thought as he watched Mani running down the dirt road back to the cheri.

Nobody tried to run after Mani. They wanted Raj.

The stinking slap of an old leather shoe burned his skin. Instinctively, Raj lifted his arms to cover his face. The men descended upon him with sharp, potent hits. They used their hands, shoes, sticks, and whatever other weapons they had been able to find.

Each blow felt powered by their resentment and stung with their fearful hatred. Soon his entire body quaked with blows from all sides, and the pain seared into his bones. He felt the sharp pain of a wooden stick bruise deep into his thigh. His head throbbed. His ears rang. His vision quickly blurred then faltered into sparkling darkness. Only pain penetrated the darkness and silence.

Raj felt himself being dragged through the dirt and mud. He slowly came to his senses, hearing vulgar shouts. He realized his shirt had been torn to shreds and had fallen off him. His dhoti trailed away in the mud. Only his undergarment remained. He lowered his hands, exposing his face, to clutch onto his last shroud of dignity. The boys continued to surround him, kicking, hitting, and shouting.

Raj felt a dozen people drag him to his feet. Some hands held him while others tied a rope around his wrists. Raj felt rough concrete against his forearms. He forced himself to open one swollen eye and found himself gazing up a concrete shaft, with electric wires high above it buzzing menacingly. He had been tied to the electricity pole in the center of town.

Commotion and chaos surrounded him. Now more than a hundred people from the town watched uneasily. They all knew Raj. They had only ever known Raj to do good. They had watched him grow up, be responsible with his education, help others, and lead the boys of the cheri to work hard for money to build a sign. They saw that the INC party liked him.

But these successes had perversely produced an underlying dislike of Raj. He was not of Anaigudi, he was of the cheri, and now the threats Raj had walked through had become reality. When the village's loyalties were tested, they followed Prakash. Intimidation by his father silenced any who were tempted to do differently.

The church bell tower watched silently from its elevated vantage. On and on, the beating continued as the pain seeped into Raj's soul. Raj had never felt more humiliated in his life, and the humiliation struck him with each blow. Nor had he ever felt so alone, so vulnerable, so hurt. He didn't know whether to snarl or to cry. Between the slaps, Raj felt a chill breeze against his half-naked body, only his undergarment still clinging to him. Raj dropped his head down.

"Please! Let him go!"

"Stop!"

Raj's heart froze. He knew those voices. It was Antony and his wife, Saroja.

The crowd enveloped the newcomers, and he heard the shouts crescendo. The crowd had been provoked and found a new target to channel their wrath upon. In between the pounds of his own beating, he could see them yelling and pushing Antony.

Then he heard a loud smack and the cry of a woman.

Antony had been struck down to the dirt, and Saroja, also struck, knelt by her husband at Prakash's feet. Red-brown mud covered her. It had been smeared onto her face, in her mouth, and on her arms. With her head bowed, she pleaded in daring self-humiliation, her beautiful black braided hair in the dirt.

Antony had been hit multiple times. His face had already begun to swell. Still, he would not relent in his begging on Raj's behalf.

Raj's eyes traced the legs of the person they knelt before. Prakash basked in his power with a stone-cold face. With every blow to Raj, he sensed his honor restored.

Desperately, Raj searched the crowd through blurred vision. Raj searched for a friend in the crowd. Vanitha? The pole was only five houses away from hers. A past teacher? The church pastor?

But the entire village yielded to Prakash's command and did not dare question his vengeance.

chapter nineteen

"We were just coming home from work when Mani told us what had happened. They would sometimes put mud on us to punish us, so this time I put mud on my mouth and over myself to plead for them to let Raj go."

—*Saroja, interview in Anaigudi cheri*

Raj wished he could die.

A hit pounded against Raj's head, and his ears were ringing again. His wounds throbbed with the hurdling rhythm of his heartbeat.

Then the mayhem became even more chaotic. Angry shouts mixed with new cries, and the blows raining down on Raj's back turned even more livid with a sense of desperation. It was as though the crowd felt threatened, and Raj strained his neck to see why. An entire third of the cheri had arrived, his father and mother leading. Together they fell to the earth at the feet of his aggressors and begged them to stop.

Anxiety and anger raged through Raj as he watched his aged mom and dad humiliate themselves. Kanni cried, and the tears streamed down her cheeks into the dust. Aandi hung his head low, his palms open in a plea. The others of the cheri began to lay prostrate with them.

"Please, let him go!" they cried. "We beg you!"

Raj glanced between his aching arms to see Antony and his wife kneeling together. Each blow on his skin stung even more deeply with his family watching. They were giving up their dignity and safety in favor of exposing themselves to the mercy of Raj's captors.

Afterward, Raj realized that the townspeople must have

been scared. Never in the town's history had there been such an organized movement of Paraiyans as the one he had begun. Before that, the townspeople had enjoyed security, knowing that the Paraiyans depended on them, not on each other. A single Paraiyan was nothing, but sixty could cause trouble. What if the scheduled castes all around the area suddenly came together? All their workers, all their means of operations would be jeopardized.

The mayhem of shouts and blows rang out from the center of the crowd while a still silence settled ominously on the fringe. The onlookers weren't participating; they weren't intervening. They were watching.

Raj clung to the concrete electricity pole and listened to his own stuttered breath. Here he hung, tied to a pole. He was the cursed boy they always thought he was. Pathetic, wretched, helpless.

Now the silence crept into the center. The winter sun had begun to set. Raj looked up through his swollen eyes to see a new figure emerging in the dusk.

Vanitha's father had stepped in to survey the situation. He commanded the hushed crowd with authority—even Prakash stared at him, waiting for validation. The crowd leaned in on their toes as they watched.

Vanitha's father fumed in a cold rage. He stepped around Antony and Saroja, then stepped toward Raj. Raj trembled under his scrutiny, becoming all too aware of his own naked exposure, still only covered by his undergarment. Then Vanitha's father glared at the young men of the Anaigudi Youth Association. His eyes bored into his son's. Suddenly Vinoth looked scared. Finally, Vanitha's dad spat on the ground at the feet of the Anaigudi Youth Association.

The crowd gasped.

"Shame on you!" he yelled at the young men. They quivered under the power of his judgment. He turned to Raj and looked over his bruises and cuts.

"This dog is standing like a hero! He should have died by now. Shame on you boys that you don't know how to hit properly."

Raj withered inside of himself.

Prakash moved toward Raj and hit him harder. The pain echoed through the bruises on Raj's back, and Raj smelled Prakash's foul breath as he leaned close to his ear and whispered, "Paraiyan filth, you dare file a case on me? Did you think the police wouldn't tell my father?"

Hot spit hit Raj's face. Then Prakash was gone. Someone loosed the rope around Raj's wrists and laid a blanket gently on his naked skin. Raj felt some of the other Paraiyans softly lift his trembling body.

"No, don't," he protested. But he was too weak to object further.

The air that filled Raj's shuddering lungs seemed too generous. He felt worthless and wretched and hated himself. He had humiliated his entire community. He wished they would leave him. He wished Antony had spared himself. He wished his parents had let him die.

Two men from the cheri supported him, and as they walked, they gently covered him in a dhoti. In the evening light, he saw Antony, a river of dried blood smeared from his brow to his cheek—but at least Antony was able to walk under his own power. Saroja, Antony's wife, walked clasped in the arms of some women who were also busily combing her disheveled hair and fixing her sari. Most of those who had come from the cheri were women.

The emotional pain overwhelmed any physical pain Raj could feel. Raj looked around at his people and then down at his bruised feet. Suddenly he questioned everything he had taught them, everything he had stood for. Maybe nobody really did care about them. Perhaps the world was right in saying they were less than worthless. They were polluting. Maybe he had better go back to the cheri, say nothing, and do nothing. He teetered on the edge of the abyss of hopelessness.

Then anger burst through his despair. He had trusted the government too naively. The government didn't care about

Raj. Instead, it taunted him with the promise of protection and a Scheduled Caste Atrocities Bureau with a fancy sign.

And yet something in him rebelled. He couldn't give up now.

"Take me to the police station," he croaked.

A shrill telephone ring echoed through the mostly empty rooms of the Thisayanvilai police station. The small, red-bricked station sat modestly on the outskirts of the town. Police Inspector Chitharanjan already knew who was on the line. He knew what they wanted. The phone had been ringing incessantly throughout the entire evening.

First, it had been the superintendent of police, his highest superior. "Have you heard what has happened?" the man had asked. The sound of his voice had been enough to set the inspector's heart racing. Just to be acknowledged was incredible and terrifying.

"It's the son of the MLA, Kumaresan. I'm sure you understand," said the voice on the line. The inspector's heart plunged. Everything in him moved instinctively to accomplish his superior's requests. But then he heard the superintendent's order. All of him cringed into a knot of moral dilemma. His duty was to his superior...or was it to the law? The matter concerned the son of Kumaresan, the man who had reigned over that region for twenty years. To file a case against the MLA's son was to file a case against the MLA. And to file a case against the MLA was impossible.

Then he saw them. A crowd of sixty-five Paraiyans, mostly women, coming toward the police station. They must have walked the entire three and a half miles from Anaigudi to Thisayanvilai just to protect this young man. The inspector's heartbeat pounded through his body. As the door handle creaked, Chitharanjan shuddered. As the door slowly opened, he stood up expectantly. In walked the young man, bruised and bleeding, and one other—his older brother, also beaten.

The young man's swollen eyes gazed into Chitharanjan's— tired, yet defiant. "My name is Rajendran," the young man said. His voice was raspy. "I would like to file an FIR."

Chitharanjan glanced through the bars of the police window at the mob of Paraiyans waiting outside. The spectacle of a single Paraiyan at the police station wanting to file a case was not something that had been seen in the past hundred years. Now, sixty-five of them set their demand on the threshold of justice. The sun had set long ago, but he knew they would not leave until the case was filed.

The phone screeched again. The inspector picked up the phone and answered. The head of *Newspaper Daily* was calling. It was one of the most prominent sources of reporting in the state of Tamil Nadu. The journalist on the phone reigned over public perception through the power of his printed pages. And Kumaresan was his relative.

Another phone call. It was the superintendent of police again.

Kumaresan's power extended far beyond his given realm of responsibility in state politics. Certainly, his ostensible power alone was frightening, but his real power extended throughout his robust network. His friends and relatives were strewn throughout powerful, influential positions in the government and society. One of these was a person who sat at the very crux of Raj's plea. Married to the MLA's own daughter was a man named Kamaraj, one of the highest police officers of Tamil Nadu. To threaten his father-in-law was to threaten him. He was not a man to be trifled with.

"Yes? Yes, sir. Eh, yes, sir."

As Chitharanjan spoke, Raj grew more and more nervous. He could tell the inspector was nervous as well.

Inspector Chitharanjan hung up the phone and turned to Raj. "Perhaps a compromise can be made?" he asked Raj. "Do you know the danger that filing a case will put you in?" He looked at Raj, imploring. "Everything can be taken care of for you."

"I want to file an FIR," Raj replied.

Chitharanjan wiped his sweating brow. "You could lose your scholarships for school. You will be in danger. Your family will suffer," he warned.

"I know. I want to file an FIR," Raj replied again.

The phone continued to ring. The pressure coming from politicians, businessmen, and influencers swelled with every call. The inspector was staring authority in the face, holding only a crummy law written fifty years ago, with sixty-five bedraggled but stubborn Paraiyans outside of his station. And one very bruised, very bold Paraiyan standing directly before him.

The phone shrieked, but this time the inspector ignored it. He stared intently at Raj.

Unbeknownst to Raj or anyone from the cheri, let alone the police, Kumaresan, or any influential person on the phone line, Raj had landed upon perhaps the one police inspector in the entire district who just might follow through on filing the case.

This man had been raised poor and low caste. He had grown up seeing the atrocities that the untouchables faced. Moreover, he and his brother had been raised under the pious supervision of a Christian mother who urged them to pray, and to hold justice firmly. He and his brother entered law enforcement to pursue this ideal. Other police officers followed their bosses for whatever benefits they might gain. Chitharanjan followed justice. And this was the man who happened to be in charge when Raj came to file a case against the son of the most powerful politician in the area.

He knew Raj's story was real. He also knew the retaliation he could face. At the very least, Chitharanjan expected he would lose his job.

The way of justice could be thwarted by simply throwing a piece of paper into the trash. A case that was not filed immediately quickly lost momentum. Even if this young Dalit appealed in the courts, Kumaresan's powerful network would have an easy time dismantling his effort. The case would dissolve into unknown obscurity. Chitharanjan and his family would be safe and secure. Everyone could go on with their lives.

Chitharanjan wiped his brow again. He had already made his decision.

"Come, fill out this report," he said, handing Raj a pen. "List every name."

Raj stared at the pen, awestruck. Then he bent over the desk and scrawled out twenty names, each of the young men from the Anaigudi Youth Association. The pen quivered as he wrote "Prakash...Vinoth..." Their images were imprinted on his mind. They were people he had grown up with since elementary school. And with every name, he could be signing his own death warrant.

Raj pushed this fear out of his mind.

"Come," the inspector said. "You will go to the hospital for the Medical Legal Certificate. You must go to Tirunelveli. Only a government doctor can issue the certificate."

It was nearly midnight when Raj and Antony left the others to drive one hour to High Grounds Hospital in Tirunelveli. There, they were inspected, and the certificate was issued. Raj and Antony stayed that night in the safety of the hospital.

The night could not fully darken their room or hide the white-steel hospital beds. Thin threads of moonlight fell through the window onto Raj's and Antony's still figures. They lay next to each other in the darkness, with the buzzing and beeping of monitors as a lullaby. They were safe here.

"Antony, I—" Raj began.

But Antony cut him off. "Don't apologize, Raj," he said. "You're a good man, Raj. You taught us how to believe in ourselves—you taught us how to hope and carve out a better life."

A warm tear slid down Raj's bruised face and gathered along his cracked lips. Raj closed his eyes as he listened to his brother.

"You taught us that if there's ever going to be real change, somebody has to be the one to do it, no matter the sacrifice.

Maybe it only takes a few good people in a hundred—a few good people to stick up for what they know to be right. If the system's bad, of course, the good is gonna rub it the wrong way. But just because it's hard doesn't mean it's not worth it."

Raj thought about those words for a long time. There in the safety of the hospital walls, they settled into silence.

Police Inspector Chitharanjan received the Medical Legal Certificate, and on January 14, 1987, he filed the case. He informed his superiors of the tense situation and the high risk for communal violence in Anaigudi. He was immediately transferred out of the district for his own protection and demoted for his insubordination. Essentially, he did lose his job and was placed in the monotonous, paperwork-filled "Missing Idols Department."

Not once did he regret his decision.

chapter twenty

The cheri awoke to the clanging of the church bell and the gongs of the temple. Their hollow sounds throbbed ominously from Anaigudi. Murmurs spread through the cheri of what the nearby town was organizing. The people in the village nervously awaited the backlash to yesterday's events.

First, word came that each of the Anaigudi Youth Association boys, including Prakash, had fled Anaigudi.

Then a man stumbled into the cheri with more news. "The leaders of the town have come," he warned. "They are waiting outside the cheri."

Dread slunk through the cheri. At least Raj and Antony were safe, still at the hospital, but they knew they would be held complicit for standing by them. The village rounded itself together. Aandi and Kanni fell into step with the rest of the cheri and made their way to the road that ran between their village and Anaigudi.

The sun glared over the dry shrubbery, cracked earth, and dusty Paraiyans. The rice mill stood menacingly silent beside them. Across the path stood Vanitha's father, along with Aandi and Kanni's overseer, the temple priest, the rice mill owner, and nearly every other important man from the town.

Vanitha's father spoke first.

"You have violated the sacred Shudras and your duty. You have humiliated our culture. You have profaned our town. Anaigudi has reflected upon your unacceptable behavior. In response, we have drafted three resolutions." Vehement mutters simmered from the townsmen behind him to back up his words.

"First, we will not employ anyone of this cheri. You are

all terminated from your service starting now."

The blow rocked through the crowd. The Paraiyans could not own land. The land they lived on, the land they cultivated, the land their animals grazed on and that they gathered from—none of it was legally theirs. They had no alternative but to depend on being employed by the high-caste landowners and receiving whatever pay they could from them. And there was little incentive for the landowners to deal with them kindly. This could be the end of their village.

"Second, you may not defecate on our land." The cruel irony hit sharply. The high-caste families had entire rooms that sheltered a clean, porcelain seat. On the other hand, the Paraiyans had but a bush or tree for privacy, a bush or tree on land they did not own.

"Third, your animals and livestock may not graze on our land." There was no other land for the livestock to graze on. The walls around the space allowed for their existence seemed to be closing in, as the stipulations became more and more restricting. They would not be able to survive more than a week under these conditions.

"Last, you may not walk through our land." Even if they were to find work in a nearby city, their commute just got a lot longer. They would have to walk the opposite direction of the next town over to circumvent the Anaigudi townsmen's land. The longer path would add two extra kilometers and lay outside of the protective shade of the plantations.

Aandi's overseer stretched out his hand expectantly. "Aandi, the keys to the machine room." Aandi looked toward the plantation, pregnant with full stems of green plantains, ready for harvest. He knew he would not get his settlement for the past ten months of work. Aandi had served his landlord since he was a child, for over forty years. The only security he had in his old age, for all the labor he had done, was the good graces of his landlord, the loyalty of his own sons to care for him, and this key. He looked so old in that moment. His bones seemed more brittle, his taut muscles thinner, his face more tired. But he did not plead. With quiet resolve, he returned the key that represented his life's work.

Raj and Antony returned later that day to a cheri thick with vapors of smoke and apprehension. The old men squatted by their homes and puffed on their beedies, thinking. Most of the men had already begun to pack their belongings. Some entire families planned to temporarily move in with relatives in other parts of the region. They did not know how long the landowners would boycott their employment, but they knew the landowners could all too easily find new laborers.

Raj hung his bruised head in his bruised hands. A horrifying reality had dawned on the cheri. Soon he would return to his studies and beckoning future, and they would be left in the enclosing abyss of their tethered lives.

The next morning, trucks full of new workers hurdled past the village, leaving behind a cloud of scorn. The landowners made it clear that those of the Anaigudi cheri were expendable. These laborers were Paraiyans too, from neighboring cheris.

"They are paying us more than we can afford to refuse," they explained, ashamed. They were just as destitute as the others. Those of the Anaigudi cheri had no upper hand to bargain with. Like discarded chaff blowing in the wind, they had to go.

It did not take long for the MLA himself to summon Raj. Kumaresan had been favored by the Paraiyan constituents in past elections, which had aided him in his political career for twenty years. He held most of his meetings in his beautiful mansion in Anaigudi. Raj was called to his modest office, located in Thisayanvilai.

"Rajendran, please, sit." Kumaresan gestured toward a generously padded chair across from his desk. His hands kneaded each other as he watched Raj sink into the chair. The bruises on Raj were turning into blotches of deep purple and green. The severity of the incident stared at Kumaresan through swollen eyes.

"Chai?" he asked, as one of the maids entered carrying a pot and two glasses. Raj consented, and the scent of sweet cardamom and ginger filled the room as they sipped carefully. Raj took in his surroundings. The office sported modest accommodations, fit for a rural politician. Outside, the honking and chattering of the town swelled as people went about their day's duties. Inside, however, the tense silence was interrupted by only the clink of a chai glass.

"I wanted to express my sincerest condolences for all that happened two days ago," Kumaresan began.

Raj shifted uncomfortably. He felt his body sink deeper into the cushion of the chair.

"I care deeply about the Paraiyans. We cannot be separated, like a finger and its nail. I have served your community for a full twenty years now. That's your entire life, I presume." He eyed Raj to gauge his reaction. Satisfied, he continued to speak. "Certainly, you have witnessed me give my life for your community. I am grateful for the Paraiyan support that has allowed me to hold this position and serve you.

"Raj, I want what's best for you. You have put so much work into your education to be the first of your community ever to graduate. I have watched you build your community. You have finished just your first year of university, correct?" He paused. "It must not be easy, coming from your family's financial position. But you have so much potential.

"You and I, we both care about your community. We both serve your community. I am in the position to do it now, and you one day will be...that is, if you are able to complete your studies. Let me take those worries away. Let me pay for the rest of your degree so that you can keep growing to be a leader.

"Think of your people and what they would face if I were not in this position. Think of where you would be if I were not in this position. Rajendran, withdraw your case against my son, and I will pay for your education and do good for your people."

Raj felt so small in front of him, and the power that emanated from him. He was frightening. But he was also wrong. Raj pulled himself out of the cushion onto the frame so that he could look the MLA in the eyes. Now he was angry.

"Sir, thank you, but I was humiliated. I have been so tortured that I wished I could die. In front of my own eyes, my brother and sister were beaten. My father and mother shamed themselves by falling at everyone's feet, pleading for me. Nothing can redeem the agony I have endured because of your son."

Raj stood up. "Sir, I will not withdraw the case." With that, Raj strode out of the office, filled with the adrenaline of defiance and utter terror.

Raj was lying in his home when his father walked in, carrying warm oil. Aandi knelt next to him and gently massaged Raj's sore body. Raj grimaced.

"Be careful, son. Take care of yourself," Aandi whispered.

Raj felt his eyes begin to burn, and a warm tear settled on the cusp of his eyelid.

"We cannot really fight them, you know. Your brothers have left for Mumbai. Tonight I leave for Chennai to find work until this blows over," his father continued. "Your mother and sisters will stay here." Jothi and Selvie passed by the house entrance, helping their father gather his belongings to leave. Their entire future had always hung by a thread, and now they too had lost their jobs. The rice mill had fired everyone.

"But you, Raj—you must keep with your studies. Forget about this incident," Aandi urged.

Raj stayed silent. He would keep up with his studies. It was all he had now. But he couldn't forget, and the case had been filed. As Raj shifted his weight, his deep bruises moaned through his body. His own pain was bearable, but the pain of his entire community was beyond anything he could take. He hated that his family was suffering. He hated that his village was suffering. And he felt completely helpless to do anything about it.

"Raj!" His friend from the Ambedkar Youth Association burst into the hut. "Raj, Sollalagan has come back!"

"What?" Raj asked, shocked.

"And not just Sollalagan, there are police too. They are here to protect us."

Dumbfounded, Raj stood up and stepped outside. Sure enough, his old friend and eight policemen had come. There Sollalagan stood, with a sad smile, reaching out for a handshake.

The whole village had come out to watch and they gave a corporate sigh of relief. If anyone could help them, Sollalagan could. They remembered his words to them all those years ago, and the embers of hope began to glow again.

"My friend," Sollalagan said, "the police inspector sent for these men to protect you and this village. You must have made quite the impression on him." He gently rested his arm around Raj's shoulder in fatherly affection. "Come, let us talk," he invited, and they strolled out of the village. A couple of boys from the Ambedkar Youth Association followed curiously and helped Raj tell Sollalagan all that had happened.

"Look, Sollalagan," one said proudly, "we stood up for ourselves, just like you told us to."

Sollalagan nodded and responded, "Everyone is talking about what happened. When I heard, I had to come. Raj, are you okay?"

They strolled to the rice mill across the street. It stood oddly quiet. No dust spewed from its smokestack. The owner must have been out looking for new workers.

Sollalagan slid the blue gate aside, and they walked through the courtyard. "There is a man who wants to help you," Sollalagan explained. "This is the only nearby place with a phone, you see, and he will call shortly."

The boys looked at each other, curious. Raj felt a shimmer of hope lace the clouds of sorrow. He felt safe with Sollalagan. If anybody could help them, he could.

Sure enough, the ring of a phone echoed through the mill.

"Yes?" Sollalagan answered. "Yes, he is here."

Raj stretched out his hand for the phone, gaining reassurance from Sollalagan. He took a deep breath. "Hello?" he asked into the phone.

"Hi, Rajendran. This is Kumaresan. Drop the case against my son, and I'll help you."

chapter twenty-one

"...no person who professes a religion different from the Hindu, the Sikh or the Buddhist religion shall be deemed to be a member of a Scheduled Caste"

—*C. O. 19. 3, Scheduled Caste Order 1950, appended to Article 341*

Raj's jaw dropped. Words failed him as he choked on shock. Sollalagan hadn't come to help him. He had come to cut a deal with Raj on Kumaresan's behalf. Suspicions hurtled through Raj's mind. *Had Sollalagan been paid? Had he been threatened? Had he been a con all along?*

The bewilderment on his face startled his friends.

"What is it?" one whispered.

"Um…" Raj shook his head to refocus himself on the phone conversation. The voice on the other line continued, "You're a good man, Raj. My offer still stands. I know you'll make the right decision." Then the line went dead. Raj blinked, trying to gather himself together. He looked at Sollalagan.

"You're working for Kumaresan?" he asked. His friends around him gasped. Raj wished it weren't true, but his hopes were quickly eclipsed by anger. He felt utterly betrayed.

"Like I said, I'm here to help you, Raj," Sollalagan replied.

Raj shook his head. "The case is already filed. I will not withdraw."

"He is a powerful man, Raj," Sollalagan warned.

"No," Raj retorted, shaking his head. He turned to leave, but Sollalagan followed him.

"Withdraw the case, Raj," he urged.

Never could Raj have imagined that Sollalagan, of all

people, would turn on him. Raj quickened his pace. His heart pounded in his ears, and the world around him blurred.

"Please, Raj," Sollalagan said.

As they stepped into the cheri, they stepped into a cold silence that watched and waited. Sollalagan stopped his pleas, aware of a disturbance in the atmosphere. Word had spread quickly.

Suddenly a broom whacked Sollalagan in the face.

"Coward!" a woman from the cheri exclaimed. Another hit him with her broom too and cried, "After all you said to us!" Soon all the women of the village stood around him, each armed with their weapon. They ran toward him.

That day the women of the Anaigudi cheri chased Sollalagan out with brooms.

He never did come back.

Over the next few days, the social boycott began to choke out the livelihoods of the Dalits. Families wrapped small rations of rice and dhal in plantain leaves for the journey ahead. Then they closed their homes and loaded their few belongings onto their backs. Many would travel to relatives who could host them until the family found work. Some journeyed ten miles away, others farther. They would not be able to return until the landowners consented to rehire them, and there were no promises as to when that would be.

Raj's brothers had set out to find manual labor elsewhere, with their sights set on Mumbai. Aandi had left for Chennai. He would return when he could and send all the money he made back to his wife and daughters. Kanni, Jothi, and Selvie would stay in the Anaigudi cheri. They would be safer there and would do whatever tasks they could find, to make ends meet.

The air wavered with uncertainty as the community began to realize the full ramifications of the boycott. Friends shook hands for perhaps the final time, not knowing when they would see one another next. Families bid goodbye to the land their fathers and mothers tilled and died on, the land they were born on. Raj returned to college, leaving behind a somber cheri.

Raj jostled into the already-crowded bus bound for Tirunelveli with about five other men and a woman carrying a bag of rice. The compartment felt oppressively cramped. People leaned in from all sides, crowding in like the anxiety and pain that already encompassed Raj. The passengers shifted as they all made their way toward open seats. It was impossible to stand or sit anywhere and not touch another person. Raj felt the shoes of the man sitting behind him press under his seat. The entire month had exhausted his emotions and his mind. His body bore the stress wearily, and it too began to slip into exhaustion. Leaning his cheek on the window, Raj allowed his eyelids to slide down. *Just for a moment*, he thought.

The screech of brakes releasing woke Raj. He looked up to realize he had just missed his stop. *Aiyo!* he thought, rubbing his eyes. The doors closed, and the bus lurched forward. Raj looked through the window in dismay as his stop slowly rolled away. He saw on the platform outside the five men who had boarded the bus with him. How strange—they were all looking at him. Odd expressions filled their faces. It was as if they knew him. It was almost as if they had expected him to get off with them…then Raj saw it—a faint glint on one man's hip—a machete!

Raj gasped. *Gundas*. Gundas were the gangsters, the mob inciters, and the hitmen. Somebody had hired gundas to kill him. If Raj had exited at his stop, he would have been murdered.

A myriad of thoughts surged through Raj's mind. He was so scared. But Raj did not want to take his luck for granted. They could still kill him. The person who hired them—and Raj was quite sure he knew who it was—could easily hire others to try again. Raj sank deeper and deeper into his seat. Their figures grew smaller behind the bus.

Months passed. Grief and anger ebbed and flowed through Raj like the waves that lapped at the Tamilian shore. As the surface of his body healed, deeper hurts and pains became exposed. He wondered if he would ever be normal again.

Whenever Raj thought back, he shuddered with the same humiliation he'd felt as throngs of people watched, jeered, and laughed while he was tied to the pole. His mind flashed back to the moment he clutched his undergarment to save what little covered his nakedness. Then he heard the voices of his mother and father, pleading for his life. Raj would wake out of vivid dreams of his captors and abusers, and the rigid fear would penetrate his heart. He often thought of his village's sacrifice for him. The landowners' boycott continued to hold strong. As guilt rained upon him, he glided deeper down the slippery self-detestation of shame. He felt caught inside of a tempest outside of his control.

He beat the ground, wishing it would compensate for those hours when he could not defend himself, nor his brother and sister. Voices of failure and doubt lingered beneath everything he did. Grief and shame and anger conceived thorny bitterness, and Raj fought the urge to give in to it. He managed his way through his classes in tortured anticipation of his court hearing.

He wanted to forgive; it was the only way he knew to get through this. Still, the battle continued with every upswell of the emotions that the flashbacks carried with them. Each ache of healing aroused old hurts, and Raj found himself having to forgive again and again.

And again.

In those months, Raj found comfort in visiting with his Uncle Selvaraj in the city. As they sat together one day, the phone rang. Selvaraj answered and suddenly exclaimed, "This should not happen!"

Raj stood up in surprise.

"Your father has been attacked," Selvaraj explained.

Fresh anger erupted through Raj. "What do you mean?"

"He was resting outside his home. Three men sprung on him. He has been beaten very badly."

The hair on Raj's neck bristled. "You're right; this should not happen." Then Raj groaned. He knew he was the real target. His father was simply an available target upon which the aggressors could channel their hate.

"We must retaliate!" Selvaraj continued. He paced back and forth, fuming with new fervor for justice. "They are using violence!" he shouted. "We'll show them we know violence. We have endured their abuse for centuries! But not anymore."

"Wait!" Raj exclaimed. "Just wait. We would be no better than them if we did that." Raj clenched his teeth at his own words, then hung his head, resting it in his hands. "If we fight the way they do, it would undermine everything we have done."

They wrung their hands and shook their heads. Slowly the rage dissipated into an uncomfortable silence.

One full year passed before positive news filtered in from the cheri. The landowners were tired of paying higher wages to bring in outside laborers. Their old landowner had rehired Kanni, Aandi, and Antony. Jothi and Selvie were back at the rice mill. Chelladurai and Petchimuthu still navigated the uncertain life of migrant laborers but could return should they choose. Tensions had settled, they said. Maybe everything will be all right after all, they said.

Near the same time, the day of Raj's court hearing finally arrived—the moment Raj would testify. Sharp footsteps echoed through the halls as Raj waited. Stately doors rose in front of him like an inviolable gate between him and fate. On the other side sat a judge—hopefully one who was committed to the arduous process of discerning justice.

The Protection of Civil Rights Act of 1955 provided a special court system for cases involving scheduled castes. This system was meant to be more streamlined and much less subject to political sway—at least, compared to the normal court system. This court was bound by powerful words which stated that "'untouchability' is abolished and its practice in any form is forbidden...punishable by law." The court system hoped to make these words reality (PCRA 1955, Article 17). However, the truth was that it struggled against tradition and against preexisting structures of power.

This act would be deemed inadequate only a couple of years after Raj's trial and would be replaced with the Scheduled Caste and Tribal (Prevention of Atrocities) Act of 1989, which was more explicit in its terms. It dealt harsher punishments to, and required greater accountability of, the upper castes.

Raj tapped his foot on the floor, anxious to know what was happening. Everything rested on this trial. He seemed to feel the weight of every second. Mani was testifying right now, so Raj was not allowed inside. He ached to know what was happening. Footsteps echoed through the hall again, and a police inspector walked past him, eyeing Raj warily. Shortly after Inspector Chitharanjan had been transferred, the authorities had filled the position with this new officer. He was a man known to be much more partial to the area's political powers, and he had come to testify in Inspector Chitharanjan's place.

Raj shifted his feet and wrung his hands. The seat had become stiff under him. Every once in a while, Raj couldn't help but glance toward the entrance. There was one person he longed to see—it was foolish, yet he could not help but hope. He wanted to see Sollalagan. Sure, Sollalagan had cracked under pressure; he had betrayed Raj. But Raj knew Sollalagan could still use his political influence with the other state parties as leverage in this case. He could mobilize Kumaresan's political opponents to support Raj. They trusted

Sollalagan. They would do it. If only Sollalagan would come.

The door opened, and Mani stepped out.

Raj jumped to his feet. "Mani!" he exclaimed. "How did it go?"

"It was all right," Mani answered reservedly. He looked away.

"What is it? What happened?" Raj probed.

"My parents are scared for me. *I'm* scared for me...and for my family." Now he looked guilty.

"What is it? Tell me," Raj pleaded.

"My family made me promise I wouldn't say anything against them...you know, them." He glanced uneasily toward the police inspector. "I think something good can still happen. You gotta understand, though, I still live there. They could do anything to me."

Raj swallowed nervously. He understood. But now the case was so weak. Mani may have just compromised everything. Before he could truly digest this new information, a clerk called him in to testify. Raj walked toward the doors. Giving Mani one last glance, he stepped in.

Standing before one judge, one typist, and one clerk, Raj repeated, "I do solemnly affirm that what I shall state shall be the truth, the whole truth, and nothing but the truth." Then he recounted the incidents that led up to the beating. He recounted the names of those involved. He did all that he could to plead his case.

Raj exited past the police inspector, disturbed. He knew the case itself was strong, yet he felt justice slipping away from him. The court would have to sift through the mixed information from Raj's Medical Legal Certificate and FIR to faulty reports, a hostile witness, and a biased government official's testimony. All he could do was wait for the second hearing.

It was not long afterward that Raj opened his door to an official letter. Eagerly, he sliced through the outer paper to draw out the contents. It was from the courts. He searched for a date for the second hearing, then fell upon the words,

"...finalized that this case will not come under the Protection of Civil Rights unit." His heart began to pound. The letter continued to advise, "you may take this case up in the normal court system." Raj's heart fell. He dropped the letter to his side and took a deep breath. He would start reading from the beginning.

In dutifully dull prose, the letter disclosed the discrepancy the court had found. It was not that the testimonies were found faulty, nor any evidence. In fact, the case could still be tried in the normal court system. The letter explained that Raj had been found to not belong to the "Scheduled Caste" designation. On those grounds, the case could not be tried through the courts provided specifically for cases based on scheduled caste violations. The letter explained that Raj was registered, rather, under the "Backward Class" designation, belonging to a higher caste. As a backward class member, Raj stood outside of the jurisdiction of the Protection of Civil Rights Act of 1955. Thus, this case must be taken up as a normal offense through the normal court system.

What is this? Raj thought. He paced his room as rage and grief churned inside of him. How could he be deemed part of the backward class? It seemed impossible.

Raj held the letter with shaking hands. It was foully brilliant. Raj could not possibly play against the other side through the normal court system. It was not only incredibly slow and laborious, such that only those with ample time and means could navigate through it, but it was rampant with bribery and nepotism. The special court system could have shielded him somewhat from political influences because it had been created with caste-based biases in mind. Raj did not stand a chance in the normal court system against the most influential politicians, businessmen, and news disseminators of his region. There would be no resolution. The case was hopeless.

❖

Raj returned to his village shortly after that, grateful to see his friends and family in good spirits. He walked past the borewell, past the little church, past the tree that he used to gather the children under to share moral-education stories with them. The Ambedkar Association sign still stood in its same place. Villagers had begun to settle back in after nearly a year away. They called out enthusiastically at the sight of him. They encouraged him and told him that not once did they regret standing by him.

It was the Christians of the community that met him with apprehension.

"We're sorry," one man told him. He and some others stood by the little cheri church at the entrance of the village. "We were angry too," he continued, as if that explained anything.

Raj tilted his head curiously.

"Angry about what?" he asked.

"Oh. About your case. You don't know?" he asked.

A million thoughts rushed through Raj's mind. "Tell me, please," Raj pleaded.

The man threw a nervous glance at the little church. "The pastor in Anaigudi...he issued an official certificate stating that you had converted to Christianity. That allowed the town accountant to reclassify you as backward class. That's how they got your case to be switched. We think the others in the town pressured him to do it."

Raj felt his stomach drop. *He must have been pressured into it*, Raj thought. But even that gracious explanation did not nullify the consequences.

In the end, the pastor had simply been the instrument the upper castes used to exploit a convenient loophole in the law. Although the very same injustices experienced by Hindu untouchables are experienced by untouchables that convert to other religions, the law asserts that "...no person who professes a religion different from the Hindu, the Sikh or the Buddhist religion shall be deemed to be a member of a Scheduled Caste" (C. O. 19. 3, Scheduled Caste Order 1950, appended to Article 341).

It was true that Raj, a member of the scheduled caste, had converted to Christianity. When that became officially recorded in government documents, every government provision reserved for scheduled castes—including university scholarships, housing, jobs, and political seats—was lost to Raj. Any grievance or atrocity committed based on his caste could not be appealed through the special court system. Raj, a scheduled-caste Christian, had officially joined one of the most marginalized and unprotected groups in India: as a convert to another religion, even the weak protections of the reservation system no longer applied to him.

He looked into his neighbor's eyes and managed a "Thank you for telling me," before a feeling of defeat overcame him.

Raj gazed at the peeling Ambedkar Youth Association sign standing next to the church in the cheri. He thought of that glorious day when the village had cleaned herself up and Sollalagan's car had pulled down the street. Sollalagan's powerful words echoed through Raj's mind: "For generations, you have worked this land. This land belongs to you."

But did it? Did it belong to them when they could be moved off it, simply for standing up for their rights? What even *were* their rights?

Suddenly Raj became furious with the idealists who had spun such beautiful lies. He had bought into it. He himself had been one of them. And now look at the pain it had caused.

The mentor he had put so much trust in had turned on him and everything he stood for. His friend Mani had abandoned him. His pastor had not protected him, gundas had tried to kill him, thugs had beaten his father. Raj felt the abuse stab at him from all sides. He clenched his fists, but there was nothing there for him to fight.

Shaking in anger, Raj strode around to the back of his hut to be alone. He didn't know what to believe in anymore. He heard the clanking of pottery and the gentle murmurs of his mother and sisters from inside. A hot tear trembled down Raj's cheek. *God, why has this happened?* he prayed. *How could you let this happen?* He looked up to see a bright lime hanging above him in his family's lime tree.

Raj felt utterly rejected. He felt alone. He plucked the lime from the branch above him and let the sweet fragrance flow through his nostrils. But this God he followed wasn't like any other god. How often had he told others about Jesus? He knew the story well. Jesus suffered. And Jesus forgave.

I was a nobody, but God made me somebody. Raj's heart throbbed under pain and the grief, frustration, and disappointment. The very word "forgive" brought nausea.

And yet, how great were the blessings that had come through following Jesus! And all the unlikely coincidences that allowed Raj to become what he was this day. He had believed once that Jesus held all things together and that Jesus was above all things. He had believed that Jesus loved him too. If God really was above all of this, then this story wasn't over. But Raj couldn't see how God could possibly redeem this now.

A shudder ran down Raj's spine and his head spun in his cognitive dissonance. He thrust his head against the tree. He couldn't follow Jesus and not forgive. And if Raj was going to get through this, forgiveness was the only way. But he could not see how he could possibly do it. Not in his own strength.

"Oh, Lord," he groaned, "help me forgive."

Raj's case was promptly shifted out of the Protection of Civil Rights court system and lingered in obscurity elsewhere in the justice system. To this day, no final judgment has been made. The cheri settled back into normal life, working hard to recover from their losses during the year of social boycott. Raj returned to college to complete his degree and continue working for the Indian National Congress party.

Indeed, his story was far from over. The simple fact that

an untouchable had filed a case, and moreover that the police investigator had followed through on that case, split open a millennia-old mentality that the upper castes were justified in violating the untouchables and that they were safe in the justice system to do so. Word spread quickly. To the Dalits, it was emboldening; to the upper castes, utterly frightening. As disappointing as the case outcome proved, a paradigm shift had begun to rumble through the region.

chapter twenty-two

1987, Tirunelveli, twenty-one years old

Smoke wafted from a cigar resting passively on a glass tray. The police busied themselves with sifting through various papers. The clinks of chai cups harmonized with the dull drone of a fan and the occasional swat of a fly. The door to the holding cells creaked open, and a policeman emerged, writing on a sheaf of paper as he walked.

"It's just another one of those political boys," he muttered to his friend. He sat down at his desk, stared out the window for a moment, and then continued to fill in the report.

Suddenly another door burst open, and a young, professional-looking man entered.

"Ah, Rajendran." The policeman stood. "I was beginning to wonder when you would come. Here, have some coffee."

Raj accepted a cup of the sweet, milky liquid.

"We have one of yours," the policeman continued.

"Well then, you know why I have come," Raj responded. These errands were not uncommon for him to make. Raj had been appointed district vice president over the youth section of the India National Congress (INC) political party. He also happened to be the leader who lived closest to the police station, within walking distance—although the party insisted that, on these errands, Raj take a hired car.

Raj had entered the playground of state-level politics. The first time he had been asked to make this type of errand, the party had arranged for one of their current MLAs to call the station to affirm Raj's request. Ever since that call had been made, Raj was greeted with a cup of chai or coffee upon entering the station, and his request was nearly always granted.

This time the INC had received a tip-off that one of their own had been jailed. The defendant and opposing party had been in some political squabble the previous night, and the opposing party had conjured up some allegations. The police played both sides, accepting a bribe to jail the person in question and accepting another bribe to let the person out. Occasionally someone was jailed over a real issue—a bar fight or something of the like—but that was rare.

Raj tapped his foot. He had other work to get to.

"Okay, okay, but since he committed a crime, we will file it as a petty case. He just has to pay twenty-five rupees, and we'll let him go. We won't file a major section," the policeman said.

"Thank you, sir," Raj replied.

The policeman smiled and wagged his head. He disappeared behind the door to the holding cells and soon reemerged, escorting a young man who had a bruise on his cheek and whose knuckles were purpled.

The young man burst into a smile when he saw Raj. "Ah, you came for me! Thanks, *anna*."

Aiyo, Raj moaned inwardly. By the looks of it, the man really had been in a street fight the night before. The offense was legitimate. This had happened only a couple of times, but Raj hated it when it did. He hated bypassing the law. Raj grimaced as they exited the station together.

Raj would soon graduate with a BA in economics, an enormous feat for him and his people. He was currently filling his time working for a nonprofit adult education project and continuing his growing role in the Indian National Congress party.

Raj toured Dalit villages and cheris to encourage them to form healthy communities, to hear their needs, and to campaign on behalf of his party. Raj played a key role in the INC as he mobilized the youth and spoke at colleges—his focus, wherever he went, was specifically with the youth vote.

Raj was popular; he knew how to talk to the rural population. Since Raj began his work with INC, the young people he met had respected him, but now, after Raj's case, they revered him.

Raj had won Dalit hearts, and the Indian National Congress leaders recognized that this made him a valuable asset. They welcomed him deeper into their ranks and provided him with a greater platform for addressing the Dalits. As they took him in, they expected him to participate in their party agendas. The more deeply Raj committed himself to them, the more doors they would open for him.

At first, it seemed a positive trade-off, even though Raj often had to sacrifice attending church on Sundays and he was required to run trivial errands for the party—like when he was sent to get people out of jail. In return though, Raj was put in the position of reaching hundreds and thousands of Dalits, encouraging them and being their voice in politics. Seeing his own people learn to take charge of their lives was extremely satisfying to Raj.

The work came with other perks too. Shiny black cars came to his door and whisked him away to his engagements. Classmates looked to him with admiration. Important people listened to him and coached him. More and more, Raj was surrounded by people of class and prominence.

It was 1988, and graduation was coming up all too quickly. Beyond it lay the unknown. Raj would need to begin applying for jobs—though he had hope he would secure a good one, because powerful opportunities were opening to him in the Indian National Congress party.

And yet, Raj felt stretched in two directions. His work with the adult education project had kindled a passion in him for social work. Raj had begun touring rural villages and teaching the uneducated important skills like writing their names and learning the arithmetic necessary to handle their finances well. Raj loved to watch their faces brighten when they understood a concept or to see their eyes light up the moment they wrote their names for the first time. Raj felt at home in this work. After all, it connected him with his past.

Yet Raj knew that if he pursued social work, he would be paid barely enough to live on. Nevertheless, the attraction of the idea percolated through his mind as he pondered the decisions he would soon have to make.

One weekend, Raj returned home to the Anaigudi cheri. His arrival provoked a stir of activity.

"Raj! Raj is home!" Jothi's joyous cry echoed through the cheri. Suddenly everyone within hearing distance rushed to greet him. Through the crowd, Raj caught sight of his parents. He moved toward them and gave his mother a huge kiss, then embraced his father. Antony and Saroja raced out of their hut while Jothi and Selvie sandwiched Raj in their embrace. Raj widened his eyes in surprise.

"Aiyo, how you've grown!" he exclaimed to the two girls.

His sisters laughed. They were now sixteen and eighteen years old. They were women, old enough to be married.

"There's a man in another cheri nearby," Selvie chattered. "Ayya and Ama are talking to his family about marriage for Jothi."

"Ah, they are, are they?" Raj responded.

Jothi smiled shyly, then hid her blushing face.

"Ah, Jothi! I must meet this young man."

"Uncle Selvaraj is here too!" Selvie exclaimed.

"Really?" Raj asked, surprised. Selvaraj had not mentioned any plans to come to the cheri to him. Before he could ask any more questions, his thoughts were interrupted by the sound of a familiar voice.

"*Mapile!*" Chitravel emerged, returning from the plantation with dhoti encircling his waist and a cloth around his head. Mani appeared just behind him, a bit more slowly and unsure. Raj and Chitravel embraced, then they both pulled Mani into the hug. Their laughter diffused any tension that still lurked, and soon they were talking just as they did in the days of the

Ambedkar Association.

Raj accompanied Aandi, Kanni, Jothi, and Selvie back to
their old hut. Antony and Saroja joined in, wanting to make
the most of what precious moments they had with Raj. The
same mud walls and thatched roof welcomed Raj with
familiar smells of cardamom, garlic, and curry leaves, and the
fragrance of cool, bare earth. The scents flooded his mind
with childhood memories. The hut felt so much smaller now
that it housed all adults.

The family had just sat down when suddenly Uncle
Selvaraj came through the doorway.

"Uncle!" Raj exclaimed, standing up to greet him.

"Ah, Raj!" he exclaimed.

"He only visits us to see you, Raj," Selvie chortled behind
him.

"I thought it would be worth coming here," Selvaraj said,
smiling. "I have something important to give Raj."

"Hey now," Kanni interrupted. "Not until some dinner."
She had entered the hut carrying a covered clay pot. As she
knelt, Jothi handed her two plates. Kanni opened the lid to
the pot, and the steam off the freshly cooked rice flooded the
room. The visitors were given full plates of rice, garnished
with a chili and some light but flavorful broth called sambar.
The family would eat whatever leftovers remained. Out of the
little they had, they shared abundantly with their guests. They
saw their generosity as no sacrifice, but as an honor and a
privilege.

Raj and Selvaraj shared news of the city's latest happenings
as they ate, and then it was their turn to get caught up on
village news. Aandi listened quietly while Kanni forced more
food onto Raj's and Selvaraj's plates.

"And so Raj is now speaking with so many villages and
cheris!" Selvaraj was explaining. "Oh, even in the city, he is a
good leader." The girls cooed with exaggerated reverence,
although their fondness and admiration of Raj were
unmistakable. "We may be seeing him on some ballots one
day," Selvaraj happily babbled on. "He is making lots of

important friends, you know…"

"And how are my brothers, Chelladurai and Petchimuthu?" Raj burst out, cutting off his uncle. He couldn't bear his uncle's praise. Selvaraj spoke with such admiration that it felt alienating and undeserved after all his family had done for him. Raj's face had become hot with discomfort.

"They are still in Mumbai, working as laborers," Antony replied. "Last we heard, at least. They've managed to find work there since they left back when that boycott began. I'm guessing they'll come back soon, though," he added, grinning. "They'll be wanting to get married some time or another."

"Like Jothi!" Selvie sang, as she wrapped her arms around her sister.

Raj smiled. He hoped the man would be honorable and treat her well.

"Raj, will you teach in church tomorrow? It's been a long time since we had you teaching," Kanni asked. The people in Raj's cheri still attended the little church at the front of their cheri.

"Yes! Raj, please," Jothi agreed. It had been some time since Raj had even been to church, with all the political meetings taking up his time.

"Yes, I would love to," Raj replied, although he began to feel even more uncomfortable. He hadn't attended church in months, since work kept getting in the way.

Raj and Selvaraj continued to eat until their bellies had been filled, then overfilled. After sufficient stories and updates had been exchanged, the two stepped outside.

"So, what is this thing you have to give me?" Raj asked.

With a glimmer of mischief, his uncle unfurled a white piece of paper. "I passed through Thisayanvilai just to get this for you, just in case—so that you have the option." He passed the paper to Raj.

"You're graduating soon, and we all couldn't be prouder. You'll need to be finding a job. You are such a leader—you have so much potential. You have led the people of this cheri in incredible ways, and now so many other Dalits as well! I could not be prouder. Ambedkar could not be prouder."

Raj smiled shyly as he looked down at the paper. It read, "Certification of Hinduvata." Below, it had been signed, "Rajendran." Raj's jaw dropped. He held a certificate claiming that he had converted back to Hinduism. One must perform a pooja, a Hindu prayer ceremony, at the temple or bribe somebody to get such a certificate. Raj felt anger begin to simmer inside.

"What is this?" Raj growled.

Selvaraj watched Raj intently, gauging his reaction, as he explained, "You are a Dalit. You know that means certain benefits, since you have completed your education. This is your ticket to get a good-paying government job. Look at your family, Raj. Look at *you*." He gestured toward Raj's skinny body and fraying shirt. "You're a smart man, and you can do so much. You just need the right label that acknowledges who you really are, a *Dalit*."

"I lost that status, Uncle," Raj growled. "And it wasn't just the conversion document the pastor gave the courts last year that did it. I gave it up the day I decided to follow Jesus."

"But you shouldn't have!" Selvaraj exclaimed. "Don't you see? It was Ambedkar's intent for *every* scheduled caste member to have these benefits. You are just as much a scheduled caste as your cousin across the street. You have certainly suffered enough because of it."

Raj shook his head. "It's not just that. I'm still thinking about going into Christian social work."

Selvaraj glanced toward the cheri church. "You can still go to church and do your Christian things. What is this one document, after all? Certainly, Jesus understands.

"Besides, you're a scheduled caste to the church. Tell me, what has the CSI church in the town done for you? How have they ever looked out for you or supported you? When we needed them, they rang their bell to summon the boycott against all of us.

"If you worked with the church, they wouldn't pay you

what you're worth. You know they'll pay you even less since you're a Dalit. You and I, we'll always be Dalits to them, no matter what the government says. The church treats us worse than the Hindus.

"Raj, this paper is such a small thing. Just do it, and you will have a secure future. You will be able to care for your family. You'll be taken care of. All the security you ever wanted is here."

Raj grimaced. "I won't—I can't do it."

But the truth was that his uncle's words enticed him. The promise to alleviate the pressure that loomed over him was alluring.

Raj tucked the folded paper into his pocket, vowing to throw it away.

At the end of the weekend, Raj stood in the back of the bus to ride the forty miles back to Tirunelveli, bound for the city employment office. The travelers were packed in tightly, steaming in their own body heat and breath on that humid day. Although all the windows were open, all the bodies prevented the fresh air from reaching Raj. He clung to his folder of papers containing his birth documents, his graduation certificates, and one Hindu conversion paper. The bus groaned along the uneven road and stopped frequently for passengers to board or for a farmer to lead his goats across the road. An elderly woman shifted uncomfortably in her plastic chair, holding a cane with both her hands.

Raj envied her the space she had sitting in the seat. Two men pressed tightly up against Raj. Raj maneuvered his hand between the men to set the documents in a grate above the seating.

"Wind is coming—that means a storm," one of the men was saying.

"Thank the gods we are in this bus," another muttered, pulling his knit hat further down on his head.

"How much longer?"

"Beats me. It will be well after dark when we arrive."

They bantered on about the weather. The man was right; a steady wind was beginning to pick up with the setting sun. Raj's feet hurt from hours of standing and shifting with the moving bus. He lifted one foot, then the other in a lame attempt to rest. He glanced furtively throughout the cabin, looking for an open seat. The bus stopped at a popular town. As people exited, he seized his opportunity to sit down, a few seats from the front. Gratefully, he inhaled the fresh air that poured in through the window.

Suddenly, the wind picked up even more. Another refreshing gust blew across him, and he sighed with relief. As the wind grew stronger, he pushed the glass window shut, latched it, then sat deeper into the chair. As he closed his eyes, a tiny thought pushed into his mind: *What about the documents?*

Raj froze.

He looked up and behind him, back to where he had been standing. The folder aimlessly flapped, empty, barely hanging onto the grate. As he watched, another gust dislodged the folder, and it flew out the window next to it.

"Stop!" Raj yelled. He climbed through the mass of bodies to the exit and yelled again at the conductor. "Stop the bus!" Every single one of his important papers that proved his birth and his education had resided in that folder.

The bus screeched to a halt, and Raj hopped off, running for the folder. The bus continued on its way, leaving Raj behind. The folder lay on the road, opened upside down in defeat. But where were the papers? Dusk was coming on quickly. A mile back, Raj encountered the first paper, white and iridescent in the dimming light. It was his birth certificate. Slowly he came upon others. A cane field grew next to the highway, and some papers had been lodged in the grass. One sat, abandoned, in the road.

One after another, Raj collected the papers. By then, it was too dark to read which documents they were, but every single paper was incredibly important. Raj looked through the grass. He scoured both sides of the road and the road itself. A lonely car drove past, illuminating another paper, stuck to a rock. Raj snatched it, then counted his pile of papers. Anxiety swelled inside as he came to the final paper. He was missing one, but he couldn't see *which* one.

Raj searched for an hour longer, to no avail. *Which one was it?* He dreaded to think. Without any one of these papers, his chances at a job would be much more difficult. He just might be able to get new copies, but even if he succeeded, it would mean an uphill battle through the bureaucracy. Defeated, Raj made his way to the nearest bus stop, hoping to catch the next one into town. It was the longest wait for a bus that Raj had ever endured. He felt alone under those stars. His only company was himself—and he was terribly angry with that particular person.

Eventually, the glaring headlights of another bus crawled toward him on the highway. Raj flagged it down and climbed on board. As the bus pulled away from the stop, Raj walked to the nearest flickering light. Holding the folder close, he thumbed through each of the documents. His birth certificate was there. High school graduation...*there*...papers of college enrollment...yes, *there*...

As he looked, his anxiety spun over what the one missing document could be. Finally, he realized what was missing: the conversion paper.

Raj exhaled a quaking breath. Then suddenly, he couldn't help but laugh. How close he had come to turning his back on God! And for what? A secure government job?

Suddenly the burdens of his future seemed trivial. Raj shook his head. He would take the unknown future, the insecurity, the uncertain way, but he would not renounce his faith. With a smile that spread slowly across his face, showing his white teeth, Raj made a plan to board the next bus, bound for home.

chapter twenty-three

1989, Tirunelveli, twenty-three years old

Three shining black cars materialized through the mirage that trembled on the horizon of the hot, dry landscape. Election excitement buzzed through the district—the 1989 state elections were about to be held, and the prospective MLAs were jockeying for support.

The DMK political party had chosen none other than Kumaresan to run again for the MLA seat in the Radhapuram Assembly Constituency. By election time, it would be a little over two years since his son had led the attack on Raj. DMK undoubtedly hoped that enough time had passed for that incident to have become merely a faint memory in the minds of Kumaresan's constituents.

Their DMK flags flapped in the breeze as the vehicles neared their destination. It was only a simple village, but the rural votes were crucial to victory. As they approached, they noticed an odd, ominous black flag that waved above the village. Curious, one man stepped outside his vehicle to read a sign underneath the flag. It read, "Your son killed our son." The man nervously returned to the vehicle. Clearly, they were not welcome in this village. Fearing greater conflict, the entourage turned around and slid away.

The cheris had not, in fact, forgotten the attack on Raj. Indeed, they were all too aware of it. At one point, word spread that Raj had died. Those stories had taken on a life of their own, and though truth and fable mixed, the message of injustice hit sharply. The hearers clung to their resentment bitterly. When the election time neared, cheris all throughout the region began to hoist black flags above their settlements. They would not even allow Kumaresan to enter.

The Indian National Congress party gladly seized the opportunity to use Raj. For a moment, they had considered sending Raj himself as the opposing MLA candidate, but then they decided it was better to have a female candidate. They nominated a woman by the name of Ramani Nallathamnbi and asked Raj to join her campaign.

However, Raj had become such a figure in this election that other parties were trying to coax Raj into their ranks. The Bharatiya Janata Party, also known as the BJP, even requested Raj to run as MLA for them, offering him a thirty-day, election-season stay at a faraway Goa beach hotel and 30000 INR cash. Essentially, they wanted him to run for MLA, but not to be involved in his own campaign—they didn't even want him near his campaign.

It was a known tactic that other parties used leaders from the lower castes like puppets. They'd capitalize on the candidate's appeal to the low-caste masses, but maintain complete control of that candidate's political decisions.

Raj didn't accept the deal.

Instead, Raj stuck with the Indian National Congress party and promoted Ramani Nallathamnbi. He mobilized thirty cars to visit rural villages and cheris. He stood before thousands of Dalits, speaking to them about their dignity and their rights. His eyes shone as he watched his people catch hold of hope.

His heart was with them. He just hoped that the party he campaigned for would care for them as he did.

Raj's influence swept through the low-caste villages, and their hearts were quickly won over. In 1988, Raj had completed his bachelor's degree in economics at St. Xavier's College. Now, in January 1989, the Tamil Nadu state elections were held.

In the end, Ramani won with 29,432 votes, beating Kumaresan by 4,502 votes. She joyfully attributed much of her success to Raj and recommended that the INC promote

Raj to youth congress secretary. She even went to visit the Anaigudi cheri, in order to give Raj's mother a garland of marigolds. Ramani would go on to have a successful first term and to win reelection to a second term as MLA in 1991.

Kumaresan took his humiliating defeat to heart. Those who live in Anaigudi say that the failure overwhelmed him for a time, sending him into a deep depression. The case against his son had, in effect, destroyed his career, and he saw the sun setting on his influence. He retired from politics. His son Prakash, who he had spent so much time preparing to carry on his political legacy, had met the end of his career before it could even begin. And Prakash never was able to live in Anaigudi again.

Kumaresan and the townspeople of Anaigudi proper had been forced to realize that their low-caste counterparts held some actual power, in that the Indian Constitution granted them human rights. Though it was rare for the law to function justly, the possibility of consequences like this election loss stood as a strong deterrent to caste-based abuse. It quickly became known throughout the region: the scheduled castes held influence in the form of their votes, and the law *could* protect them, even if imperfectly.

In the wake of celebrations over Ramani's victory, the party followed her suggestion to promote Raj to youth congress secretary. It was a prestigious position, as most youth congress leaders often went on to become ministers for the party, the highest positions in state-level politics.

At the next common meeting, all the party leaders assembled to announce Raj's new position and to congratulate him. The room contained some of the most influential people in the area: the Indian National Congress MLAs, taluk presidents, state ministers, and national members of parliament.

Raj stood in honor before them, dumbfounded as they

cheered. The sturdy walls of the meeting place magnified their shouts. It was deafening.

Raj trembled, bewildered with joy by this reception. For all that had transpired in the previous years, he never could have imagined this moment. He had been born a pariah Dalit from a mud-hut cheri. The higher castes had beaten him to keep him down and then thwarted justice with the power their status provided them. And yet, the higher castes could not stop the power of Raj's story. That story emboldened Dalits throughout the region to exercise their right to vote. Together, their votes had brought the downfall of the most powerful politician in the area.

Such a severe injustice had birthed an even more powerful and longer-lasting justice. Upper-caste citizens now respected the law and feared the consequences for abusing the lower castes.

Lower-caste citizens felt, even if ever so slightly, some acknowledgment and protection from the law. Violence against Dalits would continue to decrease in the region. It was a start.

The INC leaders crowded around Raj to shake his hand. With every touch and smile, they inducted Raj into their realm. They knew he was well on his way to joining their own ranks, and they dreamed of what he could do for their party.

Through the press of people, Raj suddenly caught sight of a familiar figure. The man stood outside the crowd, and uncertainty clouded his face as he rocked back and forth on his feet. He leaned in, wanting to join, but hesitating. The people around Raj blurred as Raj fixated on the man beyond.

It was Sollalagan.

Pain and pity simultaneously pierced through Raj. He had not seen Sollalagan since the day in the rice mill. Raj's mind reeled with past hurt and disappointment. The commotion around Raj pounded through his ears, and his face grew hot.

Sollalagan was now serving as a rogue community leader, a humble Dalit representative between parties.

His status was now much lower than Raj's. Raj could

humiliate Sollalagan—he could end Sollalagan's career. For all Raj had done to move past the hurt, the pain of Sollalagan's betrayal still clawed at him.

Sollalagan shifted his weight back; his eyes were searching Raj's.

Suddenly Raj gasped; he had forgotten to breathe. Air filled his lungs with fresh life. Something shifted deep in his heart. It wasn't that Sollalagan had changed, and yet the way Raj saw him completely changed. It was as if Raj's heart had split open, and he could receive the man again.

Raj pressed through the crowd. The leaders eyed him curiously as he stepped toward the man on the fringe. As Raj approached, Sollalagan looked down.

Then Raj grasped his hand and smiled.

Sollalagan looked up, understanding what Raj meant by it. "Thank you," he said. "Thank you. Please use me. Please call me. Please talk about our Dalit movement."

Raj gently nodded his head, and the crowd closed again around Raj. Mixed emotions tremored through him, then settled into peace. With that handshake, he let go of his anger. He had forgiven the friend who had betrayed him.

"Here's to victory!" One of Raj's youth leaders raised a glass of alcohol in salute to Raj.

"Here! Here!" the rest of the campaign workers chorused.

"Everyone, our new youth congress secretary!" another announced with a waving gesture toward Raj. They were ecstatic over the election results and expressed their ecstasy through loud music and inebriation. Raj smiled as the young men boisterously slapped him on the back. The men would be up late into the night drinking, as they often did during gatherings and meetings. Raj moved to slip quietly out of the party.

"Hey! Hey, Raj, where you going?" blurped one man. "Hey, I wanted to ask you something…"

"What is it?" Raj asked.

"Oh nothin'. Just wanna help you out a bit. I know you got a mum and dad who are gettin' old, you got sisters and brothers, and you gotta support them. We all know politics don't got much money in it. But we've found a way to make ends meet. Let me help you, *matcha*...let me help you and your family."

Raj shifted uncomfortably.

"You know our buddy over there." He gestured with his drink toward the youth treasurer. "He's under you, and he already runs three wine shops and two hotels. He can show you how it's done—it's easy. When you're with the government, you can get those permits like nothing."

Raj grimaced. He knew he needed the money.

And what the man had said was true: there was no money in politics—not honest money, anyway. You had to play the game, and those who played reaped enormous profits. It began with easy access to licenses for selling alcohol or owning small franchises. When a politician had attained a certain amount of power, building contracts ushered in entirely new possibilities for profit. A five lakh rupee road-building project, roughly equivalent to $7,000 USD, could be made to cost only two lakhs, and the politician would pocket the rest. The roads would be built poorly on this minimized budget and thus conveniently need to be repaired in a shorter time than if the full five lakhs were spent, and so another contract would emerge. Bribes would filter through the scheme, and the politician would quickly rise into fortune.

This dishonesty was overlooked as a "necessary evil" and lurked in the background of nearly every politician's rise to fortune. It was no secret; it was expected. Wealth meant respect, political influence, and bargaining power. Yet, in the end, no amount of acceptance or gains to be had could change the simple fact that this was a form of bribery that thrived and self-propagated through an entire political system of bribery.

Raj left the party early for a night of troubled sleep. The

political work itself was not bad. Yet he wrestled with himself and feared the current he felt swept into. He found himself treading muddy water. A whirlpool of alcoholism, nepotism, and bribery was gently easing him under—it was yet another flood he had not realized surrounded him. He did not know how much longer he could keep resisting it.

Was it crazy for him to give up a promising political career? He could help so many people with that sort of power...couldn't he? Raj wasn't so sure anymore. He felt stuck in a playground game of pulling strings, and he wondered if he would soon find himself to be the puppet, not the puppeteer.

His heart was with his family, with the people of his cheri. His heart belonged to the poor. Perhaps he could play the game, compromise himself for their sake. But Raj had begun to doubt the glittering gains of politics could actually help the poor. And even if they did, at what cost?

His mind wandered back to his beginnings in politics. He thought back to that day Sollalagan had found him outside his cheri hut and called him a leader. He had cast the beautiful vision of a model village and mentored Raj to bring that vision into reality.

And yet, none of it had actually started with Sollalagan. It had all started that day Raj stepped uncertainly into Bright Future's office and experienced kindness he had never imagined he was worthy of. That love had catalyzed a transformation deep within Raj, for he had experienced God himself in that love. That transformation followed Sujeevan's squeaky bicycle all the way back to the cheri. There, with all the children gathered underneath a tree for story time, it infiltrated every person's identity and their relationships with each other. The day that Sollalagan stepped into the cheri, the people were ready for him—but only because of the work Sujeevan had done first.

Raj drifted between questions and nostalgia. Should he pursue politics, his future would be secure but plagued by compromising situations. Should he choose ministry and social work, his future would be fraught with uncertainty but ever revitalized by proximity to the poor, whom he loved. Either way, whether in much or in little, in tempting pressures or in insecure circumstances, he resolved to stay faithful to God.

For either way, nothing would be certain except that God would be faithful in return. Faithful to care for him. Faithful to provide for him. Faithful to use him. It was oddly comforting, knowing that nothing was truly secure except that God would provide. In the end, Raj knew his heart was to return to where his story had begun. His heart was with the poor. A peace came over Raj as he slowly sank into sleep's soothing embrace.

In June of 1989, a certain letter was sent to the regional director of the staff selection commission for the police force. To the left of the Indian crest was stamped the formal words, "Member of Parliament." The letter read,

Dear Sir,

It seems that Shri A. Rajendran…has been called for a written test on the 18th and 19th June, 1989 for the post of Sub Inspector of Police…His family is personally and closely well known to me and I am very much interested in the welfare of this candidate. Hence, I shall be very glad, if you would kindly look into this matter with due sympathy and do the needful for his selection.

With Kind Regards,
R. Dhanuskodi Athithan

However, on June 18, the sheets of Raj's test lay untouched. His political influence and charisma had been proved. His relationships with the party leaders were blossoming. The path into politics had materialized before him with every step he took. His future could have been set up for him.

And yet, it was not the life he wanted.

Instead, Raj applied to work for Bright Future. From here, his career devoted to social work and ministry would begin.

IV
Life's Bloom

On 26th January 1950, India will be an independent country. What would happen to her independence? Will she maintain her independence or will she lose it again?

...Let us resolve not to be tardy in the recognition of the evils that lie across our path...nor to be weak in our initiative to remove them. That is the only way to serve the country. I know of no better.

—B. R. *Ambedkar at the Constituent Assembly on November 25, 1949*

chapter twenty-four

1991, Ramnad, twenty-five years old

"One *parotta*, plain."

"Five rupees," said the storekeeper as he slid one hot parotta onto Raj's plate. The thin, fried flatbread took up the entire dish, and oil beaded off it onto the plastic. Raj pulled apart the parotta with his fingers and gingerly put the steaming pieces into his mouth. The meal would make him feel full, even if it did give him a stomachache. Parottas were what he could afford, and they kept his stomach free from hunger for at least six hours, so they had become his entire diet. Every day he would eat one for breakfast and one for dinner.

The parotta shack was equipped with a canister of gas hooked up to a rusty, two-burner stove. The shop attendant smoked a beedi and bantered with a customer in the murky light as he casually managed a pot of thick, milky chai bubbling next to an oily skillet that sizzled with its next parotta. The sun had recently set, leaving behind purple strokes on the sky's canvas behind the silhouette of dry bushes and tumbleweeds, and the shack sat on the edge of the highway like a beacon of rest to weary travelers.

Raj watched the people and cars and bikes dodge back and forth. Light from a single light bulb illuminated people as they walked by and caught a gleam off the cars for a second before the darkness reclaimed them. How quickly they all passed by.

Two years had passed since he had opted out of his test for sub-inspector of police. That day he had said no to politics and all the opportunities it might have afforded him. Raj's stomach grumbled as he placed another piece of parotta in his mouth. He'd undoubtedly be eating better had he become a policeman. But he would also still be compelled to attend those political meetings and drunken parties, and to bail out of jail even more friends of the Indian National Congress party.

Raj did not regret leaving that life.

Instead, he had followed through with his application to Bright Future in 1989 and had been accepted. Raj looked down at his meager meal. He had not chosen an easy path.

At this point, Bright Future functioned merely as a funding agency and did its work through churches or other organizations. The churches would devote as much money as possible to the programs, and those who worked for them were considered volunteers doing ministry. That was why, according to standard practice at the time, the church dubbed Raj a "residential missionary." Under this title, they gave him a salary of 370 rupees per month. This was just enough to survive on.

Raj's tight budget allowed for two parottas each day, which, at ten rupees a day, totaled to 300 or 310 rupees for the month. Then he designated twenty rupees to buy a bar of soap for each month, and twenty rupees for a train ride to visit home and return to work once a month. He would give ten rupees to the church as a tithe. This budget left a ten-rupee cushion for any unforeseeable costs, whether it be to patch up clothes, save for a gift for his mother, or give to a friend. Not that ten rupees were much even for that—just one new shirt would cost his entire monthly salary.

A brilliant red motorbike glided past the shack. Its paint glimmered ever so briefly and then disappeared, but its roar carried on into the night. Raj grinned. It looked just like Sujeevan's bike. Warmth welled inside of Raj. Raj was twenty-two years old now and in his second year of overseeing rural humanitarian projects. Tonight, he was on his way to begin a new project. He wondered if Sujeevan had ever stopped at a roadside parotta shack on his way to Raj's cheri.

He put the last piece of parotta in his mouth and set the plate down next to the shack. This path wasn't easy, but it took him right to where he wanted to be. And with every project, he felt as if he were stepping into what he had longed to be ever since he was a boy.

His most recent project had concluded, and he was now headed out to begin the next.

Raj thought back to the day he first volunteered for this particular project and chuckled. He had been sitting in a Bright Future meeting hall, surrounded by 250 other staff members. It was announced that there would be a new project in a region called Ramnad.

"So now, who wants to go?" the program director had asked.

Raj enthusiastically raised his hand, although he soon realized that his hand was alone in the crowd.

The director raised his eyebrows and asked, "Rajendran, do you know what Ramnad is?"

"No," Raj replied simply.

"Then why did you raise your hand?" Murmurs sifted through the crowd. The director continued, "Ramnad is a region where there is no water and no transportation. The government sends its least favored officials there as a punishment, because nobody wants to go there. There are over thirty villages, and each is as feisty as the next. It is drought-prone, most places do not have electricity, and people there have lots of diseases. This is why nobody else raised his or her hand. So you can put your hand down now."

The director again called aimlessly into the crowd, "Who would like to go to Ramnad?" Now it was obvious that he hoped his call would be futile.

But again, one hand stuck up through the crowd. The director grimaced. "Rajendran, are you sure?"

"Yes," Raj replied.

The director shook his head, but he was smiling. "Thank you, Rajendran. Anyone to go with him?"

Nobody else raised his or her hand.

"Well, Rajendran, thank you for volunteering, but we cannot send you alone. I will find some others to accompany you." He paused. "It may take some time." In the end, the director did follow through and assemble a team, but that help was yet to come. Now Raj found himself here.

Raj stood, and a sense of providence emboldened him. He gathered his belongings together. Various bags of snacks hung in every place they could fit around the shop window and were lit by a dim light bulb, dangling uncertainly on a wire. Raj glanced over the plethora of snacks wistfully, then turned to commence his journey.

Tonight, he was to make his first contact with the villages in the region. All he knew was the notoriety of the region and the unlit path ahead of him.

The dark night cast eerie shadows on the dirt path. Only the dim, sooty glow of a kerosene lamp lit Raj's way. Thorny and sparse bushes crowded around the path. A rancid smell wafted from a black, still pond that reflected the stars and the shadow of a tiny temple situated on its bank. Raj's destination lay just ahead, ominous and silhouetted black against the sky.

As he entered the village, he noticed the homes rose high enough to fit any human but the doors bizarrely stood no higher than three feet. There was no electricity, and Raj's lamp gave the only light in that odd, alien village.

Raj's organization had warned him and his team to not stay in the village because of the dirty water and diseases. He had listened intently, thought about it, then promptly packed his things to move in. If this village was going to get any better, Raj knew he had to gain the people's trust, and he knew exactly how.

The villagers roused drearily to the strange light and to what was even stranger: a traveler. They slowly came out from their three-foot-high doors and gathered around him.

Though they were high caste, they had no way to know Raj's past. Raj figured it was better that it stayed that way. He was Tamilian, they could see, but he wasn't one of them. All he had with him was a kerosene lamp and a mat to sleep on…and he wore pants! Did he not even own a *lungi?* What a strange man he seemed to them, this mysterious person from the city.

Nobody would give Raj a place to stay. Even a stranger who has come to help is still a stranger. And to a community that didn't think it needed help nor wanted it, this stranger was most unwelcome. Suspicious and peeved, the villagers closed and latched their unlit homes. Only one man offered Raj a place, and it was a cowshed.

The cowshed had a dirt floor and a palm-leaf ceiling. The recently evicted cows lowed resentfully just outside. There was no door; it had open sides. And yet inside the shed, it was suffocating. With no electricity for a fan, the various insects gleefully danced around Raj's lamp as he set his things down. Mosquitos buzzed fondly in his ear, and the stench of recently cleared manure attracted many more. After a few hours of restless sleep, he could stand it no longer. In a daze, Raj wandered out to the nearest suitable ground. Outside the house stood a large tree. He put down his mat on the street under the tree and slept.

That next morning, Raj opened his eyes to a blurry light and voices around him. He got up and saw a small crowd had gathered. They were all staring at him.

"Did you hear a voice in the night?" one prickly, white-mustached man asked.

"Did you hear any shouts?" another inquired cautiously.

What sort of questions are these? Raj thought to himself. Would they not even let him sleep outside under a tree? Compared to tossing for hours in that cowshed, he had slept wonderfully.

Another one asked, "Did you hear the voice of *Jala Jala Jala?*"

Suddenly it dawned on him. Of course, he thought. "Jala

Jala Jala" was the voice of the devils.

"No, I have slept," he replied.

They were astonished. "The place you are sleeping—this is the tree where we have brought a lot of devils. Every time the devils come to prey on our people, we take the devil, write its name on this tree, and nail it."

Slowly, Raj turned to look at the bark behind him and saw, for the first time, hundreds of devil names nailed into it. Raj had just spent the night under the village devil tree.

A village elder narrowed his eyes, perplexed. "Anyone who comes near the devil tree encounters these spirits. How is it that you have slept there the whole night and are not dead?" The murmurs increased around him. "This man is foreign— maybe he is worshipping a foreign god." "So then the foreign god saved him?" "This foreign god—what power he must have."

Ramnad was the place that nobody in Tamil Nadu wanted to go to, and there were reasons for that. The villages in that area had acquired some strange customs that they doggedly defended. They earned a reputation for being persnickety about change, regardless of whether the change was good or bad.

What they did love, however, was the temple that sat on the edge of their sacred pond. The temple was very small and housed a tiny idol no more than three feet tall. Naturally, a door had to be built for the idol to come in and out for all his daily happenings. However, the priests would conduct all the prayer ceremonies outside of the temple. Thus, the door only needed to be tall enough for the idol.

It is hard to say when exactly the realization set in, but someone at some point must have realized a dangerous discrepancy. After all, no person is more important than a god. And so no door in the village should dare to be taller than the door to the temple. Every house in the village was compelled to have a three-foot-high doorway. This was their custom; this was their belief. But in the end, they really should not have built such a small temple door.

It was not long before the heat parched Raj's throat and drove him to investigate where the nearest drinking water was.

"There is no well in the village," one man informed him. "Instead, everyone draws water from a certain pond that rainwater collects in. It is much better than any well—it is holy water, blessed by our god living in a temple just on the bank."

The pond near which the temple was built was understood to receive a blessing from the god and was therefore known to be the region's best drinking water. Their holy water took on the color of the putrid mud it sat in. As Raj surveyed the scene, he watched a throng of cows lazily washing off their holy grime into it. Yellowed foam congregated at the banks and swirled around the cows. It was appalling.

What to do? thought Raj. The community was drinking it, so Raj would also drink it.

Raj's shoes sunk into the gray mud, evacuating more of the unseemly yellow foam. Grimacing, he knelt and stretched a round metal bowl as far from the shore as he could reach. Water and unknown substances flowed into the bowl, and Raj gingerly pulled it back to himself.

"Wait a day."

Raj turned his head to see another villager.

The man stepped toward him, carrying his own bowl. "The dust will settle down after a day," he continued. "Then you will have the pure water on the top."

"Thank you," Raj said, smiling. The man turned away, but Raj wondered. Perhaps the village would warm up to him after all. Raj questioned how much waiting a day actually improved the water quality, but it was better than drinking the mud that came with it. Raj took a sip when the dust had settled. Not the same as proper drinking water, but it was okay.

The next day Raj passed a small group of women on his way to draw more water. They were waiting at a distance from the pond, even though everyone else approached it to take water. Raj hadn't seen these women in the village before. He had a good guess as to why but asked them, nonetheless.

"Sir, we cannot go and take water. We are from the cheri...we are scheduled caste, we are not supposed to enter."

Raj shook his head and ticked his tongue.

There is a belief throughout India that if an untouchable contacts a body of water, they pollute it for the entire community. Often, they have a segregated well. But it is sometimes the case, as it was in this village, that those of the scheduled caste had to wait for someone of a higher caste to draw the water for them and give it to them. But would anyone actually do this?

Raj watched as two high-caste men passed the women by to take what they needed from this precious water source. They took it and then left, passing by the women again without so much as a glance. As he continued to watch, more men and women alike entered and left.

Raj felt his heart sink under an unbearable weight. These women could well be his own sisters or his mother. Here these women waited—not allowed to get the water for themselves, but rather forced to rely on the good nature of those who disallowed them access to water in the first place. Raj watched the cows rolling and spitting in the pond. The difference was quite striking: an animal, being a god, was eligible to enter the water, while these Dalit women could not even approach the water. *What humiliation,* Raj thought. Raj took their bowls, filled each with water, and returned them to the women.

The water truly was an abomination. So, Raj's first job was to petition the government to build a well. The people of the village, however, were not happy, and a host of surly responses were given.

"But we are taking holy water. There is a god in that water. We don't want to take any other water. Who asked you to bring this well?"

Raj tried to persuade them, saying, "It is from the

government, free only." But still they were dismissive. The drastically better quality of the water, the prevention of disease, and the closer convenience that the well presented were no match for the fear of their god. They feared that the god of the pond would punish them for taking water from the new well.

Nonetheless, Raj had a plan. He knew how he could convince the village.

chapter twenty-five

Raj wrote a petition anyway, and before they knew it, the government bored a well. It all transpired before the town could mutter a protest. As the government's boring equipment rolled out of the village, everyone congregated curiously around the well. They came as near as they dared, just close enough to see clear sparkling water descend from the pump and fill Raj's cup. Suspense petrified the crowd.

The cup had been filled and now approached Raj's lips. He took. He drank.

They grimaced.

They waited for their god's judgment to unleash its wrath upon Raj…yet amazingly, nothing happened. Raj happily drained his cup and filled it again. A strange, unspoken sense settled through the crowd that maybe, just maybe, it was okay to drink this water. Tense muscles relaxed as their fears began to soften—just a little bit.

But, Raj was a foreigner. Maybe their god's rules did not apply to him. So they were still not convinced.

Next, Raj petitioned for a borewell in the Dalit community—since the different castes would not take water from the same place, there had to be two.

The reception of this second well could not have been more different from that of the first. The Dalits rejoiced. Instead of coming and waiting for somebody to draw water for them every day, they could draw water for themselves! They enthusiastically took from the new well. And, slowly, rumors that the Dalits were using their well trickled into the high-caste village.

As Raj lived with the higher caste, he regularly took his

water from their well. In his time living there, he had befriended two families who, trusting Raj, dared to drink some of the well water too. As these two families continued to drink and thrive, objections to the well started to dwindle.

The families explained to their neighbors, "It is good, clean water! And we do not need to wait a day for it to become clean. This water can be drunk as soon as we take it!"

Slowly, the rest of the community began to join in.

Then, at last, all the people of the town drank clean water from the well.

Raj had finally accomplished one of his community development goals. However, the next challenge loomed ahead and, once again, the barrier to its implementation lay in the people's belief that they could not welcome any luxury that their god did not also possess.

If the temple had no electricity, neither would the village.

Each night lay its dark blanket over the village, and all activity would slow, then cease. The snakes loved it, but all the children who wanted to play after school or do their homework did not.

Raj again approached the government, but this time to petition for access to electricity. A single light was installed in the center of the village and children started playing and studying around that streetlight. While the town begrudgingly allowed for this one community light, they would not take light for their own homes. They were afraid again. They thought that if their god was in the dark, they would be safest in the dark with it.

By that time, Raj had revamped his cowshed. He had a screen for a door, concrete as a floor, and had successfully waged war against the mosquitos. The kerosene lamp that he entered the village with still sat faithfully among his few belongings. It was a meager living place but far improved from that first evening. Still, he had one more item to check off on his list for home improvement. Sure, the entire village might be content without electricity, but he wanted some. So, Raj approached the owner of the shed.

"Sir, this is your home and it is your property that the shed sits on. I would so love to have a small light inside the shed, but I cannot request the government to provide electricity on property I do not own. But you can ask them. I have all the papers ready for you. Will you sign them?"

The man squinted his eyes at the paper. He furrowed his brow then answered matter-of-factly, "No. I do not need electricity. I am happy with my home—I will not apply."

"Please, sir?" Raj pleaded.

Just then, the man's wife walked in. Wives tend to have a certain power of persuasion with their husbands, and this wife adored Raj.

"Surely you can let this young man have some electricity," she retorted. The man stiffened uncomfortably. At the shake of his head, his wife persisted. "After all he's done for us, you can't sign a paper?"

"But—" the man protested.

"Now, really." She clucked her tongue disapprovingly.

Finally, the man relented begrudgingly. "You can take power, but I do not want it. You take the meter."

Raj installed the second light ever in that community in his little shed. From that point on, when the sun would set, the community would gather around Raj's home. Children cried in excitement at the glowing novelty and played games there late into the evening. Parents conversed and relaxed in the cool of the night. The community had never gathered together like this before. Raj watched them fondly. Their excitement brought him back to when he and the other boys in the Ambedkar Association, wide-eyed and hopeful, would discuss their important matters late into the secret hours of the night.

The Ramnad villagers enjoyed Raj's light but were wary of acquiring their own. After all, they did not want to risk any god's wrath. They questioned whether Raj's acquisition qualified as a proper test—being that he was a foreigner, with a foreign god.

In the end, they made an experiment. They selected a

candidate out of the villagers most supportive of Raj and equipped that man's house with electricity. Then they held their breath. The man flipped on the switch, and with buzzing electricity, the bulb illuminated.

The candidate indeed suffered the full consequences of his electricity: light.

Raj woke extra early one morning. He filled a bucket outside with cold water and splashed it over his body, then, with a shiver, scrubbed all over his skin with his only bar of soap and rinsed. Raj threw on his nicest clothes, climbed on a bicycle, and started to ride. Today was Sunday, and he was going to church.

As Raj pedaled out of the town, he passed by the village devil tree, its bark mangled by so many devil names that had been carved into it. Raj chuckled, thinking of his first night in this village. How much it had changed!

A colleague had informed Raj of a tiny church in a town ten miles away from where Raj stayed. The journey would take him one and a half hours one way. Dry, splintered brush lined his path as a solemn guide. The sun slowly climbed the sky, and her heat began to dance up from the ground. The scent of earth rose all around him. The next town emerged on the horizon, and soon Raj could faintly hear church music. He must be near.

Somebody from Raj's cheri once asked him, *Why in god's name would you ever bother going back to a church?* Raj wiped his brow. It was true that the church in Anaigudi had done nothing to help him when he needed it most. Everyone in his cheri had heard the church bells ringing with the temple bell the day the landowners enforced a boycott against hiring his people—the high-caste Christians and Hindus had worked together. That thought still made him sick.

And yet, Raj loved God, so he couldn't help but love God's people. Since God forgave him and showed him grace,

Raj chose to forgive. It had not been easy to relinquish resentment and let himself trust again. But choosing to show grace for the church by finding Christians and building community with them helped him forgive. This grace for the church would bring him unexpected blessing today.

The church stood in the center of town. Though a modest building, it was filled near to bursting with music and people. Raj's bike squealed to a stop. He stood for a moment, glancing up at the tall doors.

Just then, a young man rode up on a bicycle and squeaked his brakes to a stop. Some of the village children had been running alongside him, and they all rushed to a stop too, gasping for breath and giggling. The man looked just about Raj's age. He was tall, with a shock of black hair on his head, light skin, and a huge smile.

Raj stood with a stupid grin on his face. He felt as if he were glimpsing his own past, gathering the children from his cheri to tell them Bible stories.

"Hello, brother," Raj exclaimed, offering his hand. "Are you a part of this church?"

The man smiled. "Thomas is my name. Yes, I am—in fact I live just behind the church with the pastor and his wife while I study."

Raj burst into a smile and said, "I am a social worker for Bright Future. I live and work in some villages nearby. We just started the project, so I will be here for quite some time. I'll need a church while I am here."

The two men looked at each other, grinning. They had each just found their new best friend.

After the service, Thomas rode with Raj all the way back to the village Raj stayed in. And to the children's delight, he stayed all day long, playing with them and Raj. At last, they collapsed in the shade of Raj's refurbished cowshed and continued a conversation they'd begun earlier in the day.

"I tell you, Raj, she is beautiful!" Thomas sighed. He was a man in love.

"What's her name?" Raj asked.

"Esther. Our families are only talking now. I will be finishing my classes soon enough, and then we will be married."

Raj hadn't ever put much thought into getting married, and for the first time, he felt a pang of longing. He looked back at his cowshed and tried push the thought out of his mind.

"Do you like school?" Raj asked.

"Sure. My dad is the real academic, though. He studied all the way in America—electrical engineering. He has his master's degree just like I soon will, but he reads more and knows more than I ever will."

"America?" Raj asked, astonished.

"He's a devout Christian man, too. He'll pray for an hour every morning before he starts anything. He started a ministry called Appreciate Technology for Rural India. You would like them. What you've done in this place"—Thomas gestured to the lights, then at the children playing beside the village well—"it's pretty similar to what his ministry does."

It was no wonder Thomas was smart but also kind, being the son of such a great man, Raj thought to himself.

"It sounds like you come from a great family," Raj said.

"Yes, lots of educated people, business people—it's a lot to live up to." Thomas grinned. "My family is a part of the Nadar community," he added.

"What?" Raj's jaw dropped, and sudden nausea came over him. The Nadar community was the same community Kumaresan and Prakash belonged to. Thomas's family must have been distantly related. Raj quickly tried to pull himself back together.

Thomas looked at Raj curiously. "What about your family?" he asked.

"Oh—" Raj looked away. "I come from a poor village family." That was all he could bring himself to share.

❖

Work in Ramnad gained momentum. When one village heard the news from another, they grew curious, and then they grew jealous. Word spread quickly of the new wells in the area, and soon other villages wanted the same. Often they would approach Raj with unquenchable curiosity.

Raj would build a friendship with them, then guide them through how to petition for borewells and electricity. He taught them how to make drainage ditches to avoid water stagnation and how to handle other sanitation issues. Everywhere he went, he encouraged the children to go to school.

The entire of district of Ramnad was beginning to change.

"Thomas, I keep coming across the same thing," he told his friend one day, as they were walking together after attending church. "Again and again I have felt it in my own life, and now I see it in every project I do, everywhere I go."

"Well, what is it?" Thomas asked.

"It's a kind of poverty, I guess." Raj slowed his pace, thinking. "I see economic poverty, educational poverty, spiritual poverty, but I also see…oh, I don't know what to call it! *Justice poverty*. In these villages, everyone is poor, but there are those who are the poorest, and they are kept in that place. I saw it in my own village too." Memories flashed in his mind—of himself, naked, strapped to that pole; of his mother, pleading for money to pay for his school; and of his uncle, turned out of the corrupt police station for making arrack. Raj pushed the images away and focused on Thomas instead.

"The poorest of the poor are kept in that place, sometimes by force, sometimes by a group of people in power who will not give them any other opportunity. It is as if their chances are sabotaged, and they are convinced to think it *should* be so." Raj glanced at Thomas uncertainly, wondering how his new friend would react.

"The government has laws to help these poor—especially the Dalits," Raj continued. "But when you come out here, those laws don't seem to do much. Some of these Dalits, if they do well in school, or become any sort of leader, they are targeted, beaten."

Thomas shook his head sadly. "I have only heard of such things," he replied.

"I feel so often that the poor are alone. Even when the laws are there, the people in the government are not." Raj shook his head. "No, I cannot say that. I have seen a good man in the government. It was not easy for him, but that man gives me hope."

Thomas listened, gazing off at the horizon.

"I have wondered if justice for the poor is possible," Raj continued. "If the government were protecting the poor, maybe this would change."

Thomas turned his gaze to meet Raj's. "I admit I do not know much about poverty," he answered after a time. "I have learned a lot from you, Raj. And I'm starting to see things I never saw before, now that I am friends with you."

Raj worked three years in Ramnad. Throughout the region, he did development work in thirty-two different villages, helping 5,000 families.

He had arrived unknown, unwanted, and with nothing more than a mat and a dull kerosene lamp. Yet for all of the initial tension that change brought, Raj couldn't have left more loved. By the end of his time, he left like a king.

Many pleaded, "You are part of every family now. How can we leave you?" And they didn't leave Raj, not during the entire two-mile-long walk in the night to the bus stop.

As Raj stepped onto the bus, he turned to see their tears. In the crowd, one person held his tiny kerosene lamp in homage.

chapter twenty-six

1993, Bangalore, twenty-seven years old

"Raj, would you pray at my wedding?" Thomas asked one day, as he and Raj sipped chai in the sitting room of their pastor's house. "You are one of my closest friends."

"I would be honored!" Raj exclaimed. "Don't worry, brother," he added jokingly, "I will impress the bride's family."

No money or effort had been spared when it came to this wedding. Months earlier, both families had extended countless invitations, many by personal visits. The venue, the gowns, the flowers, and the catering were all to be at a magnificent scale.

As the sun rose on the wedding morning, final preparations flew into place, and guests began to arrive at the venue. The bride slipped into her wedding sari, and her mother lovingly wrapped and pinned the long pallu of the sari in cascading pleats. Then her family gently fastened gold ornaments on her: bracelets, earrings, and necklaces given to her throughout her childhood in preparation for this very moment.

Like the unfolding of a symphonic chorus, she emerged at last in full splendor. Following Indian Christian tradition, the bride and groom stood together in front of glimmering drapery on a stage flooded with marigolds and recited Christian wedding oaths before a pastor. The guests rejoiced as Esther and Thomas embraced. Now the couple also cried with joy.

The guests filtered into a reception hall that was already

redolent with the scent of warm food. The bride disappeared for a moment, only to reemerge in another sari, equally as splendid as the first.

Raj sat down at the wedding table across from Thomas and his bride, surrounded by their closest friends and relatives. On the far side of the table, Thomas's and Esther's parents happily laughed together.

"Ah Raj," said Thomas, "you must meet my younger sister. Evangeline, this is my dear friend Raj." Turning to Raj again, Thomas proudly added, "Evangeline is just about to finish nursing school."

Raj met Evangeline's curious eyes. Wavy hair framed her caramel-skinned face. "It's a pleasure to meet you," Raj said shyly.

Evangeline smiled and replied, "Now, are you the one praying?"

Esther chimed in, "Yes, he is! Please, Raj, do not keep us from this food any longer!"

"Yes, yes." Raj chuckled and stood to his feet. He prayed a lovely prayer that asked for all the blessings for the bride and groom, including a happy marriage and—of course—many children.

Thomas and Esther moved to Bangalore, where Thomas had just started a job. Raj's wedding prayer was divinely answered when Thomas and Esther found out they were expecting their first child.

Meanwhile, Bright Future asked Raj to transfer to another project to be "manager in-charge" in a new location, overseeing more child sponsorship and economic development programs through the Hoskote Mission Medical Center. Raj's work had proved successful in Ramnad, to everyone's surprise, so they hoped he would facilitate a similar transformation here. The hospital happened to stand just outside Bangalore, and it was not long before Thomas and his wife insisted that Raj come and live with them, paying a modest rate for his room and board.

Raj used the opportunity of living in a large city to take evening classes at a law school. During the day, he would do his work for Bright Future, visiting families and encouraging the community. In the evenings, he would pour through books of laws, searching for how he might help the poor find their place in the justice system. His own unresolved court case fueled his quest to seek a better way for the poor, and into the late hours of the night he searched for enlightenment about his own story, looking for any way that his case could be brought back into the special court system.

Raj visited his own home once a month to check in with his family. He tried never to venture into the town, although on one particular weekend, he had no choice. He had to mail a letter, and the only post office for miles was inside Anaigudi.

A familiar dread fell over him. Five years had passed since he had been beaten. The thought of entering that town raised the hairs on his neck.

Raj started the short walk into the town around noon. The hot, heavy air of May was oppressive. Most people were inside working or napping to avoid the sun's intensity. Good, Raj thought.

The post office was only a few hundred yards into the village. He could avoid Kumaresan's house, the CSI church, the bus stop, and the dreadful electricity pole.

The only thing he could not avoid was Vanitha's home. It stood directly across the street from the post office. Vanitha was likely away; how many years had it been since he'd seen her? He did not know. Vanitha's father, now—*that* was who Raj dreaded to see.

Raj gingerly stepped along the dirt path through the town. Finally, he saw the tiny post office from around the corner, and, all too soon, Vanitha's house rose menacingly from just across the street.

Beads of perspiration gathered on his forehead and melded into a drop that slid down his cheek. Raj realized he had been holding his breath. He exhaled slowly. He had as much right to go to the post office as any other person. And he would be fast. He turned his back to the intimidating structure of Vanitha's house and stepped toward the post office, which was a tiny, concrete building with a blue door. It looked as though the structure itself could only hold two people at once. A red, cylindrical container hung on the concrete wall just outside, with an opening for letters to be shoved through.

Raj remembered how the schoolboys used to call him "post office box" and thought of his old tattered school shirt. Raj shook his head at the memory. How things had changed! He slipped his letter into the container.

"Raj!" a voice whispered from behind him. Raj felt his heart stop. In fact, maybe it did, because every other muscle in his body froze too. "Raj!" the voice whispered again. It was cautious but full of anticipation.

He knew that voice oh-so-well.

Raj turned to see her. Her dark hair shone under the hot sun. A red bindi was set just above her brow. She wore a long kurta that delicately shrouded her womanly figure.

"Raj! I am so happy to see you! I did not know if I would ever see you again." Her voice wavered with forbidden emotion. She paused, staring at him as if there were too many words to speak.

"Vanitha?" Raj whispered. He stepped toward her in disbelief. Suddenly an ancient and unnamed longing surged through Raj. Then he saw a golden thali glimmer around her neck. His heart plunged.

"You're married," Raj said.

She looked at him shyly. "Yes," she responded. "I—well, my family—has known him for a long time. Our families made the arrangements just as I was graduating, and we were married soon after." She looked away for a moment. "He's a good man and treats me well. I am grateful for that."

Raj nodded. "I...I am so happy for you," he replied, although his voice cracked.

"Raj, you are looking dull. You must take care of yourself. What are you doing now?"

"I am a social worker," Raj replied.

"Oh, that is wonderful! You always have been a social worker, you know. Even when you were a boy."

Raj smiled.

"Raj." Vanitha's voice was quiet, and she looked around nervously. Then her eyes turned back to Raj, imploring. "Raj, I had a baby last month. I am here with my mother so she can help. Would you...I mean, may I...may I show him to you? Please? Wait, and I will bring him."

Raj managed a smile, despite his confused emotions, and replied, "Of course."

Vanitha quickly tiptoed back to her home. Raj stood in the path, alone and bewildered. If anyone saw him here, he would be in trouble. If anyone saw him with Vanitha, he would be in even more trouble. If anyone saw him blessing Vanitha's baby...well, then he would just be happy to survive and still be able to walk!

His heart pounded in the thick silence and the stifling air around him. As he waited for Vanitha, Raj couldn't help but see her brother beating him that day he had been tied to the electricity pole. He couldn't help but remember her father condemning him.

He and Vanitha had never spoken of that day.

It felt like this friendship was from a different time. To pick it up again now, after all that had happened, felt like escaping back into a past that never was.

The beads of sweat on his forehead turned into rivers down his neck. Raj looked around nervously. Anyone could be watching from the dark windows around him.

Suddenly Vanitha ran back out into the street, with a tiny, swaddled figure in her arms. Raj peered uncertainly over the blanket and saw a small, sleeping face. The baby had the same innocent glow that his mother did as he slept in her arms. Vanitha's deep brown eyes were filled with warmth and love as she doted over the child. She looked up at Raj, entreating.

"Raj, will you bless him?" she asked.

Raj smiled and nodded. "Yes, I would be honored."

"I hope he grows up to be like you one day," Vanitha said.

Her sincerity shook Raj. He gulped, then said, "I will do as you ask." Then he touched the baby and prayed, "Jesus, bless this baby. May he be like you, Jesus. Watch over him and protect him."

"Thank you. Raj, I will never forget you—not ever in my life," Vanitha exclaimed in a hushed whisper. Then she was gone.

Raj turned to go back to the cheri. As he walked, his steps slowed with new intentionality and boldness. The odd encounter had somehow brought a sense of release.

He breathed in the hot air, feeling a fresh vitality, and continued his way back to the cheri—not once turning back.

"Oh Raj, you would be perfect together!" Esther exclaimed one evening. She stood from the table to clean a dish, revealing her pregnant belly. "My whole family is looking for a husband for my sister, but I have found the one."

Raj laughed. He sat at Esther and Thomas's table, in their small kitchen, under the unnaturally bright light of a fluorescent bulb. Leftover chapati lay next to a cooling pot of rice and curry.

"Esther, please," Raj said. "It is like I said the last time. You are my sister. I couldn't possibly think of marrying the sister of my sister—she is my sister also."

Thomas listened, shaking his head as he chuckled. "If he said no the first twenty times, I think he will say no the next twenty."

Their conversation was suddenly interrupted by a knock on the door.

"Ah, my sister!" Thomas exclaimed, standing up. He ventured to the front door and opened it to reveal his sister, a tall, slender woman with long, wavy hair.

"Evangeline, come in," Thomas said, opening the door wider.

"Thank you, brother," she replied, stepping in. She held a bag that made it look like she would spend the night.

Esther called from the kitchen, "Come, come, I will heat the rest of the dinner up for you!"

"You'll be staying in here," Thomas added, ushering her toward a back room.

Raj watched the new arrival curiously from the kitchen table. She glanced over to him with her deep brown eyes and smiled before she disappeared into the back room.

Raj felt his face grow hot, embarrassed she had caught his glance.

Thomas reappeared. "Evangeline just graduated from nursing school and found a job at Manipal Hospital here in Bangalore, which is good news for me. I'll get to see her more often."

Evangeline emerged from the back room, smiling. "And I will get to see my little niece more often! Or nephew—I'll take either," she added, winking at Esther.

Evangeline was taller than Raj remembered her being at the wedding. In fact, she was a tad taller than he was. Her hair delicately fell over the creamy skin of her left shoulder and there was a certain dignity in her posture.

Raj realized she was quite beautiful.

And then he realized that he must have been looking at her in a funny way, because she quickly looked away from him.

Esther reentered the room with a warm plate of rice, curry, and chapati. "You remember Raj from our wedding, right? He is working just outside Bangalore now and lives with us."

"What do you do?" Evangeline asked.

At least this was easy for Raj to answer. "I am helping the villages get clean water and electricity. Many are poor laborers, so they do not have these things. I also help their children stay in school by finding sponsors for them and encouraging the parents to send their children to school."

"Sounds like important things," she replied. "I just started at the hospital, but already I have had patients come in because their water is bad." She shook her head.

Then Esther served them cups of chai, and the four of them sat around the table to enjoy it together.

Raj took a sip of his drink. "You are a nurse, you say?"

Evangeline nodded.

"What is that like?" he asked.

She smiled and began to share about all the people who came to the hospital, and soon they were so immersed in conversation, they even forgot about the chai.

Eventually, Thomas stretched his arms with a wide yawn and announced it was time to go to bed. As the women shuffled to their rooms to change, Thomas turned to Raj.

"My family is also looking for a husband for Evangeline," he said.

Raj almost dropped his chai glass as his heart unexpectantly jumped.

Thomas continued as if he hadn't noticed. "Perhaps you can help us. Could you look for a suitable husband for my sister?"

Raj's heart fell as fast as it had jumped. Raj was a village boy, and Thomas knew that. But Thomas didn't know Raj was from a scheduled caste.

"Of course," Raj replied, trying to recover from an even more unexpected disappointment. "I have many friends who are good men. I will ask her what sort of man she would like, and I will look."

Thomas smiled at him and put his hand on his shoulder. "Thank you, brother."

chapter twenty-seven

Evangeline frequently stayed with her brother and sister-in-law, and she and Raj became good friends. Raj learned that Evangeline had a long history of suffering from ulcers, and he jumped at the opportunity to help her—it turned out that a simple ride to work lessened the pain she experienced each day.

As they rode to her workplace each morning, Raj would ask her all about the kind of man she was looking to marry, and then he would run through the list of his friends who might fit her parameters. Then they would laugh as Raj's bike squeaked to a stop at the hospital door, and she would leave. Raj would continue on to the Hoskote Mission Medical Center.

Esther's belly swelled as the months passed, but Evangeline's ulcers also swelled, becoming much angrier than they had ever been—aggravated by her long shifts at work. Esther gave birth just as Evangeline began the process of transferring out of her job in order to move back home with her parents, two hours away in Dharmapuri.

The transfer occurred at a welcome time because Evangeline was able to take care of the baby with her parents so that Esther could still work—a common practice among the tightly knit families of India. Although Evangeline no longer worked in Bangalore, the child gave a happy excuse for her to visit Thomas and Esther nearly every weekend— which meant Raj got to see her too.

By 1994, Raj had completed his work with the Hoskote Mission Medical Center and had been appointed project manager for another group of rural villages in a region just outside Bangalore called the Kolar Gold Fields. He slowed his evening law classes, devoting his time to the people he worked with. He couldn't help but be drawn back to working with the poor, even though he was dedicated to his studies.

One weekend, Evangeline visited with the baby. They all sat together, Esther and Thomas fawning over their baby and Raj and Evangeline sipping chai, watching.

"What of this man?" Raj asked Thomas. "He is of the same caste, he is an engineer, and everyone in his village speaks highly of him."

Thomas shook his head. As hard as Raj searched for a husband for Evangeline, Thomas did not find any acceptable. In fact, Raj sensed his interest in the search was waning.

"There is a small nursing school opening in Dharmapuri," Evangeline said.

Thomas looked up, curious. "Is there?"

"I interviewed for a position last week, for principal of a small nursing college," she replied, and then she paused.

"And?" Esther asked.

Evangeline burst into a smile. "They've hired me!" she exclaimed. "I am in charge of admitting students for the first batch. I am the only nursing staff, so I will have to do a lot of the work from scratch and hire some doctors to handle certain medical and surgery-related subjects, but I have the job!"

Raj went to bed, telling himself he was happy for Evangeline. He tried to push away the thought of the hours that would come with her new job, of how her visits to Bangalore would be less frequent, and, well…who exactly *were* these young doctors she would be working with?

He knew the answer, of course. *Those doctors will be educated and respectable men. Every one of those men will be exactly the sort of man her family would want her to marry.*

Raj shook his head against the thought, trying to ignore the inexplicable longing that had knotted in his chest.

❖

In August of 1995, Raj returned to Bangalore after a work retreat to discover that the house was locked up. His key was in Esther's purse, which had journeyed by Esther's side two long hours to Dharmapuri to see Thomas's parents.

Raj grimaced at the thought of traveling all the way there. He hopped back on his motorbike unenthusiastically to ride two hours to fetch his apartment key.

Raj arrived at the house of Thomas's parents exhausted. The home looked welcoming enough: humble and well kept. Still, Raj hesitated. He had never been to the house of Thomas's parents before. Had this been in his hometown, Raj knew he wouldn't have been allowed inside except, perhaps, to clean it. A shiver ran down his neck as Raj pushed that thought out of his mind.

He trudged up to the front door, rubbing the side of his leg to get the blood going through it again. He gave a confident knock and heard the latch loosen on the other side.

The door opened to reveal an older, regal face. It was a face that Raj had only seen at Thomas's wedding, but Raj's heart raced. This was Hezekiah Ponnuraj, father to Thomas and Evangeline, respected academic, businessman, and Christian leader.

Raj quickly introduced himself and added, "I stay with your son and his wife in Bangalore."

The man must have been over six feet tall and he towered over Raj. His demeanor was that of an educated man, thoughtful and learned. He peered at Raj through a pair of spectacles, their lenses glinting. Raj was intimidated—and yet, there was a gentleness about Ponnuraj. After a heartbeat or two, Raj relaxed under his kind gaze.

"Come in, come in. Thomas and Esther are inside."

Raj thanked him and awkwardly stepped in.

"But first," Ponnuraj continued, "may I have a word with you?"

"Of course," Raj said, and he followed the man into a study, slightly bewildered.

Books upon books lined the walls of the study, exuding the pleasant aroma of aged paper. One corner of the wall displayed a certificate that read, "Masters in Electrical Engineering, Cornell University." It was the den of a renowned man, the outer display of an inwardly intricate mind that lingered over deep thoughts and drifted at its own studious and measured pace. Raj's breathing felt loud and obnoxious in a room like this. So he stifled his breath as he sat delicately on a chair.

The man sat across from him, studying him.

"Thomas has told me much about you," he began. "He has told me about your work with Bright Future and that you are a good man."

Raj gave an embarrassed smile and attempted to mutter an awkward thanks.

"You have become a good friend to my daughter as well, I see. Thank you for what you have done in looking for a husband for her."

Raj nodded shyly.

"I think we have found a suitable man—if he accepts the marriage offer."

Raj forced a smile, "I am so happy for you. I am sure he must be a great man, if he is good enough to marry such a woman."

Ponnuraj chuckled. "Raj, *you* are that suitable man. I want to give my daughter to you. I want a good man who will take care of my daughter, and I trust you."

"You would have me as your son-in-law?" Raj asked, astounded. *It cannot be*, he thought. Raj would have collapsed in surprise had he not been already sitting down. Suddenly embarrassment flooded Raj, and he looked to the floor.

"Sir, I am not worthy," he began. The reality of his life crashed into the joyous feelings he had for Evangeline. "You must know I—well, I come from a very poor village. My whole family lives in the village. We are...we are plantain plantation workers."

And then Raj found he could not bring himself to share

anything more.

Ponnuraj nodded and sat pondering for a moment.

Raj slowly looked up and was surprised to see the same kindness in his eyes as earlier.

"Thank you for telling me," Ponnuraj replied. "I am glad you are an honest man. My family knows who you are today, and that is what is most important."

Raj left with his heart singing. Over the next month, Ponnuraj sent men to Raj's cheri to speak with the people and see what sort of man Raj was as he grew up there. They returned with an overwhelming response from Raj's cheri, affirming his good character and his leadership skills.

Evangeline excitedly consented to the proposal, dismissing the warning that she would be marrying into a village family that had only pit toilets and open-air bathing to offer her during her visits.

"It's not what I am used to, but I'll manage," she announced to the apprehensive women in her family. Little did she know, but Raj's sister Selvie had already begun to scrape her resources together to construct a proper bathroom. They built a shower with a western toilet next to their mud hut, just for Evangeline.

The first time Evangeline met Raj's parents was when they announced their engagement in September of 1995. Kanni and Aandi did not know what to make of it all and were very shy. However, despite their apprehension, their pride in their son shone through.

It was during this period that Evangeline's father must have learned that Raj was from a scheduled caste.

But he never brought it up.

On December 27, 1995, Raj's heart tingled with love, anticipation, and anxiety. He watched some women drape marigold and jasmine garlands around the church's podium and imagined himself standing there within a few hours, next to his new wife.

Thomas entered with thunderous steps that echoed through the church's chambers. He slapped Raj on the back and asked with a grin, "So, how are you feeling?"

Raj laughed as he nervously ran his fingers through his hair and the new beard that he had grown just for this occasion. "My family should be arriving soon. I sent a bus to bring them here. Almost one hundred people from my village are coming! I cannot imagine what this must be like for them. My parents, brothers, sisters, cousins—they will never have been to a wedding so extravagant before."

Soon enough a bus appeared, lumbering over uneven pavement, and it screeched its brakes to a stop just beside the church.

Raj pressed through the crowd of arriving guests toward the bus. His heart pounded. Rambling thoughts flooded through his mind: *This is the first time her family will meet my whole village. This is the first time her family will truly see where I came from, truly see me...What will they think of us?* Time seemed to slow as thoughts Raj had held down for months surfaced. *Could people like this really, truly be okay with a man like me joining their family?*

The bus door opened and Raj climbed inside. His own excitement and apprehension seemed to fill the bus. As he looked around, the children met his eyes with young excitement—but everyone else had settled into silence. Some of the men he'd grown up with and who had been part of the Ambedkar Association had come, including Chitravel, who flashed a smile at Raj. Jothi and Selvie sat beside their husbands. Jothi nervously held hands with her husband while Selvie looked through the window excitedly. Chelladurai and Petchimuthu also sat in the bus with their young families. Aandi and Kanni were at the front, sitting quietly. Raj knew their calm expressions were but a thin veil over their pounding hearts.

Finally, Raj turned to Antony and Saroja, sitting in the front on the other side. Their three daughters sat behind them, restlessly oblivious to the apprehension that filled their elders. Antony gazed back at Raj and slowly nodded his head. That gaze, that assuring nod, wielded a certain power that kindled fiery confidence in Raj. Antony knew some of the most painful moments in Raj's life. He had been there with him, had suffered with him. Raj looked around. Everyone on this bus had suffered with him. These were Raj's people.

Waxy, wrinkled, weathered skin had been scrubbed clean. Sunburned eyes were framed by freshly oiled and washed black hair. The women had wrapped themselves in their best faded saris and wore any precious gold they owned. The men had clothed themselves in stiff suits. It was the most respectable gathering of Anaigudi cheri residents that Raj had ever seen.

The doors of the bus opened. Raj gave them one last reassuring nod, straightened his tie, and turned outside. Bright flowers fluttered in the breeze and joyful shouting swelled around Raj as he stepped out of the bus. Young women had lined either side of the door, holding bunches of marigolds. Raj immediately knew these must be Evangeline's nursing students. They formed a walkway between them, and around the outside of it, happy onlookers crowded around. At the end of the line was Evangeline's family, waiting to receive him. They were beaming.

Kanni stepped out. Her eyes peered uncertainly through her thick glasses, then widened in astonishment.

"Oh Raj," she managed as she clung to her son's arm. One by one, the people of Raj's cheri stepped into the crowd. New cheering erupted with every new figure that emerged from the bus.

Raj walked up to Ponnuraj and they clasped hands. Ponnuraj turned to Aandi and Kanni and bowed his head.

"Welcome," he said.

Soon Raj found himself standing at the front of the church, the pastor on one side and Thomas, his best man, on the other. Two figures appeared at the opposite end of the hall, and the five hundred guests stood and began to sing a hymn.

The crowd turned to a blur as she walked down the aisle. It was as if light emanated from that veiled figure and gleamed from her pink and gold sari. Her long, braided hair flowed from beneath the veil. Ponnuraj walked proudly beside her to the rhythm of the hymn. Aandi and Kanni stood quietly, mesmerized by the procession.

Raj rocked back and forth on the balls of his feet, stifling a tear. Such a beautiful and caring woman would be his wife! He was a cheri boy. She was a princess.

As her veil was removed, Raj felt his heart give way. Raj gently raised a golden thali, and, with shaking fingers, fastened the gleaming necklace around her neck.

The pastor's words echoed as if he were speaking from a far distance. Raj was fixated on his bride.

They said their vows to one another. Garlands heavy with flowers were brought before them.

They each placed a garland around each other's neck, and then they were man and wife.

chapter twenty-eight

1996, Bangalore, thirty years old

Shadows danced across crumbling walls in the murky night. The mid-winter air was chill. A man stoked a fire in an aluminum bin, then held his hands to the warmth. Alcohol lingered in the vapor he exhaled through his dry, cracked lips. He coughed, then pulled a knitted cap over his head. Fifty degrees Fahrenheit was frigid to anyone in the tropics.

Tall concrete structures rose around him, in abnormally close proximity to one another. The government had built apartments for this city slum, and now the inhabitants crowded themselves even more tightly into the small living spaces. Next to him lay a large mound of sand, ready to be used for yet another building that was going up close by.

Another man, dressed in a lungi, with a towel around his head, sprawled out in the sand, sleeping. An open storm drain flowed one street away: a stinking gray river of drowned rats, human feces, and the rest of the city's waste. Occasionally the breeze would shift, gathering its sickening odor in furls and tossing the stench all around.

Skinny chickens and goats rummaged through the streets and skinny children followed after them. More men slunk through the shadows and joined the first man around the fire. The glow of a freshly lit beedi appeared, then another and another as the men began to smoke around the fire.

Conversation flowed in elegant Tamil even though they were in Bangalore, the capital of the state of Karnataka where the official language is Kannada. These men were immigrants and quickly bonded through their mother tongue. Every night, they would come and talk.

"The store owner down the street allowed me to take some arrack if I promised to pay him back next week," one said.

"Ah, but will you?" another chided. "Aiyo, these store owners know how to get us."

The other men chuckled with him.

"I gotta have some rest for my sore bones after pouring concrete all day!" the first man protested.

"You're just gonna have to pay him with extra later. He'll choke it out of you," another grumbled.

"But we all do it...what else could we do?"

"Hey, folks, I got paid today!"

With more chuckles, another teased, "Oh, from your politician friend you won't tell us about?"

"I don't talk about *that* work," the man retorted.

His companions huffed jealous laughs. Finally, one roared, "Ah well, let's celebrate anyway! Light 'im up another beedi!"

A garbled moan arose from the man sleeping in the sand as he shifted his weight and rolled over.

"Aye, so the man's not dead," one jeered, gesturing toward the sand pile. It was hard to tell with people who slept on the streets.

Across the way, a door opened, and a woman stepped out toward the men.

"Ah, Akon, it's your wife," one said as the man identified gave a long, exasperated sigh.

"I'll deal with her," he assured them, and he slunk toward her around the mound of sand.

The woman strutted toward him with fire in her steps. She spoke first. "You worked all week. Today is payday." She was angry. "Where is the money? Where is our food? Why are you here drinking? What of our children?"

The man growled, reciprocating her anger.

"We need the money," she insisted. "*I beg you.* I clean houses all day long, but I do not have enough to take care of the children. We are out of rice. What am I to do?"

"Woman, don't you talk to me that way," he snarled. Suddenly he lost his balance and nearly stepped on the man sleeping in the sand pile. "Aie, you drunkard!" he roared at the figure in the sand. Then he turned back to his wife. "Leave me alone, woman!" He flicked his hand dismissively. "See this man!" he yelled, gesturing to the man in the sand. "At least I'm not him. You should be happy." With that, he walked away.

The drunkard in the sand still lay there pathetically, face down in the dust. But his eyes were open—he had been listening to everything.

In fact, he wasn't drunk at all. It was Raj, disguised in order to gather a true assessment of the slum's needs.

Raj was about to begin Bright Future's first development project in the slums of Bangalore.

In January of 1996, just weeks after getting married, Raj set out on a new mission. For the first time in India, Bright Future was directly overseeing projects, rather than acting as a funding agency as it had in the years prior. Raj transitioned into the role of project manager on a yearlong contract, with the promise that he would soon be brought on as an employee. Raj, with an enthusiastic team of fifteen under him, was to oversee community development in ten slums in Bangalore.

Slums began with squatters taking the land around the sewage storm drains or other undesirable places. They would build shantytowns for themselves and search for work as maids, street sweepers, construction workers, or street salesmen.

Slums were illegal occupancies, which meant the government could evict the dwellers at any moment—and this would sometimes happen if the land proved valuable to politicians. However, more often than not, the government would leave the slums in place or replace the teetering structures with concrete apartments in an attempt to condense the poverty-stricken population into a smaller area. When this was done, the apartments quickly filled with families, often with up to ten people living in a ten-foot-by-ten-foot room.

Raj stepped through a narrow alley in the slum. Chickens clucked, and a goat lazily stared at him as he stepped through debris. He had changed since the night he was here and now wore pants, a t-shirt, and smart-looking glasses. The odor of sewage permeated the air as he turned onto another narrow street, and Raj wrinkled his nose. Children played idly in the dirt collected over the concrete paths from construction dust and other debris. Some teenage boys clustered around each other and eyed Raj suspiciously.

Raj shook his head. Alcoholism sank its dirty fingernails into the men before they were even men. Girls were taken advantage of and then deemed "spoiled" before they were even women. Families who moved to the slums from rural towns in hope of a better life quickly found themselves trapped.

Helping this slum would be no easy feat.

The urban economy operated differently than the rural villages, taking its cues from a much more sinister playbook. Drunk, rupee-less men could have extra cash or even a new bike appear overnight as payment for their mysterious criminal activities, and this kind of temptation to crime often proved too much for them to resist.

Raj knocked on a wooden door of a sheet metal shelter that faced the alley. It was the house of the woman he had seen a few nights before, angry with her husband. The sandpile lay not far from her door. Around them, tight concrete apartments stretched four stories high. Laundry blew on lines strung between the structures above him. A cat peered out at him from a concrete staircase in the story above. Raj thought of Evangeline, and his heart longed for her. His mind would often wander to her throughout the day. Raj sighed and knocked again.

The door opened just enough for Raj to see two suspicious eyes.

"Can I help you, sir?" The words were in Kannada, the language of that state, but were thick with a Tamil accent. Raj smiled.

"Ah, hello," he replied in Tamil. He saw the eyes widen. Then the door opened. A young girl stood before him, and a five-year-old played on the dirt floor behind her.

"You are Tamilian," she said curiously. "Any man dressed like you around here is from the government. From Karnataka." Her head tilted, and her eyes squinted. "You are not one of them."

"Madame, I am a social worker."

She smiled at the familiar sounds of his Tamilian words. He spoke like her caste, too. The look on her face turned from suspicious to trusting.

"Tell me," Raj continued, "how old are you?"

"I am twelve. I am taking care of my little sister. My mother will be coming home soon from work."

As if on cue, Raj turned to see the woman from the other night shuffling to the door, wiping her brow and tucking her maid apron into her bag.

"Who is this?" she asked her daughter, eyeing Raj with the same suspicion.

Raj quickly introduced himself and then asked, "Madame, would you consider sending these children to school?"

"Aiyo!" She frowned. "They only teach in Kannada. My children must learn Kannada before they can learn in these schools. And the teachers—sometimes they come, sometimes they don't. Sometimes there is no power, no light, so the children can't even read. The schools here are very bad. I don't make my children go."

Raj nodded his head understandingly. "Would you, madame, send your children to school if it were better?"

She looked at the child in her arms, who she'd just picked up. "Yes, I suppose I would. But good schools cost money we don't have. And I need my kids to work. When my

214

youngest, Annu, doesn't need to be looked after, Sangie, my eldest, will join me in cleaning homes. We won't get by otherwise."

"Imagine your child completing high school. Think of what kind of work they could get then. That would pay more than they ever could make now."

She looked at him with tired eyes. "But how would they ever do that?"

"It is possible," Raj replied. "I will help them."

The mother looked at her five-year-old and then at her small, meager apartment. When she looked back at him, her eyes were glossy. She answered, "I hope you do."

At the end of the day, Raj assembled his team to debrief what they had found.

"Most families, they are not interested," a young man named Hruday explained. Like Raj, he had come out of intense poverty from one of the poorest states in India, Odisha. "They are like the others—they can't understand the importance of education."

"Even if it were paid for, and better-quality education, they do not want it," another worker explained. His name was William, and he was a passionate man with an immaculate mustache.

"They will have to trust us first before they will want to listen," Raj said, thinking hard. "There is a community hall in this slum that is unused. Let us start with hosting games and cultural dances for the children and become their friends. I will tell them my story."

A woman named Jothi nodded and smiled. "You are right," she agreed. "The mothers will trust you then."

Jothi was an expert seamstress. She had chosen ministry instead of marriage a long time ago, and her joy in devoting herself to others seemed to bubble out of her. Her thin, elegant frame looked delicate on the outside, but she was not to be underestimated. Her strength and fervor carried her into the most challenging situations to help others. She had met Raj during a past project and now worked with Raj wherever he went, teaching women to sew so they could support themselves.

Raj looked around at his team with a surge of confidence. This team was passionate, committed, and hardworking. The task before them would be difficult, but he knew they could do it.

Raj ended the night well pleased. He could see it all before him: children coming to the community hall after school to learn, eat, and play. As Raj rode back to his flat, Bangalore whisked by. Outside of the slum, the scenery fluctuated between tightly situated buildings with even tighter apartments above, to kingly highways lined with ornately trimmed trees and lavish estates left by the British. These estates had long since become military training grounds, filled with trees and their refreshing scent. Smaller, slum-like shanties intermingled with the growing cosmopolitan expanse that yearned upward.

Raj arrived at his modest apartment and began to pack his bags quickly. Today was Friday, and his heart swelled with uncontainable joy at the anticipation of being with Evangeline. He would drive through the night, 175 kilometers to Dharmapuri, and spend the weekend with his wife. Then, every Sunday evening, he would face the heartbreak of having to leave her and take the 175-kilometer ride back. Evangeline's job as vice principal of the nursing school in Dharmapuri was a good job, and they were grateful she had it. Still, they prayed for a position for Evangeline to open in Bangalore so that they could truly make a home together. Week after week, their hearts yearned for each other. And the days rolled on.

Over the next three months, Raj and his team succeeded in befriending many families in the slum. Through these friendships, they cast a beautiful vision that these families had never imagined before, of their children going to school. Slowly families began to pledge that they would send their children to school if sponsors were found. Raj settled into the rhythm of the work. Good things were beginning to happen in the slum.

One day Raj made his way home, pleased with the day's work. It seemed so quiet and lonely as he walked through his door. Two more days before the weekend...his phone rang, and Raj's heart leaped.

"Hello?" he asked, hoping it was who he thought.

"Raj!" the excited voice of his wife answered.

"Yes?"

"Raj, I couldn't wait to tell you in person," Evangeline replied. "Raj, we're going to have a baby! Raj, I'm pregnant!"

"This is wonderful!" Raj cried out, as his heart swelled with love for this new tiny being.

Evangeline continued, "When you come this weekend, we will go to the hospital together and see for sure."

Raj had never felt such joy in his life. The Lord had just given him the most wonderful wife, and now a baby?

His heart was so full. It was a double blessing. And he knew his whole life was about to change again.

chapter twenty-nine

Raj and his team secured sponsorship for five hundred children over the next few months. The numbers steadily grew, and Raj visited the after-school programs frequently.

One evening, after the sun had set over the cinder block jungle, the children were finishing their tutoring time at one of the project's locations. Outside the little room, dogs barked, motorbikes whirred, and people shouted. Evenings in the slum were no quiet affair.

"Annu, where is your older sister today?" Raj asked one of the children.

Annu was six years old, with bright brown eyes. She looked up from her book where she had been tracing Kannada letters. "Sangie went to work with Ama today. Ama says that our dad is sick...I haven't seen him for some time."

The hair on Raj's neck prickled. He had never met their father, but he remembered him from that first night. It had sounded like their father, Akon, was a gangster.

Raj walked with the girl through narrow and winding paths back to her home. It was on the outskirts of the slum, directly across from the storm drain. The area reeked with the stench of feces and dead animals that occasionally floated along in the river of gray water. Metal, plastic, and cinder block shanties lined the drain. These shanties had been built after the government constructed more stable apartments throughout the rest of the slum.

Annu slipped past a cloth doorway and then poked her head back out.

"Wait here," she said.

Soon enough, Sangie emerged, looking forlorn. She was

twelve years old, but the worry in her face made her look older.

"Raj, sir, I am sorry I missed school. Please, sir."

"Sangie, Sangie, what is the matter?"

"My father has been missing these past few days. My mother...well, she got angry with him. He spent all his wages from this last week on arrack, and now we don't have any money for food. Not even a bag of rice. And we don't know where he is or when he is coming back. I have to work. I cannot go to school."

A tear welled in her eye and slid gracefully down her cheek. "My mother is bringing me with her to clean homes. Together we work faster, we clean more homes. We make a little more than if it were just her. We can get by with that."

"Oh, Sangie." Raj sat down on some cinder blocks stacked next to her home. He took his glasses off and wiped them on his shirt, thinking hard.

Should she choose to stay in her work as a maid with her mom, she would not only miss her exams—should she stay working long enough, she would soon be pressured to marry. He had seen it all before. "Our girl needs to be protected," the family would say. "She must marry now, or else she will never marry and not be protected." Why would she never marry? Because everybody knew, but nobody said, that a young girl working as a maid cleaning homes was all too likely to be subject to rape, and no man wanted to marry a raped woman.

Raj's heart broke at the thought. In an effort to protect the girl by having her marry, her prospects of a better life through education would be extinguished. Her husband could very well follow in the footsteps of nearly every other man there and, rather than protect her, spend his earnings on alcohol and turn abusive. Her life would be bound to the slum and, in a cruel irony, she would be more vulnerable than ever before.

A wave of compassion moved through Raj. He could not let this happen.

"Sangie, you're a smart girl. You know that if you make it

through high school, you will be able to take care of your family much more than you can now."

"I know!" she exclaimed. "But I just can't. I have no choice."

"How much does your family spend on one bag of rice every week?"

Sangie and Annu looked at Raj, puzzled.

Raj continued, "And how often must you borrow money to do this? Or buy medicine when you are sick? How much extra do you have to pay back on that money?"

"Twenty percent," Sangie replied. "They make us pay back at twenty percent. And we must pay back. We must also pay back my dad's loans for arrack and for when Annu got sick last year." Sangie looked down at her feet. "You see, Raj? I have no other option."

Raj knelt down so he was at her eye level. "Sangie, come back to school. We will help your family. And I will help so that this does not happen again. There are many others in the same situation—they think there are no other options, but I will show you a way."

Raj stood to leave and, when he turned, found himself staring directly into the face of an angry man.

It was the girls' father, Akon.

"What are you doing here?" the man growled, outraged. Alcohol reeked in his breath, and his words were slurred.

"Appa!" Annu exclaimed.

"Move away from him, girls," he said, lunging toward Raj. "I said, what are you doing here?"

Raj took a step back with his hands up. "Please, please, I am only here to help," he said, in soothing Tamil. "Your girls here are very smart. I have been helping them with—"

"Get out of here," the man slurred.

Raj took another step back but kept his gaze on the man. Akon's clothes were disheveled, and it looked as if he had been sleeping outside for some time. His eyes were red. He looked like a man just trying to survive.

"Do you like mutton?" Raj asked.

Taken off guard, Akon stepped back and squinted at Raj, puzzled. "Of course, I like mutton. I'll eat any meat I can get."

Raj smiled. "There is a meeting tonight in the community hall with other men. One family has prepared one kilogram of mutton. Please, come." With that, Raj nodded to the girls and left.

That evening, Raj waited in the community hall with his teammates Hruday and William. Attracted by the smells of the savory meat, the men of the slum started to trickle in. This was only the third meeting they had conducted, but many of the same faces returned. Raj hoped Akon would come, but at last, he had to start the meeting without him.

"Good evening," William began, speaking to a tired-looking group of ten or so men. "I want everyone to thank Prabhakar for providing our mutton soup tonight, which we will eat shortly."

Excited murmurs ran through the crowd.

"Now, I see some new faces, so here is how this group works. We meet every week, and each time one of you is responsible for the food. We ask that this be your only contribution. Now, you may wonder how you can ever afford to buy meat like this. Well, Prabhakar, will you share?"

The man who provided that night's meal stood up. "Two months ago, I decided to stop drinking alcohol. I would use it to help my hurting back after construction labor, but it had become too much. I was always in debt. Now that I have stopped drinking, I save the money I used to spend on alcohol. It is really actually a lot of money!" He laughed nervously. "I can buy meat now. I am even saving money to buy a cart, so I can sell vegetables in the city and not work in the sewers anymore."

A chorus of murmurs ran through the group.

Raj stood and exclaimed, "Prabhakar, you have become a businessman!" And he slapped Prabhakar on the back. Turning to address the group, he continued, "You are all welcome to join, and we will help you get off alcohol. We are together in this." Raj moved toward the mutton soup to begin serving the hungry men.

Suddenly his eyes caught a man emerging from the shadows—Akon had come after all. As the man came through the line, he had a new expression on his face.

"I want to join. I want to leave alcohol, and I want to leave this work I have been in. Can you help me?"

"Yes," Raj replied. "Meet me tomorrow at the hospital across from the slum. They have an alcohol addiction center that will help you get off alcohol. Then we will all work on you staying off alcohol." Raj paused, because the man still seemed uneasy. "Akon, today is the start of a new life for you and your family."

Sure enough, Akon came to the hospital that next morning. He moved with determination, although there was fear in his eyes. Even though Akon had showed up and seemed willing to accept treatment, as Raj parted from the man to go on to the next part of his workday, he felt a sense of foreboding.

Then one night it all made sense as Akon's wife burst into the after-school program.

"Raj, you must help!" she pleaded.

Raj followed her immediately. She led him to where Akon lay, bleeding in an alley not far from his house. Some other men had gathered, concerned. His breath was stuttered, and his teeth clenched.

"I told the syndicate I would not work for them anymore," he croaked, and then he coughed.

Raj looked around at the other men. "Come, we will take you to the hospital," Raj said.

The hospital saved his life, but after that incident, Raj wasn't sure he would see the man again. He suspected that Akon would return to the gangsters.

To his surprise, Akon had a different idea about his life. He returned even stronger, more determined to better himself and his family.

And the gang did not touch him again.

Over the next several months, more children were sponsored, and more men joined Raj's club, which still offered mutton soup once a week in exchange for them giving up their alcohol addictions. Raj stayed true to his promise to Sangie by showing her family how to avoid debt for their groceries. This time, he and Jothi gathered the mothers of the slum together rather than the fathers.

"Today, we are starting a cooperative," Raj announced to the small group of women. "How much do you spend every week on rice? Forty-five rupees? When we buy together in bulk and distribute the same amount, it will cost each family only fourteen rupees."

The women perked their heads up excitedly. "How will we do this?" one of the older women asked.

"I have already contracted with the wholesale rice distributers. I will do the same for dhal and oil. These things do not go bad, so if we ever order too much, we will order less the next time. Nothing will be wasted, only money saved."

The women chattered excitedly. They were already beginning to dream.

"This is good and all, but I am in so much debt," said Sangie and Annu's mother. "I do not know what I can do. It feels like too much."

Raj nodded. The families in the slum not only lacked skills in arithmetic and so could not know just how much extra they were paying back on loans, but, in their desperation, they often had little choice but to take loans at incredibly high interest rates.

"I know this is hard. My own family has suffered under debt. But if you work together, you can keep each other out of debt. I call it a self-help group because you are helping each other directly.

"If we practice sharing groceries, you will all be saving

money. Now, if this money is stored together, as a group, you can give each other loans at a normal interest rate, one or two percent. That is much less than twenty percent, yes?"

The women nodded.

"The more participants, the more this money will grow. If one of your families enters a time of crisis, like a child gets sick, the money will be enough to loan immediate help. The money generated by the low interest of the loan will go toward a bookkeeper, one of you women, I hope, who will manage these transactions.

"These loans can also be used to start a business." He turned to his companion. "I want you all to meet Jothi. For those who are willing, Jothi will train you to be tailors."

Jothi stepped before the women with a disarming smile. "I will make expert seamstresses out of you," she said. "Imagine if one day you do not have to be a domestic worker or a street sweeper—you will be businesswomen!"

Once the women's self-help groups were underway, they quickly grew in numbers, as did Jothi's tailoring classes. The slum was beginning to change. It seemed that new hope was growing in every alley and apartment.

One day a call came that Raj had been anticipating for nine whole months. His wife had started labor. Immediately, Raj left Bangalore, and by the time he arrived in Dharmapuri, it was time for Evangeline to go to the hospital.

Exhilarated with nerves and excitement, the young couple rushed to the hospital. It was a small structure, built barely large enough to serve the small town. They checked Evangeline in, and nurses wheeled her out of sight. Raj moved to follow but was stopped.

"Patients only," a nurse said.

"But—" Raj stopped, bewildered. "I must be with my wife. Our child is being born!"

The nurse smiled apologetically, pitying his desperation.

"Your wife will be fine with us. This hospital is just too small. There is not space to allow husbands inside."

Dejected, Raj found a pile of sand outside the hospital. He shivered. It was a cold night. Raj channeled his nervousness into praying—it was all he could do. He watched the stars slowly drift through the night sky into the warm glow of the nearing morning.

"Sir?"

Raj looked up to see the nurse.

Her smile calmed him. "Congratulations, you have a boy."

Raj and Evangeline named the child Samuel Stephan Anburaj: *Samuel* after a pastor Raj had befriended while working in Tamil Nadu and *Anburaj* because it meant "king of love." The name also brought together the names of Raj's and Evangeline's fathers, Aandi Anbalagan and Ponnuraj.

Evangeline stayed under the attentive care of her mother and father at first. Then, after three months, she came to Bangalore with Raj. Raj was overjoyed at having her with him all the time. Together, they delighted in their baby boy as he smiled and made all sorts of new noises. Then he began to crawl, then walk. Eventually, Evangeline found a job as vice principal in a nursing school in Bangalore—their prayers had been answered: they were now able to stay together as a family throughout the weekdays too.

Each morning Raj would drop her off at her work on the way to his own and then pick her up on his way home. They reveled in the time they had together as they ate dinner. Then Evangeline would ask Raj to sing. With his soothing voice, Raj sang Tamil love songs into the evening. Their baby's face lit up as he heard his father's voice lifted in song. The mundane was enchanting to them, for, at last, they were together.

Two and a half years after Sam's arrival, their second child was born. It was another boy, and they named him Daniel Anand Premraj. *Premraj* also means "king of love," and Raj prayed that both his sons would grow in God and in love.

Their family was now complete.

HAYLEY BENNETT LYLE

chapter thirty

2003, Bangalore, thirty-eight years old

"Raj, I am looking over these numbers, and they are incredible!"

The man speaking was Vijay Kumar, a short man with gentle eyes behind thick glasses. He oversaw Raj's project and three others. He held a paper up to his face as if holding it close would verify its validity. "Between starting in 1996 to now in 2004, oh my! Two hundred fifty self-help groups and more still forming? Four thousand women are saving money and sharing groceries!" He continued listing items off with a crescendo of enthusiasm. "One hundred fifty men no longer addicted to alcohol. Two thousand children sponsored in their education, and twelve hundred of them have gone through high school and received a diploma! Raj, this is spectacular."

Raj, who was sitting across from Kumar, nodded. "The team and I have seen much success in this slum. The people are beginning to believe in themselves, I think. Now that the fathers are leaving alcohol and seeing how much they can accomplish when they save that money, they are gaining confidence, and that confidence is spreading throughout the entire community."

"Well, these self-help groups, and organizing this women's cooperative, has been especially successful. With this work, you have gained a lot of experience in microenterprise, and now you have a proven track record of performance." Kumar furrowed his brow. "Bright Future is restructuring, and they are opening a wing for microenterprise development."

"I will do what I can to help," Raj assured his manager.

"Well, not just help, Raj. They will need somebody to oversee it, somebody who understands it." He peered at Raj over his glasses. "You must apply."

Raj's eyes widened.

"They want to interview you next week. Think about it, talk it over with Evangeline. If you took the job, you would have to move your family to Delhi, most likely. All the regional directors work out of that city."

"Regional director?" Raj asked, astonished. Suddenly, Raj's world opened to new hopes and new horizons he had never imagined before. He could see it all—planting self-help groups all around the country and watching them grow, bringing people just like his own brothers and sisters, his mother and father, out of debt and into a thriving life. Raj imagined bringing his family into their first home in Delhi, giving his sons the best education, and buying the most beautiful sari for his wife.

He wondered how he could fall in love with a dream so quickly, but it all felt so right. Bright Future had changed the course of his life, and now he would get to give back in an even bigger way. It was as if all the wandering circles of his life had just conjoined in gratifying closure.

Raj's life had reached full bloom. He stepped out of that office with a joyful spring in his step. In the past seven years of his work in the Bangalore slums, the program he oversaw had blossomed like the orange flowers of the African Tulip trees that were scattered throughout Bangalore. His sons were now seven- and five-year-old boys who infused his life with delight. Every night he got to sing to his sons a Tamil lullaby, then hold his wife in his arms. Could life become any sweeter?

Raj passed through the first round of interviews, and he and Evangeline started looking at Hindi schools to enroll their sons in so that they would be ready to assimilate into the Hindi-speaking north. Meanwhile, Raj confidently prepared for the next interview.

When he arrived for it, the hiring manager stood up as Raj entered the room.

"Welcome, thank you for coming in," he began. "Your track record is impressive. I see that you have facilitated many successes in the communities you have served."

"Thank you, sir," Raj said, bashfully receiving the compliment. "All by the grace of God."

"Indeed. Let us discuss the role of regional director for our new microenterprise wing."

Raj sat on the edge of his seat. He was already sweaty from the hot day, but his palms grew wet with nervousness as he waited for the interviewer's next words.

However, the interviewer's previously welcoming tone turned slightly flat. "We have a…a better job for you, though. And we have recommended you for a position available at another organization."

Raj felt like his heart stopped. "What…what do you mean?" he stuttered.

"Of course, we have spoken very highly of you to them, and we believe the job would be a perfect fit for you," the hiring manager continued.

Raj teetered between confusion and disbelief. Why would they tell him to work at a different organization?

"What about the position I applied for? The regional director for microenterprise?"

The hiring manager shifted uncomfortably but kept a sad smile pasted on his face. "I am afraid that we have run into some complications."

"Complications?" Raj asked. Now he felt himself sinking into an ambiguous sludge of anxiety.

"Er, yes. Raj, I am sorry to say this, but…we will not be able to take you as our regional director."

Certainly, this could not be true, Raj thought. Tension brewed in the room. Raj knew there must be more going on than the manager was disclosing.

"Please, sir. Tell me, what has happened?" Raj pleaded. "I have been with Bright Future for fifteen years. I have

229

pioneered the microenterprise system that this position is created for. Please, sir, can't you just tell me?"

The hiring manager shook his head. "I am sorry, Raj. Please consider this other position. I also must tell you that we will not be renewing your contract this year."

Raj left the room in shock, feeling nauseated. It had been fifteen years of working on a yearly contract, being paid less than an employee and kept stagnant in his career by this one invisible yet seemingly unshakable ceiling. All the hopes that had dawned so vividly weeks before seemed burned to ash by this same unexplainable force. Raj excused himself to a secluded area and, sliding down the wall, held his head in his hands. *How can I tell my team, who has worked so faithfully by my side these past years?*

Then his mind was filled with Evangeline. *How can I tell her?* The thought tore a new wound through his heart.

The sound of tentative feet shuffling toward him gave him pause. He looked to his side to see the shoes of a man squatting next to him. It was a man Raj had worked with who was a senior officer in Bright Future and who also happened to be scheduled caste.

"Raj," he started, "I heard what happened." His voice wavered as he spoke. "The other managers, they…"

Raj dreaded meeting his friend's gaze but forced himself to do it. Anger and sadness mixed in his friend's eyes.

"When they found out you were being considered for regional manager, they practically revolted. They said they could not work for somebody from your background. They…they would not work for a scheduled caste member." He looked down. "And so, Bright Future cannot keep you and will not renew your contract. Raj, it's horrible, and I am so sorry."

Raj felt his will to persevere give way. What he knew but had wished not to see, had wished was not possible, could be ignored no longer. He didn't want to fight this battle, not with them. He felt nothing—no strength nor will to protest.

Raj lifted his eyes to the man's, imploring. "Is there

nothing else to do?" he asked.

The man looked away. "Not that I can see."

Light from Raj's home spilled onto the stairway through the cracks around the door and a tiny window beside it, making the night seem darker and the light seem blinding. Raj paced outside the door for a long time. He had put his hand on the doorknob and then taken it off countless times.

Raj's knees buckled as he finally sat on the step outside his tiny apartment. The day's blow stung like the thousand hits he had taken that day in Anaigudi. Torturous images flashed through his mind—the townspeople passively watching him being beaten, Vanitha's father condemning the assailants for not killing him, Prakash snarling with pleasure as he hit him, again and again.

And all of this, because he had dared to call another human being his "brother."

Now a new pain stung mercilessly, like salt scraped into old wounds. He had trusted the other managers at the Bright Future and believed them to be friends. He had let his heart open and had exposed all his vulnerabilities.

He had dared to think they were his brothers.

Again, he felt the betrayal like a knife slice, slowly splitting his gut and piercing through his ribcage, into his heart.

What could he do when his opponents were the same people he labored beside as they helped so many? They had openly approved of him and then, like cowards in the shadows, had brought him down. Was caste so important to them? Or was he actually convenient competition, ready to be disposed of? His heart wrenched with that thought.

He longed for a hug from his wife and some reassurance that it would all be okay. At the same time, his anger frothed like muddy water in a bucket, with nowhere to go. *Will this ever end?* he silently cried out. *How many obstacles have I already overcome due to my caste? And still there are more?*

Suddenly, shame and guilt overwhelmed him. Evangeline was a high-caste girl; she should never have to know the hardships Raj faced because of his lower caste. He knew how life was in a scheduled caste. But his wife was the one he longed to provide for. He wanted to make the best possible life for her, and now he had proved incapable of it. That incapability threatened to swallow him further into shame. He never wanted Evangeline to suffer because of him. Raj hung his head again, resting it in his hands.

The light from the window grew dark with the shadow of someone looking through it. Then Raj heard a young voice exclaim, "There he is! I told you papa would be home soon."

Raj grimaced. The door opened, and two small boys with wild hair came and flung their arms around him. Raj looked up to see Evangeline coming. She wore a long, loose-fitting dress, the one she would always change into after work. Raj swallowed his tears back. She smiled at him, then tilted her head. She came close to sit beside him and tucked her arms around him.

"What is the matter? You look so sad," she said.

Raj looked deep into her eyes, searching. He saw only love. This woman had cared nothing about his caste, nor had her father, nor the whole family for that matter. There was God's love in that love.

Grasping Evangeline's hand, he stood up and stepped into his home. He began to tell her all that had happened. She put her hand over her mouth in shock, shed a tear, then pulled him into a warm embrace.

Raj's shattered body started to breathe courage again. It was the smallest breath, but in shallow breath after breath, it would grow strong once more. The slightest ounce of resolve flickered within Raj.

The Lord saw all things, knew all things, and had taken Raj as his son. Whatever the setbacks, whatever the obstacles, they could not touch that. And as hard as they tried to yoke him into the belief he was lesser, they could not touch that truth.

Courage was getting up again. Courage was every time he had stepped back into Anaigudi, every time he chose to go to church, and now every job he would apply to.

In 2003, Raj left Bright Future. He would apply to many jobs before a nonprofit named Samuka Initiative hired him as national field director for all of their operations in India. Raj began to oversee Samuka's eighteen projects focused on child sponsorship and education and on community development. These projects were spread throughout the country, from north India to Sri Lanka. These programs gave relief to impoverished communities through child sponsorship programs, from the children of poor tea farmers in Sri Lanka to the children of sex workers in the northeastern state of Nagaland. He also oversaw hostels for orphans and children in difficult circumstances, including one specifically for deaf and dumb children.

Raj regularly visited the projects and used his own expertise to pioneer self-help groups for mothers to encourage each other and microfinance one another's needs, as well as tailoring co-ops, and he also provided guidance in accessing government resources for clean water and electricity.

Raj's work frequently called him away from his family for extended periods of time to tour the children's programs and orphanages and to assess the progress within the communities Samuka served. The projects flourished under Raj's attentive care. Meanwhile, he gratefully took whatever time he could get with his family.

One day, after Christmas in the following year, 2004, Raj was taking in the joys of being home after working out in the field for many days in a row. Daniel and Samuel were six and eight years old and were tossing around the presents they'd recently unwrapped. Evangeline stirred byriani in the kitchen, and the savory smell of it permeated the whole home.

Then terrible news came: a tsunami had just devastated India's eastern coastline. Indonesia, Thailand, Sri Lanka—all of them were devastated. Tamil Nadu's death toll was steadily rising. Roads, homes, and cities were wiped out. Emergency relief was needed immediately.

Raj dialed the president of Samuka Initiative. "Sir, we must go. I need three lorries with bags of rice and dhal, medical supplies, and sheet metal to build shelters."

The chaos was deafening.

Four days after the tsunami, Raj arrived in Tamil Nadu with supplies and a team. They had been directed to a small fisherman's town named Kallar. It had been completely wiped out. Most of the victims had been women, children, and the elderly.

Raj couldn't have imagined what he was stepping into, and it was worse than all he could have imagined. The dead were still being found. Children were still missing. Unidentified victims, strangled by the sea and sucked down the coast, lay unidentified in a line on the shore. Shock, anger, and grief commanded the living.

The small coastal town of Kallar lay in muddy rubble. Two miles inland, still undiscovered at that point in time, lay the decimated Dalit settlement of backwater prawn farmers. Both villages' people struggled, immersed in anguished desperation. The Dalit settlement would struggle on for four years before relief arrived. Until then, hope was just a distant dream.

Raj stepped out of his truck in Kallar. The door shut with a loud clap, but it did nothing to penetrate the commotion.

"Who is your leader?" Raj asked. "We have come with supplies—we are here to help."

V
New Kallar

I think God has a special place for the poor always. I see it in my own life. How God has faithfully walked with me throughout my life. The Lord is really loyal. In the culture, the system, the community, everything is away from God—in spite of that, we can follow God. We cannot become complacent; we need to follow God. And God also is sustaining us.

—*Raj, Interview I, July 16, 2018*

chapter thirty-one

2011, New Kallar, forty-five years old

The warm turquoise water lapped against the shores like soft silk dancing with the breeze. The palm tree fronds blurred as Raj zoomed along the road to the fisherman village of Kallar on a motorbike. The year was 2011, and Raj had journeyed all night to get to his destination.

Despite how many years had passed, rubble from the tsunami lingered like a painful memory among the young bushes and newly constructed homes. The road was newly paved and divided the sandy coastline from the muddy inlets where the reconstructed prawn fields lay. Raj turned his head left to watch a few of the fishermen's boats return beneath the pink dawn. On his right, spigots sprayed up water in oddly square inlets, indicating the locations of the prawn farms. The muddy water caught the morning light in a purple glow.

It had been six years since the tsunami had struck, six years since Raj began to help rebuild Kallar. Two years had passed since he had discovered the untouchable community. Raj shuddered, remembering the moment he had followed those two ragged children to their home. He would visit the school and child sponsorship program that he had started for them today, after he visited Kallar.

Raj mulled over the situation as he rode. *Are the fishermen able to sustain their businesses? It has not been easy for them. Are the women's tailoring co-op and self-help groups still working?*

The piles of rubble grew more prominent on the coastal side of the road. *Old Kallar*, Raj thought to himself. Raj saw where he had first met the villagers and the place where they had set up their emergency shelters just after the tsunami struck.

The scars still lingered, but old Kallar was practically deserted now. Now a wall of giant, dark rocks concealed the breaking waves along the shore. These rocks and others like them had been placed as barricades along much of the coast of Tamil Nadu to weaken the impact should another tsunami ever arrive.

Over the last six years, Raj had witnessed an incredible transformation in the community, from children stepping into self-confidence and believing in themselves enough to nurture their potential through schooling, to women taking their first steps as tailors and businesswomen, to men saying no to alcohol and beginning to help their families steward their earnings.

Raj swerved from the coastal road onto another that took him inland. Samuka Initiative had partnered with Bright Future to construct homes for every family three miles inland, out of a fear that another tsunami could destroy the village if it were built in the same place. Now Raj was headed there.

Raj's bike sputtered to a stop at the entrance. A wall circled the village, and a sign arched over the entrance saying, "Welcome to New Kallar," in Tamil. Raj stretched his back, aching from the long train ride he had taken through the night, then set off for the nearest house. He always started by visiting each family individually.

"Madame, you are looking so happy today," Raj said as he stepped into the first house. Inside stood the once-distraught woman in the yellow sari. Today, her face was bright, and her smile spoke of life and joy.

"Raj! It is because I sold another kurta this week! Sister Jothi here has taught me well." Jothi sat next to her, smiling and nodding approvingly. She had arrived to check on her tailoring students the week prior. The woman excitedly held up some cloth next to her sewing machine. "I just bought this with my earnings. Now I can make more." Her face relaxed into a large smile. "Sit," she ordered as she slipped away into her kitchen.

Raj sat obediently, turning to Jothi. "Jothi, you have done such good work."

Jothi burst into a smile at the words of praise.

The woman returned with two hot *dosas*. The thin, sour crepes were folded gracefully on the plate, fresh and crisp. In line with Indian hospitality, every family Raj visited would insist on giving him the best of their food—and they adored Raj, which meant they gave not just well, but abundantly.

"Eat," she ordered, smiling. Then she pulled out a small metal bowl with a spicy sauce called chutney. "I ground the coconuts this morning," she said, dishing it out beside the dosas. Raj's stomach grumbled happily as he grasped the chutney with his dosa.

She watched Raj eat with contentment and quickly moved to refill his plate with more dosas and chutney as he finished. Raj thought about that moment eight years ago when he had encouraged her to eat by having her make food for him, and he smiled.

Sometimes the grief of a present situation eclipses any thought of the future, any notion of life beyond the miserable present. And sometimes, a person just needs a friend to help them look ahead. A friend with a hug and a prod that beckons them to join the throngs of those who have seen life for all that it really is—the joy and the anguish—and who defiantly cling to hope all the same. *How the people of Kallar have come together for one another through these years!* Raj thought to himself.

"Our sister here is leading the women's tailoring co-op now," Jothi announced with pride. "She has become a good leader, teaching these women how to be leaders in turn."

The woman bowed her head bashfully. "Thank you, sister Jothi."

"How wonderful!" Raj clapped his hands. "You are a leader, sister. You are doing good for your community."

Raj parted with them to visit the next family. Uniform concrete homes stood in rows, small but sturdy. Across from him, New Kallar's community hall stood freshly painted. Raj strolled down the road between one row of homes. Some inhabitants cultivated gardens outside their homes, and Raj stopped as he passed by one green, scaly custard apple that poked out from behind a low wall.

"Sriti, how are you?" Raj called through the open door behind the wall. A cry of delight rang from the house, and a woman ran out to meet him.

"Raj, you are back! Please, sir, come inside." She ushered him in, and before he knew it, another dosa with chutney lay before him, this time with a cup of the woman's best juice. This woman had also lost someone dear in the tsunami: her husband.

A young, curious face poked through the door. It was the woman's daughter.

"How are your studies?" Raj asked the girl. "Remember you must stay with your studies and work hard. Then one day you can go to university."

"I have been working very hard, sir," she answered.

"Tell him what you decided," her mom prodded.

The girl stood tall and announced, "I want to be an engineer."

Her mom stood proudly next to her. "What do you think of that? Her father would be so proud. We would never have thought we would have somebody so educated in our family."

"How wonderful," Raj replied. "I think you will make a great engineer."

News of Raj's presence spread quickly through the village, and other heads started to poke through the door to give their own invitations.

"The Kumraj family is not here," one man explained when Raj stopped at an empty home. "They have saved enough money to rebuild their original home in old Kallar."

"They have?" Raj asked.

"Yes. But me? I am happy here. I have a new business selling chips and chai. My family will stay here. But many families have been wanting to move back." He shook his head back and forth. "It is just, you see, that we are fishermen. It is hard when you live here and barely make enough off of your catch to live and for your family. But when you live so far inland, you must commute, and a fisherman cannot afford that. They cannot even afford bikes."

Raj nodded understandingly.

"We lost everything in that tsunami," the man continued. "We have rebuilt our boats, our businesses, and now we rebuild our homes." He paused and looked to the ground. "Our lost children, our wives, our mothers, and fathers. That we can never rebuild."

The man looked out toward the distant sea. "But old Kallar, that is home."

Raj put his hand on the man's shoulder and felt his sadness. "Kallar has shown such perseverance," Raj said. "You did lose everything, and now I see your hard work. You men have rebuilt your businesses. Your women have become tailors and businesswomen, your children are in school. You inspire me."

In a moment of rare vulnerability, the man let a tear roll down his cheek, and then he hugged Raj.

Raj spent most of the day walking through the town to greet each family. By the time he reached the last house, it was late afternoon. The sun was intense and hot on his skin. He could just make out the ocean glaring in the sun to the east. He ran his fingers through his dark hair, longing to be on the beach and to feel the breeze tickle his neck.

The town found itself in a difficult place. They were fishermen by trade, yet to pick up their business after the tsunami meant they would have to commute to the shore every day. These fishermen could not afford that. To move back to the coast required money to rebuild, but if they could not fish, they could not get money. It took time, but the wealthier people of the village had slowly started to move back to old Kallar, and others were beginning to follow. Meanwhile, many chose to stay in New Kallar and find new trades.

Six years, Raj thought. His head ached from the previous night's bumpy train ride. His heart missed his wife and his sons. These days, Raj devoted all his energy to his job as National Field Director for Samuka Initiative. His life was on the road, spending days with each of their eighteen child sponsorship projects around the country. Raj knew that his physical presence at these projects significantly raised the morale and sped up the progress of the people these projects served. He knew that what he was doing was important, especially for the children he worked with.

Still, Raj missed his family. Samuel was now fourteen years old, and Daniel was twelve years old. They were good boys, growing into strong, good men. He was so proud of them. Raj's heart suddenly wrenched. He traveled so much that the past weekend had been the only time he got to spend with his family this month. Now it would be another month before he would get to see them again.

Raj strolled out of New Kallar toward the untouchable village. *At least my sons have a mother and a father who love them…and are alive.* Raj's heart broke for all children who were part of the sponsorship programs. Even if they had parents, those parents did not take care of them. They did not have a future unless they stuck through school all the way. Raj's heart opened wide for these children. They too were his sons and daughters, and he was their father.

"*Appa!*"

Raj raised his head at the voice of a small boy—he had arrived at the edge of the untouchable village. The gate to a small building opened, and children ran out to greet him.

"Appa! We missed you!" another child cried as she flung her arms around Raj. Suddenly Raj was surrounded by children. He peered past their faces and arms to see their teacher shaking her head indignantly but smiling all the same.

"Children, children, you are in the middle of your tutoring!" Raj exclaimed. "Go back to class, I want to watch you learn."

"Appa, look at my drawing!" A girl exclaimed, shoving a paper in his face.

"Raj, sir," an older boy said. "Raj, will you play a game with us?"

But Raj's arms were already full of two girls who had snuck into his embrace.

"All this last month, my brother was saying you would not come back," one boy said.

"Ah, Anuj." Raj bent down to greet the little boy. "You are always in my heart. How can I forget you?"

The teacher called, and the children ran back to the little house. Each child had a sponsor who funded their school fees, a meal once a day, clothing, and most importantly, their after-school tutoring. What a contrast they were to those first two ragged and scared children Raj had followed back here. The children were looking much better than before—healthier, cleaner, and brighter.

But the surrounding conditions were not.

Raj took in his surroundings. Unlike New Kallar's strong, concrete homes, this village was composed of haphazard huts made of rotting wood, with thatched roofs. The huts teetered on muddy land amid the brush and the brackish inlets.

Raj looked around at the shabby huts. No parents came out to greet him. Just like when he first came two years ago, the parents stayed inside—scared, or untrusting. Raj ran his fingers through his hair, remembering the challenges he had faced to help this place.

After stumbling upon it four years after the tsunami, Raj had organized relief efforts that poured into the Dalit village. The village had seemed incapable of receiving the rations at first, for there was no leader to direct any of the efforts. But the children had crowded the relief workers, curious and hungry.

Then Kallar protested. The rations were for them, they

had said. These people were not fishermen, and it had been specified that the relief rations were for fishermen.

In their protests they did not, of course, elaborate on the fact that the people of the Dalit village were not allowed to fish, lest they "pollute" the ocean water.

Raj had initially brought the scheduled-caste children to the beautiful community hall in New Kallar to study with the other children. After all, the untouchable children had no other place to go.

But one day Kallar's leader had sought Raj out and said, "Rajendran sir, you know we are so happy with you. You are one of our sons with us. But please, sir, we are uncomfortable with these children coming."

The fishermen tolerated the mixed-caste schooling for a time, but their tolerance could not be sustained.

After that, the one after-school program became two. Raj always ensured the Dalit program had more staff, to compensate for the additional obstacles to education those children faced.

One of these teachers poked her head out from behind the gate.

"Raj?" she called and then came toward him nervously.

"Pooja! So good to see you!" Raj exclaimed. "What is the matter? Why do you look sad?"

"There is a young girl who hasn't attended school for a couple of weeks—Aarthi. She is scheduled caste from this village. Sir, everyone knows you and respects you. If you went to see her, I'm sure she would come back. If she misses any more school, she's not going to be able to pass her exams."

"Okay, I will go," Raj replied. It was not uncommon for the poorer children to be held back home, just as it had been with his brothers and sisters and with the children in the slums.

Raj biked through the muddy paths of the untouchable village. The air was humid, saturated with the smell of fish and prawns. Raj frequently stopped to ask the way to the girl's home. With every knock on a door, a villager was happy to direct him, yet it was odd that they seemed nervous to give any details on her situation. Raj began to sense that the situation might be more dire than he realized.

Raj came to a dilapidated hut and knew this must be the girl's home. As Raj parked his bike, he could smell the vapors of brewing arrack. Then he heard the boisterous chattering of drunk men. Raj's heart sunk. He could guess that the alcohol had something to do with why Aarthi had been missing school.

He took a deep breath, then knocked on the door.

"Hello?" he called through the rusty-hinged door.

It opened slowly, and out of the dark, musty room, a masculine voice shouted, "What you want, boy?"

"I am looking for Aarthi." Raj cringed as bad breath and alcohol wafted out of the hut. "I am with the school. She has missed the past two weeks and is in danger of failing her classes. Where are her parents?"

An oily laugh echoed from behind. "Dad's dead. The arrack got to him finally."

"And her mother?"

"In jail, busted for making arrack."

"And the girl?"

The question was answered by silence.

chapter thirty-two

Anger surged deep inside Raj. He was not going to go anywhere until he knew where she was. Raj lowered his voice threateningly. "I asked you, where is the girl?"

More silence betrayed uneasiness in the man. Raj stood in the doorway, indignant. Finally, the man answered. "I don't know where she is now, but she'll be back. Maybe she's gone to fetch water."

Sure enough, soon a young girl, no more than thirteen years old, struggled up to the porch carrying four bike tire tubes. They were empty but stank of alcohol.

"Are you Aarthi?" Raj asked.

She passed by him, not even glancing up at him, but simply asked, "How much do you want?" And, as she stepped into the hut, the men cheered rowdily—but hushed themselves as Raj entered behind her.

His eyes adjusted to the light, and he saw a group of old men, clad in their lungies and happily intoxicated. At the sight of Raj, they awkwardly shuffled their feet and studied their empty cups.

"I have not come for arrack," Raj said.

The girl's eyes widened, and she stepped back, glancing over at the men.

"No, no, I have come to see how you are doing and to ask why you have not been in school these past few weeks."

Her eyes relaxed and became glassy—soon, tears dripped down her cheeks. She set the tubes down, and Raj gently led her outside.

"What has happened?" Raj asked. "Tell me everything."

"I want to come back to school, but...but if I don't do

this, my family…"

She searched his face, and finding a friend in his sad smile, she began to tell her story. "One of the landowners here…he had my father make arrack for him. My dad would make it there in the back, from all the waste he would gather.

"Maybe he enjoyed it for a bit. He would fill up tire tubes with the stuff to hide it, then bring it to the different rich people in the night so he wouldn't get caught. They seemed to like him for it. And he would get paid too…a little bit.

"Once he tried to stop making arrack. I remember that the landowner came here then. He was angry and said something to my dad. My dad never tried to stop making it after that, and he started drinking more himself. By the end, he was always drunk. He got so thin. He couldn't speak clearly or think clearly." The girl looked down. "He didn't feel like my dad anymore, not toward the end."

"I am sorry," Raj said.

"He died a couple of months ago. That same night he died, the landowner told my mom that my dad had taken a loan from him. It was a pretty big loan. She wouldn't be able to pay it off…so, she had to start selling the arrack." The girl looked back up at Raj with wide, fearful eyes.

"I don't know when my dad took the loan or what it was for, but it's there. We don't have a choice now. I feel like even selling arrack doesn't make the loan any smaller, it's so big. But we must, and now…I must.

"The police came in a couple of weeks ago and took my mom. They do that every once in a while. She was supposed to just go to court to pay a fine for making the alcohol, but they've locked her in this time. I'm the only one here who can make it now. If I don't, we'll lose everything or worse. I don't know what that man would do to us, but I am so scared." Tears had begun to flow down her cheeks again.

Raj shook his head. "This is not good, not good."

"When my mom got put in jail, the owner came to me. He told me if I didn't keep on selling the arrack, he would hurt my mom and me…because of the debt."

And then she burst into sobs.

Raj shook his head grimly. The debt was always the manacle of the lower castes. It held his parents in bondage to the plantation, and it shackled this girl to arrack. By now, Raj knew this debt was nothing more than a construed ploy to exploit the family and that it was against the law.

But the law was only as strong as the people willing to enforce it.

"Aarthi, will you let me sort this out for you?" Raj asked. "I promise you I will. And, in the meantime, go back to school. Your exams are soon, and you need to pass them to be able to stay in school."

Disbelief came over her face, and she shook her head. "What about—"

"I will take care of all of it," Raj assured her. "If anyone gives you trouble, send them to me. I am going to talk with your mother now. I will come back tomorrow." Raj stood up, then looked toward her hut. "Do you have a friend you can stay with? No need to go back there tonight," he told her.

Raj revved his motorbike and headed immediately for the police station. Anger burned through his veins. He knew this story because it was all too familiar and happened all over the country.

But at least in this instance, he could change the ending.

The police station emerged in the distance. It was almost dusk now, but the station's sign was neatly lit up. Raj parked his bike, then made his way toward the door and took a deep breath.

Then he burst through the door. "Where is the mother of Aarthi?" he demanded.

An officer holding a cup of chai startled, and the drink splashed down his nicely pressed shirt and into his lap.

"Raj, sir!" another officer exclaimed. They sat there, petrified for a moment. Then the first officer scrambled to wipe the chai off his pants.

Everyone there knew Raj—they couldn't help but know the man who had spearheaded the rebuilding of so many communities around them. And they all respected Raj—he had helped them rebuild too.

Now they were terrified.

"Where is the mother of Aarthi?" Raj asked again. "You have held her in jail for a week now when the law clearly states that within twenty-four hours of arrest, you must present the arrestee to the court. Even if she is responsible for the felony, you cannot keep her without informing the court."

The men glanced over to their commanding officer, who twisted his mustache anxiously. He knew that Raj knew the law. He knew that Raj was loved in the region. And unfortunately, he also knew that Raj chose to help the poor— which was quite inconvenient to their operation.

He stumbled out of his chair to stand and replied, "Ah yes, yes. She...er, voluntarily accepted to spend time, so..." He wobbled his head, grimaced, and shrugged. "We took her in. We are sorry."

Raj scowled. "Do you know what state her child is in?"

The officers looked at each other uncertainly.

"We both know how this works around here," Raj continued, "and you have no business letting a young girl be in the situation she is in."

Raj looked deep into the eyes of the head officer. "By law, you have no right to hold her mother. You must release this woman immediately."

They released Aarthi's mother that night.

Now Raj had one more person to visit in the town if this situation were to truly be reconciled: the landowner.

After making sure Aarthi's mother was in good condition, he left for the owner's home. By now, it was deep into the night, but the moon shone brightly on the smooth walls of the house. Raj weaved through the backwaters and finally came to a well-lit manor. Colorful chalk patterns called *rangoli* embellished the pathway to the house. A black steel fence surrounded the place and cast foreboding shadows in the moonlight.

Raj shook his head. He wanted to finish this.

"I can file a case on you because of this," Raj explained, his voice stern. He stood in the parlor of the manor, facing the owner. The owner listened as if he were annoyed to be talking over such a matter so late in the night. However, his focused attention foiled his show of indifference and betrayed his apprehension.

"This man worked for you for years, and only you gained the benefit out of it. He worked so many years, and you did not pay him the right wages. You threatened him with this debt when you yourself have not honored his payments of this debt. You held an illegal debt over him to contract him into illicit labor."

Raj thought of his own father, Aandi, as he spoke, laboring under debt bondage until the day his body gave out. How many times had his mother pleaded for money out of desperation, money she would have had if she had been paid justly?

"Now you have forced his wife to continue making arrack, and now his daughter. And all these people coming for the arrack are misusing them, abusing them. Verbally and physically, and you are not taking care of that." Raj had leaned in close to the owner. He looked straight into the man's angry eyes.

"So," said Raj, as he raised his chin to look his adversary directly in the eyes, "I must file a case against you. And you will be put in jail."

The owner gave up on his pretense of not caring. He knew the respect Raj commanded in the area. He shook his head. "Oh, sir, you are not a man I want to come up against. Please," he pleaded. "what do you want me to do?"

Raj nodded, satisfied the man would do what he asked. "From here on out, neither Aarthi nor her mother will make arrack. I want the girl to be in school. If she is not in school, you will feel the consequences." Raj paused, thinking for a moment. "They have labored for you unjustly for so long. You must do something for this family. You will buy the family a sheep and a cow. That way, this family can start a new life." *And be free of you*, Raj thought to himself.

The owner consented.

Raj rode home in the moonless night, at peace. He had done what he needed to do. As Raj arrived at his sleeping place, one of the homes in Kallar, his mind was filled with action items for the week. Tomorrow he would help Aarthi's mother clean the house and get rid of the arrack. Maybe Jothi could teach the mother to sew. Aarthi would come back to school. His heart grew warm again with hopes for this family and their new future.

"Raj," a voice called out as Raj stepped inside his resting place for the night.

"Yes?"

"Raj, well, I don't know how to say this, but…"

"What is it?"

"Raj, your brother Antony, he is dying. It's his kidneys."

chapter thirty-three

"Kidney failure. He needs dialysis, or he will die," the doctor announced, "dialysis for the rest of his life, I mean."

The doctor wore a tired expression, and he kept glancing at the clock as he spoke to Raj's family. He stood for a moment longer to let his words sink in gently.

Raj looked around at his family—they were a sad lot in this hospital. One professional from the city, and the rest rural farmers, with weathered faces and well-worn clothes. Raj imagined what the doctor must think of them all. *Maybe the man from the city can afford dialysis for his brother, but not the rest of them.*

Sure enough, the doctor sighed and said, "We can put him on dialysis immediately...but it will be costly and difficult to maintain."

Next to Raj, Antony sat solemnly in his hospital bed. Saroja and their three daughters encircled him. Their daughters were now twenty-four, twenty-one, and eighteen years old. Near them, Evangeline wrapped her arm around Kanni. Aandi could not come, for in his old age, his legs had become weak. This left Raj as the man in charge.

Raj hung his head low. The life savings of one sick man, uneducated, laboring his whole life for one-fourth of the amount considered the international poverty line, was a grim total. Combined with his wife's earnings and those of his old mother, also at twenty-five cents per day each...it wasn't close to enough.

And even if you added in what one well-educated man made on a nonprofit salary, the math still gave bleak results. Raj was the only one who would have had any chance to afford such care. Perhaps he could have done it had he pursued government work.

But he had sacrificed that sort of luxury a long time ago.

Now the weight of his sacrifice hit him in the gut. In all his years of serving he had never felt so inadequate. There was nothing he could do to rectify the situation. Had he unwittingly sentenced his brother to death? His rational mind answered "no," but still, he could not bear to look his brother's family in the eyes. Through his peripheral vision, he saw Saroja praying, with her arms around her children.

Raj felt two hands slide around his. Kanni was staring into Raj's eyes through her thick glasses. Her eyes and mouth stayed taut and stubborn against the grief of losing her son.

"Raj, it is up to you—you make the call," she said.

Raj lowered his head. He could not bear to say it. He could only shake his head in resignation. The doctor nodded, interpreting this answer correctly, then turned and walked away down the ward.

The family circled more closely around Antony's bed. He looked so weak and tired. Burdened with swollen feet and ankles, he could sit up in the bed but could not walk. Without his kidneys, his body would slowly intoxicate itself and gradually shut down.

Saroja touched his head as the tears rolled down her cheeks. Antony's daughters crowded in close to him. Kanni stood next to Raj, grasping his arm for support. Raj's other hand clasped Evangeline's. She squeezed his hand reassuringly.

The room offered humble accommodations. One chair other than Saroja's had been put by the bed. Raj led Kanni there. As Raj sat her down, Antony looked up at him.

"Raj," he whispered, "take care of my family." His voice was tired, but his plea was strong.

Raj mustered a whispered, "Yes."

Saroja threw herself into prayer with gasps and cries. Her three children joined her, and together they pleaded to God to heal Antony.

Twelve hours passed.

The golden sun departed and cold night shuffled in. The whitewashed walls and shiny metal of the beds and intruments cast an alienating sense through the room. Even the smallest of sounds—a foot shuffling, a cough—would echo off the steel. The white lights flickered an unnatural coldness. It was the families that brought life to those corridors—and it was life in all its realism. Laughter and smiles bubbled in the good moments. Weeping penetrated most.

By now, Saroja had lost her voice from her cries yet she still prostrated herself before the Lord in silent pleas. Groans too deep for words resounded through her whole being. She sat next to Raj, slumped over her thin plastic chair, murmuring.

Raj watched Antony's rising and falling chest. It fluttered, then fell, again and again. His arms were tense as if bracing his soul for the inevitable. His jaws clenched, then relaxed in resolve. Raj fixated on his brother. Slowly, those familiar eyes turned to meet his.

"Raj—" he spoke. The words cracked through his parched throat.

"Yes, Antony, I'm here."

"Raj..."

"Antony, I am so sorry. I am so sorry I can't—"

"Raj, thank you."

"What?"

"I can have peace knowing you are here to care for my family. I wouldn't ask for anyone else."

Raj stifled a cry, and his face grew hot as tears began to pour down.

"Raj," Antony spoke again. "You gave me life. You helped me see the world new and taught me to fight for that new world." Antony opened his hand, and Raj clasped his own around it.

"My children have gone to school because of you. One will soon become a nurse. They won't have to labor in the

253

plantations as I did. They will be able to take care of each other, just as you take care of us. Saroja will be safe, she will be looked after. I…I can leave in peace." He never spoke again. The silence spread as his breathing slowed. Dusk had turned to night, but even the buzzing cicadas seemed to hold their breath. Just an hour before midnight, Antony's hands grew cold.

Raj collapsed, resting his head on Antony's still chest. Choking on his own breath, with his arms spread and palms open, Raj wept.

Raj rode a motorbike along the familiar dirt path. Evangeline's arms wrapped around him, and her sari trailed in the wind. Their two sons rode silently on another bike behind them, in dress pants and collared shirts.

Sadness hung in the hot air. Nostalgia welled in Raj's throat as the scents of tamarind and plantain trees flooded his nostrils. Soon the cheri church emerged. Next to it, the Ambedkar Association sign stood rusted and faded but just as proud as that first day Raj and the cheri boys put it up. The cheri well glistened, wet from recent use. Beyond it, the same dilapidated mud huts lined the dirt road. *Home.*

The family gently reunited with their cousins, aunts, and uncles. A group of men came around Aandi and softly picked him up. Saroja stepped out of her house with her children and nodded solemnly. Then the procession began.

The funeral was held in the graveyard less than a mile from the cheri. People wept, shared cherished moments, and embraced. The sun eased below the horizon, gleaming fiery orange for just a moment and then light gold. Antony was buried and a cross placed above him. Engraved in elegant Tamil, it reads, "A. Anbalagan, June 15, 1956–June 26, 2011." He was buried as *Antony Anbalagan*, proudly taking the Christian name his father had chosen the day he had been baptized.

Aandi was gently lifted again to be carried back. Kanni walked closely beside him. Her thali still gleamed around her neck in the setting sun. Raj quickened his steps and put his arm around her. She answered his gesture with a grateful look from her sad, piercing eyes. Her hand slowly lifted to touch his.

The family pressed itself into the old hut. In Raj's childhood, the hut had been crowded with the family of eight. Now the room burst with the adult children, their spouses, and their children.

Grief lingered alongside a new peace. The family was happy just to be back together. Evangeline chattered with Jothi and Selvie, patting Saroja's hair. Chelladurai and Petchimuthu shared about their jobs driving truck lorries and their dreams for their children to go to college. Daniel bantered with his cousins while Samuel knelt next to his grandmother, telling her about his last semester in high school.

Aandi rested on his bed. His skin covered the thin protrusions of his bones like a waxy film, and his eyes had begun to turn milky. He watched his children and grandchildren around him. Underneath the veil of the moment's sadness, pride glowed.

Raj crossed the room to his father. Aandi smiled and whispered, "I want you to use the pen, not the *manvetti*." Raj grasped his father's hand, nodding his head.

"Look, Appa, now all of your grandchildren will graduate high school," Raj said. "Some already have university degrees. Others will soon have degrees."

"My, that is something," Aandi replied, sinking back into his cot with a smile.

Raj stole outside and sat under his family's lime tree. The welcome cool of the night had begun to descend. A lost butterfly fluttered to the tree and rested beside an old cocoon. It stirred at the sound of shuffling feet behind Raj.

"What is it, Dad?" Samuel asked. Daniel stood beside his brother, watching curiously.

Raj lowered himself to the ground and ran his fingers through the dust. "You know, I used to not be allowed to walk through the town with my sandals on?" he mused. "Antony—he was there for me, standing up for me in one of the most painful moments in my life. And now look, the abuses are so much less."

Raj reached to touch a young lime growing on the tree. "These pains in our lives...I see that God has brought something good out of them."

Raj faced his two sons with a glimmer in his eyes. "Did you know my name was not always Rajendran? I was born *Natarajan Aandi,* the name of a Hindu god combined with grandfather's first name—'worthless.' Today it is *Rajendran Anbalagan,* 'the king of the way of love.'"

He shook his head as he smiled and then said, "I did not choose this name, no.

"But let me tell you how it became mine."

epilogue

In 2013, Raj concluded his work with Samuka Initiative and moved to an organization named Global Rights Network to pursue the question he had wondered about his entire life, *Could there be justice for the poor?* To further this pursuit, he helped found and serves as president of a grassroots nonprofit named Maarga.

Maarga is located and operates in the Bangalore slums giving holistic community development. Maarga runs an after-school tutoring for children in the slums, which brings enrichment to the often substandard education available to them. Young women are offered workshops for mental health, since they are extremely vulnerable to abuse. In addition, Maarga trains women in how to entrepreneur tailor businesses and train as beauticians. The organization is now reaching beyond the slums to assist farmers in sustainable agriculture, taking a holistic approach to solving the social and economical needs of the marginalized.

During the COVID-19 pandemic, Maarga distributed lifesaving supplies to undocumented inhabitants in the slums who do not have proper identification to access government provisions. The heart of Maarga runs in the same veins as the heart of this book. If you feel moved to action by this book, please consider supporting this organization. You can learn more at maarga.org.in.

Raj has worked with the Global Rights Network since his conclusion with Samuka Initiative where he focuses on fighting the same system of debt bondage, called bonded labor, that Raj's own family was trapped in. Although this system is illegal, it is by no means eradicated.

Raj has successfully pioneered a network of partnerships with grassroots community groups to work together in identifying the worst cases of bonded labor, initiating police rescues, and advocating with government officials. Together, they champion the growing number of police and government officials who defend justice for the poor.

Raj served with Bright Future for a total of fifteen years. Raj worked in four projects in over forty-eight villages and slums, touching around 50,000 lives. Raj served as the national coordinator for Samuka Initiative for nine years, overseeing the child sponsorship and education of 2,000 children and the aid given to around 3,000 families through community development programs. This impact could never have happened had Raj not been enabled to complete eighth grade and high school himself, through child sponsorship.

Today, Evangeline continues to teach nursing. Raj and Evangeline's two sons, Samuel and Daniel, are adults, living in Bangalore and Chennai. Raj still wishes he had spent more time with his sons during his time-demanding work with Samuka Initiative.

In 2012, Aandi passed away, a well-respected and well-loved man. Aandi lived a long and rich life for a landless laborer. Raj and his family requested a portion of land to bury him in, on the estate that Aandi had worked his whole life. The landowner consented and gave them a plot of unused land alongside the road, where Aandi's grave lies to this day.

Kanni passed away in December of 2020. I had the honor of interviewing her in her home in Anaigudi cheri, sitting underneath her photos of Aandi, all of her children, and their families. She now rests next to her husband.

Saroja, Selvie, and Selvie's husband still stay in the Anaigudi cheri and work as daily wage laborers. Chelladurai and Petchimuthu each live in the area, working manual labor jobs. Jothi lives in Bangalore, working as a cleaning maid at a university.

Aandi and Kanni have a total of fifteen grandchildren. Thirteen have completed their studies through high school.

Three hold bachelor's degrees and three hold engineering degrees. One has studied through nursing school and works as a nurse.

Chitravel works as a conductor for a government bus and Mani works as a laborer; both have families. Selvaraj has retired from his government job and lives outside Tirunelveli. He is still very active in advocacy for Dalits. Sollalagan has also continued to advocate for Dalits, and his daughter works as one of the district judges in Tamil Nadu.

Rates of alcoholism and domestic abuse have significantly dropped in the Anaigudi cheri since Raj began the Ambedkar Association. In 2018, the government built homes for the Anaigudi cheri, finally replacing the thatched mud huts. A wall still stands between the Christian and Hindu sides of the cheri, and their church and temple are still standing as well. The same Ambedkar Youth Association sign, the school, and the homes in the town—all still stand as they did back in 1986. The electricity pole also still stands in the same place.

Not far from there is the home of Vanitha's family. As Raj and I strolled past, one of Vanitha's brothers, curious about the town's American visitor, invited us in and served Raj and me refreshments. Raj introduced himself as a student of their mom, Teacher Thangam, and we got to meet her. If they did recognize Raj, they never said anything.

Vanitha lives outside of Chennai and runs a business. Evidently her family never told her about what happened to Raj. The first time she learned of the incident was when Raj and I reconnected with her about this biography.

Inspector Chitharanjan retired as deputy superintendent of police and resides outside of Tirunelveli with his family. His choice to file Raj's FIR, as well as his Christian status, have most likely contributed to him not being promoted to superintendent of police. Still, as he said to me in an interview, he has not once regretted filing the case.

To this day, Raj's case has not been heard in the public court system; however, caste-based violence has significantly decreased in Anaigudi.

Kumaresan's political career ended with losing the MLA seat to INC candidate Ramani Nallathambi in the 1989 election. Prakash never entered politics. Since Raj married Evangeline, who belongs to the same caste as Prakash, Raj is now a distant relative of Prakash. One could even say that Prakash is indeed Raj's brother.

GLOSSARY

FAMILY TERMS
Ama: Mother
Ayya: Father
Appa: Father
Anna: Brother (older)
Mapile: Brother (younger)

CULTURAL TERMS
Lungi: A short cloth tied around a man's waist for informal occasions.
Dothi: A long cloth worn around a man's waist for more formal occasions or to work.
Sari: A three part formal women's outfit composed of a skirt, blouse, and long cloth draped and fastened around a woman's waist and over her shoulder.
Arana Kkayiru: A black rope that is used to secure the dothi and store things, functioning like a belt and pocket.
Betel Leaf: A leaf plucked from vines native to India, used to make beedies or an after-meal treat called paan.
Beedie: A makeshift cigarette.
Aarack: An alcoholic drink from south Asia that is very high in alcohol content. In rural areas this alcohol is created through wastes and battery acid and has been known to be very harmful to drink.
Toddy: A drink made from sap of a palmyra tree. The later in the day it is taken from the tree, the more alcoholic it will be.

SOCIAL TERMS
Scheduled Caste, Untouchable, Dalit: Each of these are terms for a

segment of society

Scheduled Tribal Caste/Adhivasi: Communities living in rural parts of India that tend to live indigenously off the land and suffer similar social obstacles as the Scheduled Castes.

Paraiyah: A group of people in south India who belong to the scheduled castes in India.

Dravidian: Having ancestry in the indigenous South Asian Hunter Gatherers and having dark skin, eyes, and hair.

Aryan: A term used by the Indo-Aryan people of the Vedic period in Ancient India as a religious label for themselves. The term tends to describe the lighter features of people from north India.

GOVERNMENT TERMS

Taluk: A subdivision of an Indian administrative district.

Panchayat: A village council.

Dravida Munnetra Kazhagam (DMK): Translated Dramudian Progressive Federation, particularly in Tamil Nadu, and adheres to the social democratic and social justice principles of C. N. Annadurai and Periyar E. V. Ramasamy.

Indian National Congress (INC): A political party that has its roots in Mahatma Ghandi's social movements and is one of the major political parties that operates on the state and national level in India.

Bharatiya Janata Party (BJP): A right-winged political party that operates on the state and national level in India, defined particularly by its agenda to assert India as a Hindu nation.

RELIGIOUS TERMS

Poojary: A low-caste officiator of Hindu ceremonies.

Pooja: A Hindu prayer ceremony.

Brahmin: The highest caste in India, whose ancestral duty is priesthood.

Alagu Kuthuthal: A Hindu ritual in which a volunteer has a long rod pierced through both of his cheeks. He will keep the rod through his mouth for a week.

Sudalai Madan: A god of the graveyard, worshipped by

rural,low-caste communities in south India.

Church of South India (CSI): A liturgical church prominent in south India that arose from the union of protestant denominations such as Anglican and Methodist after Indian independence.

APPENDIX I

LAWS OF MANU VIII 410–420

410. (The king) should order a Vaisya to trade, to lend money, to cultivate the land, or to tend cattle, and a Sudra to serve the twice-born castes.

411. (Some wealthy) Brahmana shall compassionately support both a Kshatriya and a Vaisya, if they are distressed for a livelihood, employing them on work (which is suitable for) their (castes).

412. But a Brahmana who, because he is powerful, out of greed makes initiated (men of the) twice-born (castes) against their will do the work of slaves, shall be fined by the king six hundred (panas).

413. But a Sudra, whether bought or unbought, he may compel to do servile work; for he was created by the Self-existent (Svayambhu) to be the slave of a Brahmana.

414. A Sudra, though emancipated by his master, is not released from servitude; since that is innate in him, who can set him free from it?

415. There are slaves of seven kinds, (viz.) he who is made a captive under a standard, he who serves for his daily food, he who is born in the house, he who is bought and he who is given, he who is inherited from ancestors, and he who is enslaved by way of punishment.

416. A wife, a son, and a slave, these three are declared to have no property; the wealth which they earn is (acquired) for him to whom they belong.

417. A Brahmana may confidently seize the goods of (his) Sudra (slave); for, as that (slave) can have no property, his master may take his possessions.

418. (The king) should carefully compel Vaisyas and Sudra to perform the work (prescribed) for them; for if these two (castes) swerved from their duties, they would throw this (whole) world into confusion.

419. Let him daily look after the completion of his undertakings, his beasts of burden, and carriages, (the collection of) his revenues and the disbursements, his mines and his treasury.

420. A king who thus brings to a conclusion. all the legal business enumerated above, and removes all sin, reaches the highest state (of bliss).

APPENDIX II

CALCULATIONS

Chapter 3: Kanni, Aandi, Antony's wage in 1986

According to the Reserve Bank of India, the INR to USD exchange rate in 1986 was 12.7782. 3600 INR in 1986 is $281.73 at the 1986 conversion rate. Using the 133.7% inflation increase in the US since 1986, $281.73 would be about $658.26 today.

Chapter 19: Residential Missionary Salary

In 1986, 3600 rupees was equivalent to $281.73. When divided between 3 people, then by 365 days in a year, this amounts to $.2573 per person per day. In 1990 the International World Bank would declare the international poverty line to be $1 per person per day.

about the author

Hayley Bennett Lyle resides in Southern California. She is co-CEO of Elyon Technologies along with her husband, Micah, and oversees the user experience design wing of the company.

Hayley lived in India for a full year before beginning to write this story and returned for another month for field visits. She loves to be immersed in cultures different from her own, cultivate friendships there, and learn from them. She is grateful for the opportunity to steward this incredible story.

Made in the USA
Middletown, DE
11 August 2024

58933022R00170